TO CURSE THE ROOT
A Christian Alternative to 12 Steps

Rev. Pamela Sheppard LMSW

1663 LIBERTY DRIVE, SUITE 200
BLOOMINGTON, INDIANA 47403
(800) 839-8640
WWW.AUTHORHOUSE.COM

© 2006 Rev. Pamela Sheppard LMSW. All Rights Reserved.

No part of this book may be reproduced, stored in a retrieval system, or transmitted by any means without the written permission of the author.

First published by AuthorHouse 01/26/06

ISBN: 1-4259-0766-0 (sc)

Printed in the United States of America
Bloomington, Indiana

This book is printed on acid-free paper.

DEDICATION:
"To My Angel, Sent From God"

This, my first book, was begun in 1995 and completed in 1996, self published and first printed by Brentwood Press in 1999. At this ,its second printing, the year is 2005 and nine years have passed. Nine years ago, I only knew about addiction as a licensed therapist and an ordained minister and not from any personal experience as an addict. Even though I grew up in Harlem, in New York City where addiction was pervasive, there were no addicts among my relatives. In fact, I did not realize that my own father was an alcoholic until after his death in 1988. Therefore, I was totally oblivious to the trouble, trials, tribulation, and testing that I myself would go through for the next nine years as the wife of a heroin addict. Consequently, I am amazed at the truth that I was able to write about this subject by revelation of the word of God alone. Therefore, my utter ignorance of the addict's daily life tells me that "To Curse the Root" is truly the inspiration and revelation of the Holy Ghost.

As I was putting the finishing touches on this book in 1995, I had also developed a Christian model of recovery that I field tested in a local county jail in the month of October.

In the very first session of my group counseling program, I met Richard, a Puerto Rican parole violator---a heroin addict who was cleverly planted in my midst by a religious demon to attempt to destroy me. Once released from incarceration on August 14, 1996, Richard came and joined himself first to the new church that I had just begun two months prior to his release, and then ultimately to me as my third husband. In my third book entitled "FACES OF THE RELIGIOUS DEMON," highlights of my victory over a legal, yet demonic soul tie is described in some detail. For now, suffice it to say that as the wife of a man addicted to heroin, I had to use every principle that is outlined in "To Curse the Root" to survive my nine year ordeal in what I believe now to have been "an unholy union."

Therefore, today I can now affirm from personal experience that every revelation in this book has been tried and tested by me , its author, and I have edited this second printing very minimally with the major change being in the subtitle and various additions. The subtitle in 1995 was "A Thirteenth Step to Recovery and Spiritual Empowerment." I now find that subtitle to be too vague, perhaps misleading. Although I certainly believe that the unsaved need AA to live and survive sober, I have found that those who are Christian may very well be hindered by such a model. Therefore, I have changed the subtitle to "A Christian Alternative to 12 Steps."

Ironically, this book was first inspired by an angel whom I once believed was from the Lord when I began this book in 1995. In a dream a decade earlier, a being who identified himself as "an angel sent by God" declared "AA is not God's program. You must not hire anyone with AA background in the Christ centered program that the Lord shall establish for you to co-direct."

There is certainly a mixture of truth in this prophetic word that has been confirmed by the last twenty years of both personal and professional experience with people involved in 12 Steps programs. However, today I know that the angel who gave me this dream in 1985 was NOT an angel sent by the Lord Jesus Christ because of the second point that the angel made in that dream---that my next husband and I would run a residential rehabilitation center. In 2005, I realize that it never was the Lord's will that I develop and direct a Christian residential rehab for addicts and ex-offenders, just as it was not his will that my former husband would be its co-director. GOD DOES NOT LIE. THE DEVIL IS THE FATHER OF LIES. Therefore, the angel that came to me in 1985 was a religious demon, sent to distract me from my true calling in Christ Jesus which is to "set the captives free."

I indeed married an addict in recovery whom in the beginning I believed would serve with me in ministry, but today I know without a shadow of a doubt that Richard was sent by a religious demon to discredit, shame and destroy me. I hold no ill will toward my ex-husband because I accept the fact that I have not been wrestling with flesh and blood but with principalities and powers. Therefore, I dedicate this book to the angel that Jesus Christ assigned to me for my guidance and protection---the one who prepared the way that kept me safe, the one who consistently and supernaturally exposed and disarmed the enemy so that my victory would be assured. When, you, my angel are judged by the Church, you will receive high honors and acclaim for your skill and wisdom in delivering me out of the lion's mouth. I believe that Jesus has given me the liberty to thank you personally with this dedication.

LET THE LORD JESUS CHRIST OF NAZERETH BE PRAISED!

Table of Contents

INTRODUCTION: MY SPIRITUAL BACKYARD xi

PART ONE: PLOWING 17
- CHAPTER #1: THE LANGUAGE OF THE SPIRIT 19
  - THE NATURE OF THE GROUND 19
  - MY WALK IN THE SPIRIT 23
  - I HAVE A DREAM! 31
  - SPIRITUAL PERCEPTION 35
- CHAPTER #2: THE SOUL AND THE FLESH 41
  - I THINK, THEREFORE, I AM! 41
  - "I FEEL, THEREFORE, I AM!" 44
  - "I CHOOSE, THEREFORE, I AM!" 47
  - "I SENSE, THEREFORE, I AM!" 49

PART TWO: WEEDING 53
- CHAPTER #3: THE "I AM!" 55
  - BREAKING THE "I AM!" 60
  - ESTEEM, PRIDE AND VANITY 64
  - THE BREAKING OF AFFECTION 68
  - THE BREAKING OF DESIRE 72
  - THE BREAKING OF FEELING 76

PART THREE: SOWING 83
- CHAPTER #4: THE SEED AND THE SPIRIT 85
  - SPIRIT FOOD 85
  - BIRTHING A VISION 88
  - DEVELOPING OBJECTIVITY 94
  - POWER-PACKED WORDS 96
  - CONFESSION CAN BRING RECOVERY 99
- CHAPTER #5: THE SEED AND OTHER SPIRITS 104
  - THE DEVIL MADE ME DO IT! 104
  - ALCOHOL--A SPIRIT OR---A SPIRIT! 109
  - THE SEVEN WALLS: FINDING MY PURPOSE 111
  - AN ENEMY HAS DONE THIS! 115
  - THE THREE "R'S": REPENTANCE, RESURRECTION, AND REBIRTH 118
  - REPENTANCE 119

FALSE RELIGION AND 12 STEPS 121

PART FOUR: TILLING 125
CHAPTER #6: THE LABOR AND THE REST 127
THE SPIRITUAL RECIVIDIST 127
GIANTS IN THE LAND! 129
ENTERING THE PROMISE LAND 135

CHAPTER #7: WATERING THE SEED 140
A THIRST FOR RIGHTEOUSNESS 140
RECEIVING THE TRUTH 142
DISEASE OR SIN?! 143
THE WASHING AND THE CLEANSING 148
THE ATONEMENT OF BLOOD 149

PART FIVE: FRUITBEARING 155
CHAPTER #8: NURTURING THE INNER ROOT 157
WALKING IN THE BLESSINGS 157
REJECTING THE WORLD 158
LOVING GODS WORD 161
MEDITATING GOD'S WORD 164
BRINGING IN THE SHEAVES 167

CHAPTER #9: THE WAY TO DELIVERANCE AND GROWTH 169
DYING TO LIVE 169
KNOW YOUR ENEMY! 173
PREPARE FOR BATTLE 177

PART SIX: RECOVERY IN CHRIST WORKBOOK 185
THE RIC PROGRAM 185
A PORTRAIT OF A RECOVERED PERSON 189

KEY #1: REPENTANCE 196
Background 196
Key Scriptures 202
Study And Reflection Outline 205
Workstudy Exercises 209

KEY #2: RESURRECTION 215
Background 215
Key Scriptures 221
Study and Reflection Outline 222
Workstudy Exercises 232

KEY #3: REBIRTH 236
    Background 236
    Key Scriptures 244
    Study and Reflection Outline 250
    Workstudy Exercises 257

KEY #4: REVELATION 261
    Background 261
    Key Scriptures 271
    Study And Reflection Outline 274
    Workstudy Exercises 280

KEY #5: RESISTANCE 284
    Background 284
    Key Scriptures 292
    Study and Reflexion Outline 297
    Workstudy Exercises 308

KEY #6: RENEWAL 312
    Background 312
    Key Scriptures 321
    Study and Reflection Outline 325
    Workstudy Exercises 332

KEY #7: RESTORATION 333
    Background 333
    Key Scriptures 343
    Study and Reflection Outline 345
    Workstudy Exercises 348

APPENDIX: 352

FOOTNOTES 368

INTRODUCTION:
MY SPIRITUAL BACKYARD

Consider my backyard that grew weeds every summer. Every month, I chopped them down and a month later, they all grew back, stronger than ever. Why? Because they should have been pulled up by the root! My first house was built in 1988 on a piece of land that had been a vacant lot for several years. Weeds and "ghetto trees" flourished year round, as the lot had been the surrounding neighborhood's garbage dump. When the foundation was laid, apparently the weeds were not pulled up by the root, and so, they stubbornly and proudly continue to stand their ground each year. Yet for the last seven years, I have steadfastly persisted with my unskilled efforts of weed control.

Comparable to my back yard, weeds have been growing in the hearts and minds of people. These weeds are the product of our beliefs, attitudes and behaviors for several years, where even our identities and gender expectations have become "a garbage dump." The neighborhood of our families, peers and the world at large have continued to dump their opinions, desires and hang-ups in the unprotected garden of our minds--and these seeds have grown into strong and flourishing weeds, with unyielding, stubborn roots. Once a weed has been identified, we must curse the weed at its root, or else it will continue to feed on and be nourished by those attitudes, beliefs and actions that have fed it and caused it to be embedded in the mind and in the emotions.

Cursing the root is painful. It requires digging down deep, pulling and tugging at the weeds in order to get to the root. The process is similar to AA's Twelve Steps: However, the first step in cursing the root is that you must acknowledge not only that you have a problem, BUT that the ability to overcome it is within your the power through your repentance and your belief in the resurrection of Jesus Christ and the ministry of the Holy Ghost!!! The Lord desires that those who are in recovery not only from addiction but also from other demonic bondages and those who are seeking spiritual maturity to reap a rich harvest for His glory. However, fruitbaring is hindered if the ground has not been properly prepared or tilled.

The Holy Spirit as the gardener or landscaper plays an important part in tilling the ground of our souls. As we become spiritually empowered, the Holy Spirit will teach us how to become the gardener of our spiritual garden. How can we till the gardens of others, if our own gardens are filled with weeds? How can we remove the mote from our brother's eye if we have a beam in our own?! Once we cast the beam from our own eye, it is written in the New Testament that we will be able to see clearly to cast out the mote from our brother's eye. (Matthew 7:3,4) While a mote is a small particle, a beam is a long piece of heavy timber. By a similar comparison, some weeds are small flowers while others grow into trees. Once we address the major issues that negatively impact upon our own self-destructive attitudes and behaviors, then our insight will be such that armed with self knowledge, we will be able to identify undesirable thoughts, stop them and replace them with seed or "word-seed" that can germinate, grow and bring forth fruit. Likewise, we will be equipped to recognize with precision even the most apparently insignificant signs of similar problems and issues within others.

Plowing is an initial and fundamental step to planting seed. Involving the steady and laborious breaking up of the ground by lifting and turning over the soil, the plowing stage prepares a seed bed. The ground is then so ordered as to make neatly organized furrows or ridges in it. Spiritual plowing involves a renewal of one's mind through self examination. As we examine ourselves, plowing poses the questions of "'who am I,' 'what am I a product of?' and 'who has molded me?'" As we prepare the ground, we must be able to discern between good fruit or plants and harmful weeds. Very often, at various stages of growth, plants and weeds may resemble each other. A gardener must be able to discern between a healthy product and weeds that overgrow and choke out the more desirable fruit. The process of spiritual weeding involves the uncovering of and deliverance from those attitudes, thoughts and habits that have been hurtful or have hindered our growth.

Once the ground has been prepared, we must consider the seed. The spiritual seed is the overt and unconscious presentation of a specific message. In order to be a good gardener, we must be very comfortable with and knowledgeable of our seed. Planting seed must be deliberate and purposeful. The goal is to instill a commitment to attitudinal and behavioral change. Change is the harvest. Traditionally used to denote cause and effect from a negative standpoint, the old adage of "what you sow you reap" takes on a more enlightening meaning. Obviously, if we sow watermelon seed, we will not harvest tomatoes. We can expect a big green watermelon with red delicious fruit, as opposed to a red, citrus vegetable.

In like manner, if we sow negative spiritual seed, we will reap a negative harvest. Words are powerful because they are alive. Words that emanate from us are as living things, capable of penetrating a ground that has been steadily prepared to receive either good or evil seed. Most seed is scattered as opposed to deliberate and purposeful planting. As we scatter, some seed may fall by the wayside and be trampled underfoot. Other seed will take root, but weeds will choke it. Some seed will be eaten by the birds or destroyed by environmental conditions. However, some seed will get planted and will be fruitful. Therefore, sowing or planting positive words or messages will ultimately develop into blessings or positive results. (Matthew 13: 18-23)

Tilling is the process of cultivation. Cultivation brings forth improvement through care, labor and study. It is a period of refinement and enlightenment, whereby the attack on weeds is less intense, as we begin to examine "root causes." When we reach the tilling stage, we should experience a breakthrough that uncovers new solutions out of the context of our unique experiences. My spiritual backyard continues to enlighten me with fruit of spiritual wisdom. To illustrate, one summer, a co-worker gave me two small tomato plants which I planted in my backyard. This was a new experience for me. Right in the midst of some weeds, the tomato plants grew. Planted in two small feet of ground in a rather large yard, these two plants receive the most care, including sunlight, and fertilizer. One morning I observed seven olive sized tomatoes growing in the midst of the weeds. Implicit in this example is the spiritual truth that if we concentrate on our problems one at a time, we can STILL produce positive and fruitful results, in spite of the fact that we have several other problems. In other words, FRUIT CAN GROW EVEN WHEN SOME WEEDS ARE PRESENT!

The tomatoes grew because not only had they been nourished by the sun, weeded and fertilized but they had also been watered. Watering is that aspect of spiritual tilling that is characterized by nourishment, satisfaction and continued movement. Watering is a three-way flow from outside in and from inside out. While we become spiritually empowered, we will find within us a well of water from which our spiritual hunger and thirst can be nourished and satisfied. Watering equips us to establish a root within ourselves, so that our spirits become a consistent and reliable source of guidance and direction.

Finally, fruitbaring and pruning are both intuitive and practical. The field of our spirits should become like good soft soil through which we can run our fingers. Soft soil provides accessibility to the content of the most important aspects of our lives which is often deeply buried underground in the top soil of our intuition. This book is based upon the premise that we know more intuitively than we can rationally understand. However, from a practical standpoint, the Holy Spirit is never in a hurry to bare fruit in us. Fruit can be described as our dedication to a high pursuit of growth, character, wisdom, righteousness. responsibility, satisfaction and excellence. Fruitbaring and pruning go hand in hand because we must constantly cut back and eliminate excess foliage by submitting ourselves to the triune God. The one who bares fruit is the one who knows how to CURSE THE ROOT!

PART ONE: PLOWING

CHAPTER #1:
THE LANGUAGE OF THE SPIRIT

THE NATURE OF THE GROUND

Plowing is a fundamental preliminary step to planting seed--- a process which involves the steady and laborious breaking up of the ground by lifting and turning over the soil to bring the underground "top soil" to the surface. To reach the top soil, the gardener must first contend with the clay and the sand. In the course of our discussion, the ground or soil represents one's personhood. Many schools of thought propose that man is a three part being. Psychoanalysts like Sigmund Freud use different terminology to describe man's triune nature: the id, the ego or conscious mind, and the superego or subconscious mind. Psychoanalyst Carl Jung coined the terms the "shadow", the "persona" and the" collective unconscious." However, the scriptures refer to man's three parts as body , soul and spirit. The intermingling of the soul and the body is called "the flesh."

Regardless of the terminology, the general concept is that the essence of man is more invisible than it is visible. The outer body and its outward actions are all that is actually visible. We can see the dust or clay of the earth, the weeds and the fruit, but we cannot see what is underneath the ground unless we dig it up and turn it over. Underneath the ground, we will find roots. Roots run deep. They are the power source that give life to either weeds or fruit. They are the origin of all thinking, feeling, and believing. If we are rooted or grounded in a particular belief system, ultimately the root will bear fruit. To illustrate, it is written in scripture that the love of money is the ROOT of ALL evil. (I Timothy 6:10) In support of this adage, a lust for material things can rule a person's thoughts and feelings to such an extent that he or she will literally "DO ANYTHING!"

In keeping with our agricultural theme, the outward man is the clay of the earth. According to psychoanalytic theory, outward man has a dark side that is ruled by his lusts and passions. The nature of man's flesh is to be disobedient, willful, unruly, rebellious, hedonistic, in a constant search for immediate gratification of his senses. In other words, "I see it, I want it, I MUST have it." The body is instinctual--- motivated by biological urges and appetites that can only be temporarily appeased. KEY WORDS FOR THE FLESH ARE "LUST" AND "DESIRE!" However, man's outward nature is believed to be balanced by his inner nature of rational mind, willpower, emotions and feelings--- faculties of man that constitute his personality. As the instrument of our thoughts, the mind is the source of information, understanding and reasoning. Likewise, "I think, therefore, I AM!" The willpower is the faculty for decision making, with the power of choice. It expresses either willingness or unwillingness: ie. "I will or I won't!" The instrument for our "likes or dislikes, is the faculty of emotion. Without emotion, man is insensitive, and cannot feel joyful, angry, sad or happy.

As the seemingly endless stretch of a sandy beach point to immeasurable time, man's inner nature is an enduring and perpetual mixture of the world's influences, both parental, societal and cultural. As sand is a mixture of clay and bits of rock that have disintegrated over centuries, man's inner nature is also mixed with influences from his outer physical nature. The urges and appetites of the outer man combine with the thoughts, attitudes, beliefs and feelings of the inner man, producing such qualities as "self centeredness, selfishness, self exaltation, self pity, self loathing, self esteem, self love, self-hate, self gratification, self-recrimination, self-righteousness, self-satisfaction, self importance and self-seeking, to name but a few.

The inner man is the source of self consciousness. Two more names for the inner side of man is "THE SELF" or the SOUL." "THE SOUL" is the life that each human being lives. As the soul or inner man is joined to the body or outer man, it becomes man's "LIFE". Our lives are simply an expression of the common life shared by all human beings, that each of us receives at birth. All that this life possesses and all that it may become is a product of intellect, thought, attitudes, ideals, love, emotion, discernment, choice and decisions. These are but various aspects of the inner man ,the "SELF" or the "SOUL". As I have compared man to the elements of the ground or soil, we proceed further with this metaphor by comparing man's innermost nature to topsoil. As weeds can flourish in sand, so too can unhealthy attitudes and negative emotions produce and cultivate destructive behaviors. To produce good fruit, a farmer or gardener turns over in plowing both the clay and the sand of the ground to reach the top soil. Unlike the sand, top soil produces good fruit. The top soil of man's ground is his innermost nature. Without plowing under the clay and the sand, topsoil is invisible as it is buried. So, too, is man's innermost nature. Psychology refers to this side of man as the unconscious. Another word for the unconscious is "the spirit."

As the outer body functions with the five senses of sight, sound, touch, smell and taste, and as the inner body or "SOUL" senses with the faculties of reason, awareness and feeling, the innermost body or the spirit senses with balance, intuition, and creativity. The spirit is balanced in that it enables all persons regardless of age, race, gender, national origin, intelligence, education, or social background to begin where they are, and to progressively draw their lives into focus by establishing a personal relationship with God. The removal of demographic barriers offers a broader bond for identity that is not based on racial blood ties or on territorial affinities. In fact, the same opportunity for growth is available to empower each person. In the spirit, we can discover our life goals and purpose at our own timing and on our own terms. Unlike the soul, the spirit is intuitive because insights can be obtained and believed without visible evidence. Very often a person thinks of a certain activity that his mind tells him that he has a right to perform. For example, in our present day society, the tendency is to believe that sex is a right of every human being and that the sex act should be performed whenever one desires. The outer voice says "I feel the urge." The inner voice of the soul says "I desire it, I want it, and I'll do it." Yet somehow, in the innermost depth of his being, there seems to arise an unuttered and soundless voice strongly opposing what the mind, emotion or will has considered, felt and decided. If not deadened or muffled, the intuition of the spirit can come to one's aid with a sharp warning, that is totally in contradiction to the mind.

With a voice of its own, intuition has the capacity to provide wisdom, revelation and understanding from within itself. Thoughts, reasoning, feelings and emotions may run amuck with worldly opinions, making it difficult to tap the spirit's resources. However, taking time to ponder, dream and meditate can make one's innermost voice audible, making sense out of confusion. The innermost, unconscious side of man is creative in that the spirit carries the true seed nature of each person. Motivations, habits, and defense mechanisms are often unconscious and invisible. Nevertheless, through dreams and fantasies, the innermost nature of man has the capacity to creatively reveal and resolve the personal contents of life. Through signals and intimations, each person can become aware of his potential to overcome his current circumstances.

MY WALK IN THE SPIRIT

I began to study the language of my own spirit in 1974. Prior to that time, I had no conception of a "spiritual" side. In fact, I considered myself either an atheist or an agnostic. I did not believe in the existence of God, but I qualified my disbelief with an attitude of nonchalance. In other words, if it turned out that a He actually existed, I did not care. In 1974, I began to study and practice relaxation therapy, which is an introduction to hypnosis. Almost immediately, I was bombarded by spiritual experiences of various kinds. I believe that my practice of self hypnosis opened the veil to the hidden side of my nature in particular, and to the spirit world, in general. In the first three years, I documented in a diary about 3000 dreams. Sometimes I would dream, remember and document as many as 10 different dreams in a night .

In those early years, meditation, hypnosis and dreams were appetizers that stirred a hunger within me to know the truth of existence and creation. These appetizers also stimulated a desire to investigate the reality of life after death and whether or not God really existed. I began to study astrology into the wee hours of the night. Consumed by what I believed to be cosmic or planetary predictors of the course of human life, I initiated a study of the astrology charts of the deceased. Within the sample, emphasis was placed upon the lifespan of those who had died a violent death. On one particular occasion, I even went to the graveyard to obtain the exact date of a man's birth and death from his tombstone, in order to construct charts of these dates for my study. Later that same night, as I marvelled over the charts that I had constructed, a friend suggested that I try to contact my "deceased subject" in a seance. I laughed. I did not believe in such nonsense.

However, that very night I held my first séance in the summer of 1974, never expecting that I would enter into a supernatural realm of which I was totally unaware and ill prepared to contend with. As six (6) people,--- three(3) children and three

(3) adults--- gathered around my friend's dining room table in the dark, we began by making fun and nervously giggling. We thought we were playing just another parlor game. As we settled down and got quiet, to my amazement, when I raised my head and focused my eyes toward the center of the room, a spirit materialized in front of my face! It manifested in the form of a head of a man, at least 3 times the size of a normal human head. Its substance or essence looked like a thick cloud or a dark room filled with cigarette smoke. However, the "smoke" formed itself into a perfect shape of a man's head, with a "V" shaped hairline, sideburns, a chin beard, wearing an old-fashioned ascot around his neck. The room had been darkened by pulling the socket out of the walls while the lamp had been lit. The "head" could not be seen in a lit room. I inserted the plug in the socket and then removed it about three times. While the room was dark, the "head" remained. The third time that I darkened the room, the "head" disappeared suddenly. POOF!

At first, I was not afraid, only excited and amazed that my whole world of skepticism and unbelief was being turned upside down. However, as I lay in my bed in the dark that night, I began to experience a sense of apprehension. Finally I drifted into sleep, only to have an ominous experience that African Americans from the deep south have named "the haints." The "haints" is difficult to describe. Psychoanalysts would probably classify the haints as an episode of the "Three D's": disassociation, decompensation or disorientation. The haints feel like you are choking. A heaviness comes on you where you believe that someone is on top of you. I remember patting my body and the bed to see who it was that was smothering me. I tried to call for help. However, I had no voice---not even a whisper--- to give my call an audible utterance. This experience was so disturbing, that my only response was to pass out into a deep sleep. Simply put, I probably fainted.

Webster's dictionary contains two (2) words that are akin to the haints, namely, the incubus and the succubus. The incubus is defined as "an evil spirit that lies on persons while they are sleeping in order to have sex with them." The incubus oppresses women for sex while the succubus is an evil spirit that assumes female form,--- the stimulator of the so-called "wet dreams" of men. However, after I had fainted into sleep, the spirit that crossed my body that night identified himself in a dream as the spirit of the dead man whose astrology chart I had been studying. He gave me a warning. He said, "Let me rest. Leave it alone!" He did not have to speak twice. I GOT the message.

Notwithstanding, the very next day as I sat by the pool in an apartment house in Hempstead New York, I shared my startling experience of the previous night with two perfect strangers who called themselves Rosebud and David. At first, they told me that they were brother and sister. I later found out that they were not blood related. As our friendship became more intimate, Rosebud and David admitted that they had once been lovers, and now were platonic friends. Both of these people were Jewish. They listened to me with a kind of secretive, knowing ear. From their lips, I heard for the first time the term "psychic power." They invited me to their apartment to "test" the level of my "psychic power" with that dangerous toy called a "Ouija Board."

Almost immediately, two so-called deceased individuals began to move my fingers across the letters of the Ouija Board. Sophie McDonald and Mr. Voynich nicknamed "MR. V." teamed up together and became our spirit guides. Sophie had been a very close friend of mine while she lived--- a lovely, fun loving Irish grandmother who, as my secretary, had become like a mother to me. She had recently died of cancer. "Mr. V" was Rosebud's deceased father. Upon witnessing my effectiveness on the Ouija Board, Blossom and Richard suggested to me that I was a medium to the spirit world, and that the seance that I had amusingly held had unleashed the powers within me. My summoning of the dead was said to have opened me up to the deceased who dwelled in the spirit world by transforming me into a source for their communication. I did not know what a medium was, but I soon found out.

Within the next few months, this "unearthly spirit team" began to progressively take over all of my life. I did not think a thought or take an action without consulting Sophie and Mr. V. As time passed, the style of their communication went from the Ouija Board, to spiritual writing with a pen or pencil, to their coming into my body and speaking through me, by taking complete charge over my larynx. I remember the first time that I was "taken over" or possessed by them. I did not go into a trance. I was fully conscious but also totally out of control. One day, after an exhaustive session of spiritual writing, I began to feel dizzy and a little weak. There was also a tugging feeling in my throat. Suddenly, my spirit vacated my body and stood on the opposite side of the room, listening to a conversation that others were having about me. As I stood outside of myself, I can remember thinking "what in the world is going on here! Let me back into my body!" The spirits did not pay me any attention. This experience is very similar to the one portrayed in the movie called "Ghost", starring Whoopie Goldberg as Oda Mae. Like Oda Mae, these two (2) spirits leaped in and out of my body at will. One voice was masculine and the other was feminine. I had no control over these entities. They spoke and departed according to their own will. I could not call for them at my own will, nor could I make them leave.

After the mediumship, one experience seemed to follow another. Objects began to appear and disappear, less frequently as in the Poltergeist movie but with comparable methods. Not only did I travel astrally, but on occasion it seemed that I was transported bodily, car and all--with companions in the car experiencing the same phenomena. Each night that I slept, I would receive clairvoyant information about people, places and things. Through the writings and the dreams, the doctrine of reincarnation was revealed. Information was provided about my own past lives and so-called "karma" that appeared to be corroborated by my actual ancestral history. By 1976, I had

The Language Of The Spirit

left Hempstead, having returned to Albany New York. The powers came with me as others joined my intimate circle of Albanian psychics and mediums. One day, as I was involved in one of my "sessions", I moved into a realm where I came confronted by an angel of the Lord. By this time, I had been so flattered by my "spirit guides" that I was filled with ego, pride and vanity. My ambitious nature caused me to envision myself as some great psychic, of the caliber of an Edgar Cayce or a Jean Dixon. I had managed to acquire a few moments of glory on local radio and television stations, several years before the fame of "Psychic Network." I had also begun to conduct New Age seminars on dreams, hypnosis, astrology, reincarnation, telekinesis and mediumship when something new and different came forth in the writings.

I was used to words of flattery. However, on March 25, 1977, the writings declared that I was a materialistic sinner. With it came a quotation that later on I found out was in the bible. The scripture cited was "ALL have sinned and fallen short of the glory of God." (Romans 3:20) I protested vehemently with foul mouth cursing at the invisible beings, who or whatever they were. This was not my Sophie and Mr. V. This was some other being entirely. It was even suggested to me that I was headed for hell. I cursed back at the invisible writer something like "so what. If you think you have power over me, I challenge you to kill me."   At the moment that I spoke forth these fighting words, I will never forget what happened. I was in a ground floor apartment on Morton Avenue, directly perpendicular to Elizabeth Street. As I stepped out of the door, I saw a sunny sky turn dark and watched the wind violently stir up and blow down the hill all of the street litter, cans and bottles that was on the sidewalks. With a certain amount of fear and trepidation, I headed home.

I pondered the experience of mid-afternoon as I laid in the bed that night. I wondered why the spirits had so reviled me when they always stroked my ego in the past. I could not be a sinner. I was an expansive, generous and giving person. I didn't have a materialistic bone in my body, or so I thought at that time. However, once I went to sleep, I had a dream about Jesus Christ that far surpassed the 3000 of them that I had documented up until that time. It was particularly astounding because at this point in my life, I believed that the story of Jesus was a lie construed by the white man to keep the black man in bondage. For the sake of brevity the overall theme of this dream concerned His cross and His resurrection. In the dream, the Lord called me by name and said, "hand me my cross, please."

To further summarize the sequence of events that followed, the Holy Spirit so arranged my future experiences that I was put into a situation where it was brought before my face that not only was I materialistic, but that there was something in my inner nature that was defective. I was indeed a sinner. It was March 29, 1977. This revelation caused me to cry uncontrollably for several hours. I later found out that I was repenting. As I wept over the phone to one of my psychic friends whose name is Velma, I was confronted with the miraculous. Velma was not a born again believer. As I sobbed through my tears, I cried "Velma, this is not like me. I am crying and I don't fully know why I am crying. This doesn't make sense." She responded "you know why you are crying." "No I don't." "Yes you do." "NO I DON'T!" This dialogue continued until, out of my gut, I hollered out these words. "I AM CRYING FOR WHAT THEY DID TO JESUS!"

This explosive call for Christ that burst forth from my lips brought about an experience for which words are too restrictive to describe. Natural language is limited in providing understanding of a spiritual catharsis. What followed is that I began to utter a gasping sound akin to the sound of someone who is hyperventilating. With the sound came a set of contractions or "labor pains" that reminded me of when I had bore a daughter eight (8) years before. However, the seat of the contractions was not in my womb. It was in my gut where my dead spirit was located. What followed was the manifestation of a vision. I perceived a huge light, shaped into the form of a cross, shining brightly in my living room. I saw that light, shaped like a human hand , go into my body and induce "spiritual" labor.

As this experience proceeded, my friend Velma provided me with instructions while I gripped the telephone, very much like a coach in a labor room. She said "you are giving birth to your new spirit in Christ Jesus." Once my new spirit was birthed, she continued. "Go run a bathtub full of water. Baptize yourself in the name of the Father, the Son and the Holy Ghost." I did as she instructed. At the completion of my self-induced baptism in my tub, still in a state of joy that is difficult to describe, I sat down on my couch and picked up a bible that I had bought just a few days before. The book opened to the gospel of John, the third chapter which reads, "you must be born again. That which is flesh is flesh, that which is spirit is spirit."

How do I explain such an experience today? Over the years I have learned that each person's revelation of the Lord Jesus Christ is unique and special. However, most testimonies are not as graphic as mine was. Although each born again experience is supernatural, other than for crying or an emotional outburst, nothing physical usually transpires. However, since I had no minister to guide me nor a background in church or religion to inform me, the Holy Spirit used my own body to reveal to me the spiritual truth of rebirth. The Lord taught me by using my knowledge of physical childbirth. He used my very own body as a teaching tool to compare the experience of natural childbirth with spiritual birth in my very own body. As Jesus explained to Nicodemus the difference between natural and spiritual birth, by using my physical body the Lord taught me the same spiritual principle of "that which is born of the flesh, is flesh and that which is born of the spirit, is spirit!" (John 3:6) With my acknowledgement of my sinful nature and my confession of Jesus Christ as Lord that came from my mouth, faith came into my spirit and caused my mind to believe that what I had dreamed about four (4) days before was true. Jesus was crucified for my sins and He was raised from the dead.

After thirty years of "spiritual experience", it continues to be an exciting walk. As indicated, three years of my spiritual journey was a walk on the evil side of the spirit world, unaware of His divine guidance and direction, as compared to nineteen (27) years which began with partial and then full awareness of His influence. I realize now that the Lord was always there, even when I did not believe in Him. At times, the walk has been very dangerous. I stumbled into spiritual alleys and side streets that, without the protection of the angels of God, I might have either died or been institutionalized for mental illness. Of course, the first three years were the most dangerous for me. I was completely ignorant about spiritual matters, an ignorance that was complicated by the fact that I did not have a teacher to explain to me the nature of my "unusual" experiences. Furthermore, I had no faith or belief that there was a Power who could rescue me. There were three things that kept me both sane and alive. First of all, I was not prone to inebriation through drugs or alcohol. Secondly, I had an open mind. In other words, I believed that any thing was possible. Finally, there was a certain boldness and tenacity about my nature that kept me from being afraid.

My spiritual experiences have revealed to me that not only is spiritual development like a walk or journey, it is also like a garden. Just as seeds planted take time to bare fruit, the fruitbaring nature of spiritual experience is sometimes gradual and inexplicable. I defy you to try to catch the budding of a barren tree. It is impossible. One day in spring the trees are filled with twigs. Look away awhile. The trees will be filled with buds, and you missed it while it was happening. Although weeds may hinder the fruits' health and development, they do not stop the growth of fruit. However, once we commit ourselves to uprooting the weeds that have been planted in our minds, emotions, will, desires and attitudes, the spirit will become more empowered.

I HAVE A DREAM!

In the early stages of my spiritual walk, I learned that my spirit had a language of its own that was filled with symbols. For example, back in 1974, one of my earliest symbols came forth with a message of encouragement. It was a jar of peanut butter. I remember that I was in some trouble at my place of employment. I was to be confronted by a group of administrators who were conducting a hearing to investigate my part in the matter. Of course, I was concerned. The night before the hearing, I had a dream about "peanut butter." I saw myself sitting in the hearing, with a piece of bread and a jar of peanut butter in front of me. As I spread the peanut butter across the bread, I heard in the spirit, "SMOOTH, SMOOTH LIKE PEANUT BUTTER." I awoke with a feeling of confidence about the hearing. Things would go "smooth" for me, like peanut butter. It did! I was exonerated.

What did peanut butter mean to me? Well, in reality, I didn't like it, either smooth or chunky! I never ate it. I did not have a jar in the house. All I knew about it was that it came in two kinds: smooth and chunky! Peanut butter might mean something different to you. To me it means "smooth, clear sailing." This example brings me to my first point about certain symbols. Some symbols vary in their meaning based upon the life experiences of each individual. The most important goal is to receive the message. However, I have found in my experience that if a symbol is not understood, the spirit is creative enough to repeat the message either with the same symbol or a different one.

The "Peanut Butter" dream is an example of how the spirit deals with situations at the immediate surface of our lives where our immediate problems and circumstances are known to us. However, dreams also uncover subconscious levels of invisible experience that may hold the key to the resolution of the more deeper problems of personality and character. Consider yet another example. A man that I have known for several years revealed to me an interesting dream. He dreamed of a woman that he had not seen in ten years, with whom he had once been involved. The dream was outstanding because he found himself in her apartment, where huge pictures of himself were painted on the entire span of her living room wall. Figuratively, he was "bigger than life." As he discussed this dream with me, his attention was directed toward this particular woman, wondering if she could possibly still be in love with him after so many years.

When we do not understand the language of our own spirit, very often the Lord will direct us to someone who can interpret the symbols for us. I advised my male friend that the identity of the woman in the dream was not significant. She served merely as a representative of this man's attitude about women in general, and himself in particular. His spirit was telling him that he desired to be "BIGGER THAN LIFE" in the experience of ANY woman that attracts him. For years, I have observed how vanity and male pride remained a serious issue in this man's life. Even so, he refused my interpretation because it did not reinforce his own self perception. However, if my interpretation is correct, I am satisfied that until he accepts the message, this man will continue to have dreams that attempt to reveal to him the same meaning in a different form.

Many years of dreams have provided countless benefits. I have found that these benefits can be categorized in the following ways:

1. dreams that REVEAL

2. dreams that REBUKE

3. dreams that RESTORE

Dreams that reveal are those that inform, enlighten and explain. They can provide insight into personal motivations as well as the motivations of others. They can illuminate the meaning of our past, give us directions about the present and provide a glimpse into the future. A significant purpose of a revelatory dream is to present a symbolic meaning for our lives. When our spirits learn to translate the meaning of a symbol, dreams will be less metaphorical. In fact, dreams can be a helpful storehouse of specific, concrete information. For example, as described in the preface, I have receive five (5) consecutive dreams, over a span of ten (10) years, that have provided specific information about my overall purpose in life. Each dream was like an additional chapter in a book where the plot was unfolding, line by line.

Although dreams that rebuke can also reveal, their overall purpose is to present a reprimand in a way that urges, cautions, and/or warns in a dramatic style. The goal is to bring about correction. When the Holy Spirit chastens us, it is because He loves us. The more we run from the chastening, the more dramatic, even frightening the dreams may become. Every apparently frightening dream is not always a nightmare. Sometimes the Lord creatively confronts us so that we become motivated to become fruitful. This kind of confrontation is a part of the purging process. On an August morning in 2005, I myself was purged by an astounding dream. In a chapter entitled "Demonic Soul Ties" in my third book, "Faces of the Religious Demon: Unmasking the Spirit of Jezebel," I go into more detail concerning my marriage to a heroin addict. For now, to understand the dream, what you need to know is that in June of 2005, I divorced Richard primarily due to his continued abuse of heroin but I was still very much in love with him. Although I had some unconfirmed suspicions that he had been unfaithful, my ex-husband was not purged from my heart, even two months after the divorce.

So on Monday, August 8, 2005, I had a prophetic dream that clearly showed me that Richard had committed adultery. I saw him leap up hill into a tide of water, and when the water receded, he arose out of the water completely muddy. Underneath him, buried in the dirt, was a woman, also covered in mud. As I lay there in my bed pondering the meaning of this dream, the phone rang. It was Richard. I had not heard from him since he left the home several months before, so with the dream still fresh on my mind I listened to Richard intently. " Pam, you have been my best friend, my back up and I feel lost and empty without you. I really miss you. Why did our marriage have to end?" With a tear trickling down my face I replied, "There was something missing. I felt that you had another woman." His response? "Why is it that you women always blame another woman when things go wrong? It wasn't that. It was just the heroin."

After this very sentimental, heartfelt telephone conversation, I wondered if perhaps I had been too hasty. As I continued to lay in my bed, I thought to myself, "Pam, could it be that you should have given the marriage yet another chance?" Soon after I arose, about an hour had passed since this phone call when I walked into my spare bedroom, kicking a piece of paper that was on the floor. To cut to the chase, on the floor was a piece of paper—an application with a phone number on it, in Richard's handwriting. I had gone into that room on countless occasions since he had left the home and never once had I noticed this paper before. I dialed the number. It was the phone number of Richard's woman---a person who revealed to me that he had been sleeping with her for two years, while he was still married to me. Now, faced with the truth, I realized what I always knew in my spirit. Richard has always been an adulterous, deceptive and manipulative person. The truth revealed through a dream was the catylyst that broke the soul tie and I was immediately cleansed. Within one hour of the dream, I was shown that the divorce was spiritually justified and that the man that I still loved was not worthy of my continued devotion. The Lord knew that the true grounds for my divorce from Richard was indeed adultery and with this dream, He ensured that I would know the truth and therefore, never again doubt my decision to divorce him.

Rebuke and chastisement will bring both cleansing and restoration. As calm follows a storm and as growth follows pruning, we need to see the mountains when we are in the valley of the shadow of death. Dreams that restore provide us with strength, healing, assistance, help, support and relief while we are in the midst of hardships and distress. Such dreams help us not to fear evil, because the Lord is with us. To illustrate, in June 1994, I experienced a devastating setback in an important lifetime goal. I was removed as pastor from Dyer Phelps AME Zion Church, never to be reassigned to another AME Zion pulpit for the next 10 years. I believe that I was so depressed primarily because I did not know what the Lord was doing. So in August of 1994, I had a dream which showed me that God was going to intervene on my behalf and deliver me from Zion. He literally showed me that He would turn my adversaries "upside down" and set me free from their power and control. On June 11, 2005, I experienced the evidence of my 11 year stand in faith, waiting for the fulfillment of that prophecy. I was completely delivered from those who were hindering my spiritual path, a major subject of my second book, "The Making of a Prophet: A Spiritual Indictment to the Organized Church."" However, even without concrete evidence, for 11 years that dream continued to strengthen and support me.

Dreams are not the only language of the spirit. There are visions, as well as hunches. A hunch is an intuition or an inner state of simply "knowing" without "knowing why." However, understanding the symbolic meaning in our everyday experiences is another form of spiritual language that enhance spiritual perception.

SPIRITUAL PERCEPTION

It stands to reason that if God Himself is Spirit, it is understandable that He would communicate to the spirit side of our three part human natures. By comparison, our spirits are like His candles. The word of God says that the spirit of man is the candle of the Lord, searching all the inward parts of the belly. (Proverbs A candle provides light in the midst of darkness. Consider that our three parts are three adjoining rooms in a railroad flat apartment. When the front room light is lit, the middle and back rooms are dark. This is a good illustration of the condition of mankind. We are all familiar with the expression "the spirit is willing but the flesh is weak." The flesh is weak because of its perpetual activity. The front rooms of our flesh or bodies remains constantly "lit" with its continual appetites and labors. When the middle room is "lit", our mental and emotional lives are preoccupied with thinking and feeling. We are consumed with our likes, dislikes and opinions.

Most human beings spend the bulk of their time in the front and middle rooms of the house. However, those who are willing to let the Holy Spirit "light up" the back room of their spirits with His enlightenment and illumination, attempt to function at AA's step #11 and #6 with a higher power of the addict's choosing[1] The goal of Step #11 is to use prayer and meditation to "improve conscious contact with the higher power, praying only for knowledge of His will and the power to carry it out." In step #6, we seek God to remove our defects of character. Goal attainment of these two steps is to allow the higher power to communicate with enlightenment and understanding to our spirits. It is important to note that unless an addict repents, believes on the bodily resurrection of Jesus Christ and becomes saved, he will not be able to make contact with God the Father or receive the guidance of the Holy Ghost.

As our bodies have eyes and ears for the purpose of sight and sound, as we wear clothing to protect ourselves from inclement weather conditions and for the sake of modesty, our spirits have eyes and ears also. One who is spiritually blind cannot see or perceive His character. In this sense, sight is a matter of revelation and discernment. Those who are spiritually blind remain confused, misleading others. Similarly, one who is spiritually deaf cannot hear the voice of the true and only Higher Power. If you cannot hear His voice, then it is impossible to know His will.

The eleventh step of A.A. suggests that we can choose how we want to understand Him. It is clear that confusion is built into this step. Created in God's image, even we human beings desire to be understood correctly and not according to the expectation or notion of others. The triune God is not different from us in this regard. If we want to improve our conscious contact with Him, then we must know and perceive Him as HE IS and not as we believe Him to be, for He is the Great "I AM" and not our "YOU ARE!" He is who He declares Himself to be in His word. Consider the words of Watchman Nee as he enlightens us of our need for spiritual perception if we are to know God at all:

There is a knowing of the Lord Jesus which comes from human instruction; such knowledge is accounted null and void by the Lord. Only the knowledge of the Father concerning the Lord Jesus is a true knowing of Him. And God alone can impart such knowledge to men. For this reason all who have not received such revelation from the Father have never known the Son. No man can come to the Father but by the Son, and no man can know the Son apart from the revelation by the Father. This revelation from heaven is absolutely necessary. (Nee, pg 47)

If we cannot understand God the Father without a knowledge of His Son and vice versa, we will not be able to manifest His will in our lives and we will remain spiritually naked. To be spiritually naked is to have our most outstanding personality or character flaw exposed by His light. We will not gain the maximum benefit of Steps four(4) and five(5)[2], if the Higher Power does not cause us to stand spiritually naked before Him. Many times our moral inventory of ourselves is limited because we cannot recognize the nature of our spiritual clothing. We cannot know the exact nature of our wrongs if we do not discern the style of our clothing.

Therefore, if we want to know what ails us, we need first to recognize our most prominent weakness. Most likely that weakness is barely visible, as it is either subconscious or preconscious. Let us go back to that three (3) room railroad flat. Picture that there is a veil or curtain up between the third and second rooms. The veil is the clothing or covering on the spirit---the symbol of our most prominent personality trait. If you want to know the nature of a person's spirit, you must first recognize his or her most prominent spiritual feature. It will stand out so conspicuously in the spirit that regardless of every effort to clothe or hide it, the triune God can see through the veil. It is transparent. The spirit is naked.

For example, the inner and outer nature of a proud or vain person can be successfully hidden from himself and from others. Such traits can be clothed in a demeanor that is so mild, sweet and pleasant, that the true nature of his personality remains hidden. The sad reality of spiritual nakedness is that the person does not know that he is naked. To illustrate, consider an older gentleman that I once knew, now deceased. Because of his age, his appearance and the quality of his voice, every time he was described, he was called "humble." He has also convinced himself that he was humble. However, I believe that his desire to control other people was at the center of all of his actions. In fact, he was the least humble man that I ever knew. This brings me to the importance of motive toward understanding one's spirit. Motive is the driving force that reveals our spiritual nature. Just as a district attorney searches for a motive to convict a defendant, the motive is the key to spiritual perception and discernment. As a serial killer may have a recurrent motive, so does the spirit of man. A spiritual motive is a recurrent, repetitive spiritual theme that is at the root of every action that the soul persuades the body to take. Anyone who remains ignorant to his or her primary spiritual motive is spiritually blind, deaf and naked.

Contingent upon the extent of activity of the flesh and the soul is the spirit's ability to receive God's enlightenment and translate His knowledge and wisdom to the soul and the body. This is why most religious systems emphasize various forms of meditation. Meditation slows down the activity of the soul and the flesh, causing the spirit to become more receptive and active. Hypnosis is a more intense form of meditation where the activity of the spirit passively responds to the direction of the hypnotist. It is my belief that hypnosis is dangerous because it is the most blatant example of the "blind leading the blind." Since the hypnotist is blind to the invisible world of the spirit, he cannot see where he is directing his subject. It is like a blindfolded man leading a crippled person who has lost his wheelchair across a dangerous highway. The cripple sees the oncoming truck, but he cannot get out of the way without his wheelchair. The blindfolded man could get out of the way, but he is handicapped without his vision to see oncoming traffic.

To avoid such danger, it is important that the spirit not be handicapped by passivity. To be empowered, the spirit must have clear vision. It must be able to distinguish between good and evil. It must be able to engage, encourage and enlighten the mind. Our spirits must be able to engage our will to choose God's will above our own. Therefore, meditation should be active. We are not obligated to obey the Lord mechanically. Instead, we must choose and do His will in full and conscious awareness. Even if we are unaware of His will, our spirits must be free to decide to choose His will. In and of itself, such a decision will be enough to empower our spirits to know the will of the God intuitively, allowing our spirits to govern our flesh.

Motive also foreshadows the success or failure of deliverance and recovery. For example, a recovering substance abuser must avoid a tendency towards self love. I have found in treating those in recovery that too strong a motive to be alcohol or drug free has led patients to become so self absorbed that they end up in "self-love" or indulgence. For example, within their anxiety to remain alcohol free, their thoughts endlessly dwell on their own symptoms. Countless hours may be exhausted thinking about their own sobriety that they find no time to meditate on God or on what He may desire to accomplish in their lives. Likewise, within the cycle of addiction, an excessive concern for oneself may cause a person to become addicted to his sickness. We must ask ourselves, " If all we desire is that the Higher Power deliver us from pain, are we really being led by Him?" Therefore, prayer, meditation and fasting should actively concentrate on entreating the Lord to:

1. open our spiritual eyes and ears so that we can perceive our true condition before Him;

2. reveal to us the language of our own spirits that we may know His will; and

3. provide us with His strength in our spirits to choose His will, once we know it.

CHAPTER #2:
THE SOUL AND THE FLESH

I THINK, THEREFORE, I AM!

As previously indicated, the sand is a metaphor for the "self" or "soul", consisting of the mind, the emotions, and the will. As the sand changes according to environmental conditions of wind, sun and rain, the mind, emotions and the will of the soul also change according to intellect, feelings and desires. Where the mind is concerned, a though is a means to activate one's intellect. The intellect is the seat of reasoning.

As the body has a built-in system to eliminate wastes, the intellectual activity of the mind controls our thoughts. Thought life is extremely important because our personalities and characters are reflected in the way we think. The more steadfastly we fix our minds on a particular thought, the thought then becomes "an imagination." The stronger the "imagination," the closer we come to taking the action that the particular thought suggested. We can determined how close we are to making a mistake by monitoring our thoughts. In most cases, the innermost voice of the spirit will break through to the mind and tell us not to take the particular action we were about to take. However, if we are out of touch with our innermost selves, we will generally yield to the thoughts of our mind.

If our reasoning is defective, our thoughts can manipulate us in a negative manner. For example, consider the person who thinks: "I can have more than one sex partner because HIV infection will not come upon me." Such a thought will bring about an action that will ultimately produce an unexpected weed. Rationalizations and justifications are the products of an unrenewed mind. In such cases, we make excuses for ourselves by blaming others. In order to correct the thoughts of our minds, we must take the following actions:

1. open our intellect to examination by being honest with ourselves;

2. stop a thought in mid-stream and analyze it;

3. change the words of our mouths;

4. say "no" to that thought, out loud if necessary.

People who negotiate life through their minds are very often confused or "double-minded." A double-minded person is unstable in all of his or her ways. (James 1:8) Such a person will use the world's standards of money, status, clothes and of course, sexual prowess to prove to himself that he is valuable. A double-minded person compares himself to others. He has a "grass is greener on the other side of the street" mentality, and therefore, is never satisfied. This lack of satisfaction causes such a one to place impossible demands on the people who love him or her. He also seeks to fill his inner unrest or dissatisfaction with temporary sexual fulfillment. Furthermore, the double-minded will minimize or exaggerate the facts when discussing his sexual life.

People who are double-minded also tend to be procrastinators. They "reason" that something that ought to be done now, can be done later. Such a person will stay in an unsatisfying relationship because he is so consumed by his thoughts that he is out of touch with how he really FEELS. For example, his thoughts tell him that he should not forsake the present relationship until he has found a romantic replacement. "A bird in the hand is better than one that is in the bush." Out of touch with his emotions, the "double-minded" will reason in his mind that he is "in love." His feelings become so disguised, that he loses the ability to be genuinely affectionate. The thinker reasons that to be emotional is to be too "soft". In an effort to emotionally survive, he may hide his real self from others. Such behavior creates an emotional blindness, where the doubleminded person is out of touch with his own true feelings. For example, the "macho" image is rooted in masculine hardness as a way to avoid painful feelings. The thinkers need to rediscover their emotions by quieting their thoughts long enough to feel what they need to feel.

In order to renew our minds, there are some key points that should be underscored:

1. <u>We are what we THINK we are.</u> Our thoughts have power to draw both positive and negative energy. If we have practiced negative "self talk", in the same manner, we should consciously practice positive "self talk." Positive thought will bring forth positive talk. Positive talk will bring forth the fruits of victory and success. (See Part V,)

2. <u>A part of renewing the soul is to learn how to deal with what is uncomfortable.</u> In keeping with the metaphor, sometimes the sand is very "HOT" and it is difficult to walk on it. Struggles and failures supply the necessary preparation. We must learn to picture in our minds a positive outcome in "all things." Where deliverance from demonic oppression is concerned, torment can be a blessing. Torment wipes out the delusion that "all is well" and

caused the tormented one to search for answers and solutions---reasons that he would never have even considered if he had not desperately sought to be released from torment.

3. Once we discover what we need to learn about our own inner struggles, there are other people who will need our testimony and our influence so that they too can be victorious. A major purpose of struggling is that we can become consolers of those who are struggling in those areas where we have become triumphant. By planting new seeds of power into our minds, old patterns and habits will be destroyed. In a metaphorical context, the seeds are the "words of power."

"I FEEL, THEREFORE, I AM!"

The soul is the "sandy side" of our nature --- a mixture of the emotions, the mind and the will. A person who acts from the emotions cares neither for principle nor for reason, but only for his feeling. Under the power of the emotions, the mind becomes undependable. With a powerless mind, we cannot distinguish between right and wrong. Consider the person who tries to collect his emotional debts from the opposite sex because someone of that sex hurt him in a previous relationship. In this regard, some men hate all women because their mothers hurt them. Similarly, some women hate or distrust all men because some man in their past hurt or betrayed them, ie, a father, brother, friend, etc.

Rooted in emotional dysfunctions, repetitive scenarios become habitual re-plays, where similar patterns evolve in every relationship. Unable to break this emotional cycle, the emotionally disabled person cannot trust other people and therefore does not make lasting commitments in a relationship. It is difficult for such a person to accept love from others. Whether real or imagined, feelings of victimization or rejection

The Soul And The Flesh

will lead to a need to victimize or reject others. To obtain victory over such feelings, it is important to develop other parts of the soul, particularly the mind. To instill rational thinking, you as the caretaker of your own spiritual empowerment and recovery should realize that very often those that we are hating are not even thinking about us. They are simply moving on to a new conquest, and literally having themselves a "grand ole time."

The primary message in this book is that behind every outward manifestation of weakness or dysfunction, there is a ROOT CAUSE. It should also be understood that at times the ROOT CAUSE for our behavior may be GROUNDED in emotional conflicts that are not even conscious to the person who has them. For example, those who have been "love starved" may habitually behave in different ways in relationships, according to the nature of their emotional obsession. While some such persons may focus on themselves exclusively, and expect others to be focused upon them also, others FEEL so unlovable that they need a "fresh fix" of strokes every day just to feel good about themselves. SEX BECOMES THE "FRESH FIX!"

Then there are those who try to earn love by what they provide or give to their love object. Sometimes such people will stay in unsatisfying, painful, humiliating or otherwise unhealthy relationships only so that they can continue to remain sexual with someone. For "the love starved" person, sex has become an emotional crutch, crucial to survival. Such a person is self effacing, lacks confidence and self esteem, and continually denies his or her own needs and interests to satisfy the love partner.

If we trace the course of our lives and work back to its root, we fill find that our desires are behind those behaviors that have been the most self destructive. In order to satisfy our desires, we planned, plotted, schemed, and connived with every ounce of our minds, emotions and willpower. Both our intellect and our emotions remained in constant turmoil. As we struggled to obtain our desires, other people hindered us from our goals. People's inconsistent affections and changeable affirmations worked together to induce depression. When people and conditions strived against our desires or things did not turn out exactly the way we planned, we may become disturbed. When life seems unjust and unreasonable, we may become angry. Since emotions can be easily stirred, provoked and wounded, the question then becomes, "how do we handle our emotions?" First of all, we should recognize that when our emotion is negatively influenced by our surroundings, our lives will undergo a negative change. Only when we have conquered being swept away by our various emotional tides, will we become empowered to achieve a steadfast and consistent life. If we can quell these feelings, we can triumph over our surroundings and cope with changeable people and changing circumstances.

The positive side of our emotions is that they serve to stimulate and motivate action. Strong desire can be the impetus for change. However, if we depend on emotion to stir us, we will become immobile and ineffectual when we become weary, despondent or lacking in feeling. Our former behavior which was corrected during the period of energetic feeling will return to us, as the change was not permanent. Without the high emotions to motivate us, we will lose interest and adopt our former ways. Responsibilities go unfulfilled.

The way to victory is to establish a value system or a set of principles that will be followed regardless of the emotional situation. Since feelings generated by our emotions are so changeable, we should never take any actions during highly emotional times. Moreover, we should not allow any external force to create any feeling in us that is against our will. If we follow the leading of strong, negative feelings, our whole being will learn to thrive on these sensations, our willpower will be paralyzed, and our minds will become undependable.

"I CHOOSE, THEREFORE, I AM!"

Anyone who makes decisions either by the influence of the mind or the emotions is usually weak in his or her will. The will is the organ that examines, distinguishes, judges and makes decisions based upon the information received from the mind and the emotions. Choices can be enduring and immutable. Unfortunately, we can make the choice but we cannot choose the repercussion. Consider the aftermath of a choice of 15 minutes of sexual pleasure. The fruit of such a choice may produce the life altering consequence of HIV infection. By not allowing our thoughts, attitudes, opinions, habits, feelings and emotions to dominate and control us, we can learn to use our wills to resolve, choose, refuse and resist.

Loss of control is a major issue in the cycle of addictive behavior, where pleasurable feelings temporarily obliterate both physical and emotional pain. However, I received a new revelation on human willpower as I watched a documentary on the changing sexual habits of people living in the "AIDS GENERATION." My attention was drawn to the statements of a young man who gave an account of a sexual encounter in his recent past wherein he was deeply entrenched in the web of foreplay and the throngs of passion. However, when he reached for a condom, the female in question told him that she was against their use. At the point of vaginal penetration, this young man reported that he pulled himself back and discontinued all sexual activity.

To understand his choice, I reflected upon those principles involved in this man's victory over his passions and his emotions. I asked myself, "does this young man have a stronger willpower than the average person, or are there fundamental principles of a person's life that move beyond the surface level of strict discipline toward enhancing or strengthening one's willpower?" Considering the young man in this particular sexual situation, some basic truths about willpower were revealed to me about this man's belief system:

1. He BELIEVES in free love or casual sex.

2. He BELIEVES that HIV/AIDS is life threatening.

3. He BELIEVES in the effectiveness of the condom to prevent HIV infection.

4. He will not take a chance with his life, as he VALUES living MORE THAN he VALUES the heat of the moment.

It would appear from this example that a key element of having control over our will is to have a STRONG BELIEF SYSTEM. What we believe has a strong influence over choosing what actions we will take. This young man believed in promiscuity and therefore, did not hesitate to engage in sex with a perfect stranger. However, the key to the victory of his willpower was the limited nature of his options. Without a doubt, he viewed himself in a life or death situation. He had to choose life or choose death. In his mind, there were no other choices. For a non life threatening sexually transmitted disease such as herpes, he might have engaged in sex without the condom. However, he viewed AIDS as CERTAIN DEATH. When faced with death, the willpower does not have to struggle to make a choice. A quick, life-saving choice is imminent.

It is clear that one of the hindrances to the functioning of the willpower is our deceptive belief that we have "more time." Since physical death appears to be "far off", our willpower can more readily procrastinate and take chances. However, when death is a daily reality, we can learn to live toward prolonging our lives. The key is to maintain a balanced perspective about life and death. Although reminded of death daily, we can live without fear of it as we make the choices that will prolong our days. The key to whether or not we choose to live vigilantly or recklessly is determined in part by the extent of our priorities. Continuing with this example, sex was high on this man's priority list. Notwithstanding, his desire for long life was higher than his desire for sexual pleasure. Even when his

The Soul And The Flesh

passions brought him close to sexual climax, his willpower was strengthened by his DESIRE to live, and by his BELIEF that the only other option to prevent HIV infection was the use of a condom.

Even so, this man is still playing "Russian Roulette." Suppose the condom was to break during the sex act? Is his faith in the infallibility of the condom realistic or justifiable? What if the condom did not exist and abstinence or monogamy WERE THE ONLY OPTIONS? As options diminish, so do the available choices. Anyone who values life to the extent that his willpower can rise above his passions and subdue them is also capable of either abstaining or restricting sex to one partner who has been tested for HIV and who is trustworthy. Whether or not he is willing to make such a choice will be determined by what he believes. Those who believe that like thirst or hunger, sex is a biological drive that must be satisfied will find it more difficult to choose abstinence. IN ORDER TO STRENGTHEN OUR WILL POWER, WE MUST CHANGE OUR THOUGHTS, BELIEFS, OUR PRIORITIES CONCERNING WHAT WE BELIEVE, AND OUR ATTITUDES TOWARD LIFE AND DEATH.

"I SENSE, THEREFORE, I AM!"

In regards to life and death situations, our physical bodies are the vehicles for our whole life history. Our bodies are the temples of all human experience. While the meaningful aspects of our lives may be carried out in our thoughts and emotions, we can do nothing on this earth without a body of clay. Our inner life, including our minds and emotions, and our intimate relationships must pass through the clay of our flesh to reach fruition and completion. The life history of our bodies reflects as a mirror the life history of our thoughts, feelings and willpower. In this sense, our emotions, minds, and willpower are closely linked to our physical bodies. Very often, our bodies, including its various parts and functions will give us clues, insights or warning signals about our inner nature.

Those who are hot"headed", or bull "headed" are thought to be angry or stubborn. The neck and the posterior together comprise the seat of irritation for those who represent pain to us. The emotional term "pissed off" is directly related to inflamed kidneys. When we are "foot" loose, we are said to be "fancy free" or carefree. The ache in our shoulders may tell us that we are baring too many burdens. Then at times when we have run out of patience, our stomachs tell us that we are "fed up."

Within a similar framework, what we do with our bodies sexually also gives us clues into our inner nature. Sexual promiscuity leading to high risk for sexually transmitted diseases not only raises questions about how we treat ourselves physically, but also the level of inner meaning found in our outer sexual lives. For example, those who have no boundaries where sex is concerned may find that sex is their primary source of understanding and purpose, where life in general is perceived as boring and meaningless. For others, sex may mask a rebellious nature, ignoring and defying the values that they perceive as being set by those who have been unloving and judgmental.

In truth, everything in the seen world has a meaning in the unseen world. I believe the unseen world is the true world. As a case in point, we can't see the wind or the air, yet we can't live very long without it. As a microscope can reveal to the naked eye invisible atoms and cells to the physical eye, the unseen world of the spirit can reveal to our conscious minds the meaning of physical symbols. Therefore, the things that are seen are only symbols of that which is unseen or undiscovered.

The world of the spirit is where the godhead resides. For the sake of discussion, everything "spiritual" belongs to the unseen world of the Holy Spirit. If this be true, then it logically follows that if the unseen world is more real than the seen world, then everything in the seen world represents something in the unseen world. For example, if man was made in the image of

God, then our physical body is a symbol of His spiritual body. Likewise, our physical bodies are visible symbols of what our physical eyes are unable to see. Following this argument, the next supposition is that if we study our physical bodies and its various parts, we will get a better understanding of the qualities and nature of the Lord. Invariably, if I look on you, I should be able to comprehend some aspect of Him, and you should be able to perceive God when you look upon me. The major physical difference between a male body and a female body is the difference found in our sexual and reproductive organs. Therefore, if man and woman are created in the image of God, then God must be equally masculine and feminine. Therefore, when a man and a woman use their respective sexual organs to come together, they become one body or "one flesh". It then would follow that the sex act is a visible symbol on earth of the invisible God in His character and completeness as both a masculine and feminine being.

If we agree that the Lord God is light devoid of darkness and that the He is love devoid of hate, and that He is good devoid of evil, then we would clearly understand the kind of sexual behavior that would most honor Him. In this context, the term "honor" would be defined as that behavior that would best portray the true essence of His nature. The Lord demands His "images" or his symbols to accurately portray His nature and character. Consequently, any sexual act indicative of darkness, hate or evil would clearly be exposed as a behavior that is dishonorable to how the Lord intends to be revealed. We know that a symbol is a concrete, visible example of something that is difficult to explain, because it is either invisible and/or abstract. The visible thing or symbol explains, defines or stands for that which is invisible. Sometimes we say that something is "like" something else in what is known as a simile. A simile compares the relationship between the visible and the invisible. A metaphor is a stronger likeness in that the invisible thing is said to BE the visible thing.

The Bible is filled with both similes and metaphors to enable us to understand spiritual truths, particularly as they relate to sex. For example, fornication, or sex outside of matrimony, is viewed symbolically as idolatry. Those who go "a whoring" are metaphorically classified as idolaters. Idolatry is worshipping gods other than the Father, the Son and the Holy Spirit. Furthermore, the terms associated with whores, whoredoms and whoremongers are "lightness, lewdness, defilement, pollution and wine." (Jeremiah 3:9, 13:27, Ezekiel 16-17, 23:17, Hosea 4:11, Jeremiah 3:2) Whoremongers are also called "dogs" and "sorcerers". (Revelation 21:8, 22:15.) Consequently, if illicit sex is the worshipping of idols, then it would seem that sex within a marriage that has been joined by God is a positive form of worship toward the Lord. If the trinity of man---spirit, soul and body---is the temple of God, then any activity we undertake with our temple is a form of worship. According to scripture, our bodies are members of Christ and therefore, we must flee fornication which is spiritual idolatry. (Corinthians 6:13-20) Therefore, the sex act is an important symbol of serious regard to the Almighty, as it represents His relationship to His creation.

PART TWO: WEEDING

CHAPTER #3:
THE "I AM!"

As previously presented, the soul is the seat of human personality and consciousness. It acts as a mediator or "middle man" between the spirit and the body. Simply put, the soul is the seat of the self or the "I AM." Although each human personality has some innate or genetic characteristics or predispositions, the "I AM" has been trained by habit, experiences, and cultural or societal opinion. Moreover, even though the "I AM" may appear to have a mind, feelings and a will of its own, much of its makeup has been defined by those from whom the most messages have been computed or internalized in within socialization as controlled by the predominant world view.

Weeding is a spiritual process that involves self-examination and discovery, whereby we uncover those attitudes, thoughts and habits that have been hurtful or have hindered our spiritual growth. The weeding process loosens the hard soil of our soulish nature by digging deep into our spirits. Weeding draws up experiences that may have been tightly packed and hidden beneath layers of denial, procrastination and rejection. The center of weeding is the human personality. Basically there are four "different" personality types or categories: the leaders, the thinkers, the feelers, and the workers. Although most people have elements of all four types within their personality, usually one or two sides is predominate. For example, the leader who is also a feeler will tend to be dramatic, emotional and charismatic, while "a leader" who is "a worker" will be down in the trenches, working with the people. To illustrate, Dr. Martin Luther King was a unique personality because he strongly demonstrated all four types. A dynamic and fiery leader, he was an not only an intellectual and a rational thinker, but he exuded the emotional and caring side of the feeler. A willing worker, Dr. King would also be at the head of every march, enduring incarceration with the rest of his workers who were implementing the his overall plan of social, economic and political justice. He was rare because most people are strong in one (1) or two (2) personality types while he was equally strong in all four areas.

A positive trait of "the leaders" is that they tend to be less driven to seek the approval of others than the other three (3) types. Their pioneering and courageous spirits cause this type to set the pace or the standard that the other three (3) types follow. Because their nature is dynamic and adventurous, they are also people who are more capable of adjusting to change. They tend to be independent, extroverted, outgoing, and are willing to take risks. The self-esteem, boldness, and confidence they manifest attract others to follow them. On the negative side, their risk taking nature causes them to make hasty decisions. They can be impulsive, impatient, self centered, rebellious, and unwise in their choices. Their major downfall is PRIDE. In sexual matters, pride can lead to behaviors that are geared toward maintaining either a reputation or an image. Maintaining appearances may be more important to the "leaders" then gaining the approval of others. VANITY is another stronghold in the "leaders" personality. In some cases, "leaders" will find themselves remaining in a self-destructive, unfruitful, and even a dangerous relationship simply because the love partner either idolizes or esteems them above all others. Moreover, when negative, the "leaders" are usually not concerned about the needs of others or whether or not others genuinely care for them. They may also attempt to dominate or control their partner. When they don't get their way in a relationship, they may become vindictive, argumentative and even violent.

The thinkers are usually excellent communicators, for they can generally articulate or express in words their deepest thoughts. Unusual and creative, the thinkers create the ideas or concepts that the leaders commit themselves to oversee. Philosophical and insightful, the thinkers tend to analyze and debate. They can also be people who emphasize long range planning because they seek to focus on a purpose. Such people are also deliberate and circumspect in making decision. Nevertheless, when negative, the thinker can be argumentative and contentious---a "know it all" who cannot be reasoned with. Those thinkers with a "gift of gab" can be manipulative and conniving for they believe that their thoughts are higher and more intelligent than those of others, and that their ways are higher and more skillful than the average person. In other words, a thinker can take his or her partner "for a fool." Thinkers tend to have long range plans. Where love and romance is concerned, they may rationalize that a particular person fits their "romantic" or "sexual" ideal and therefore take risks in a relationship because they convince themselves that they are fulfilling their long range goals. Such distortions of reality can lead to impaired thinking. Impaired thinking of this nature may include denial, rationalizations and self-justifications that open the doors to lies and deceit. The thinkers major downfall is their desire to MANIPULATE.

"The feelers are intuitive, profound and mystical---qualities that make them more susceptible to their innermost nature that we have called "top soil." Humble and introverted, the"feelers" are more skillful at self analysis than the other three (3) types. In this regard, they are more sensitive to an expansion of consciousness through which they have the capacity to move into deeper levels of "inner knowing", bringing unconscious perceptions into everyday reality. They are capable of feeling intuitively what someone has the capacity to become. This visionary ability helps them to live in the "here and now" because they have hope in a brighter future.

However, the "feelers" also may be pre-occupied with the visionary, as they seek to move into the outer limits of non-reality and remain there. The euphoric state of drug addiction enhances this desire, where the "feelers" prefer to live in a state of mental and emotional intoxication, simply because their emotions are too painful and therefore become unbearable.

In such cases, the "feelers" may depend upon sex and drugs as a comfort from pain, for nurturing, or to cope with stress. Sex becomes the primary source of need, for which all else is sacrificed. Prone to feelings of worthlessness. the negative emotions that may be out of control can be shame, depression, and despair. "Feelers" are also susceptible to emotional "highs" and "lows". On one hand, sex may bring both feelings of exhilaration with corresponding guilt and self recrimination. The feelers can also be self-righteous, manipulative and falsely humble. They can make any of the other three (3) types into "the bad guys." Feelers are often proud of their self-effacing nature, considering themselves better than other personality types. Readily embracing the role of the "VICTIM' and driven by a need to be the one that others love to abuse, the unforgiveness aroused by hurt feelings will block spiritual empowerment and recovery.

As would be expected, the workers are the people who "get things done!" When positive, they are determined, precise, organized, practical and disciplined. Self-willed starters, they are committed to a task until it is completed. Decisive, they also know how to say "yes" or "no." Practical commonsense and worldly understanding is the calling card of the "worker." Having done all to stand, they can fight adversity and troubles with their ability to "hang on" during hard times. Since they can get things done, the other three (3) personality types depend on them. Looking neither to the right or to the left, like the proverbial "work horse", these people steadily push themselves forward with specific goals as their challenge. The "workers" measure themselves by a standard of inner satisfaction and outer excellence. To the "worker", completing a task implies strength of body and character. The "worker" enjoys involvement in a task or a relationship that is believed to be valuable. Similarly, self satisfaction is sought in a job well done.

In spite of these positive traits, the worker can be one who works just for the sake of keeping occupied or "busy", without a fruitful goal or purpose. Furthermore, the "worker" tends to develop a method or a way of doing things that is not easily changed. These folk can be headstrong, inflexible and stubborn. They can also be dull and single-sighted, working in life merely for the sake of being occupied. In love relationships, the "worker" is one who is susceptible to "co-dependent" relationships, usually with a partner who is less productive or self sufficient as him or herself. The "worker" is the person who ultimately becomes the provider, the supplier, the backbone, the shoulder to cry on, the "all in all" to someone who is shiftless, lazy and undisciplined. The worker gains satisfaction by bringing manageability to the life of someone who is out of control.

An opposite affect of the "worker" is when sex becomes a means of escape from the routine of daily life. In such cases, the out of control partner serves as a reckless fling for "the worker." The "worker" may also reward himself by frequenting prostitutes or engaging in episodic and compulsive sexual acts. In addition, the structured, practical personality of the "worker" is not easily susceptible to introspection or self examination. What this type cannot see, does not exist. Therefore, the "worker" remains out of touch with his inner and innermost nature.

Notwithstanding, "the worker" has difficulty breaking old habits and seeking new relationships. Convinced of the righteousness of his or her own situation, "the worker" rarely leaves an unsatisfying relationship. The worker's downfall is that the positive aspects of his or her personality such as STABILITY and DEDICATION can emerge as RIGIDITY AND IGNORANCE.

BREAKING THE "I AM!"

Jesus Christ calls us to His cross that we may be re-socialized by Him, through the Father's sending of the Holy Spirit. Therefore, it is imperative that the "I AM" be broken before it can be spiritually empowered. Re-socialization is a humanistic term for rebirth of the spirit and the renewal of the soul. As previously established, God is a spirit or "spiritual" in nature. His thoughts are not our thoughts and his ways are not our ways. For this reason, steps two and three of AA's recovery principles requires that we first come to believe that a Power greater than ourselves can restore us to sanity.[3] As a result, our belief in His superiority and authority compels us to a decide to turn over our will and our lives to His care.

Such a commitment is easier said than put into practice. Our "I AM"'s are very strong and rebellious. We are accustomed to attempting to solve our own problems. Even though we may have failed many times, the tenacity of each "I AM" will struggle against the Higher Power, because the soul thinks "I know more about myself than God does. In spite of our weaknesses and foibles, we have become used to them and in some cases, we even admire the very traits about ourselves that continue to keep us defeated. Notwithstanding, the things that we believe in and admire about ourselves may be the very things that the Lord finds abominable. Conversely, the things we may detest in ourselves may be the very traits that the Lord considers admirable.

In the earliest stages of our relationship with Jesus Christ, we will find that His purposes and goals differ from our own in several respects. In spite of our best efforts to line ourselves up with His will, there is very often little to no consensus between such an important matter as the nature of what needs to be changed within us. Therefore, the Lord strategically sets out to break the outer shell of the soul or the "I AM", so that the spirit can be released to agree with His will. In keeping with the analogy of harvesting ground, weeding can be painful. Yet once we yield to the process, it becomes less and less painful. In our efforts to avoid pain, our spirits will "kick against the pricks". Psychology call this kind of "kicking" a defense mechanism. In simple terms, a defense mechanism is the creative, device of the spirit to avoid the pain that truth brings. We are all familiar with the term "the truth hurts." According to psychoanalytic theory, a defense mechanism operates on an unconscious level.

In Chapter 2, it was established that the unconscious or the invisible belongs to the realm of the spirit. Consequently, the spirit has developed its own set of strategies by which to blind itself from the truth and to protect the soul from the pain of self discovery. Repression and projection are but two of the defense mechanisms that attempt to enable the soul to avoid the truth. Repression is the spiritual force that deceives the emotions of the soul by saying "all is well when all is NOT well." To protect the mind of the soul against the anxiety of responsibility, projection is a spiritual state of denial that operates by blaming other people and circumstances for virtually everything. In each individual case, it is the task of the Holy Spirit to break the power of the spirit's unconscious defense mechanisms that protect us from the truth of God's ways and purposes. Very often, it is difficult to yield because we do not understand the Lord's methods of breaking or weeding.

When the hand of God is upon us to break us, each personality type will struggle with God in its own unique manner. The feelers will cry, have temper tantrums, and organize a pity party. They cry, "Why me, why me, why me!!!!" However, the unheard response of the Higher Power is "Why **NOT** YOU!"

Ultimately, the breaking of the feeler will bring them to a point where in spite of how we feel about, we surrender to God's intents and purposes. After the thinkers have done their share of complaining, they tend to either bargain or compromise with the God in an attempt to "negotiate" a solution. If the Lord will just ease up on the breaking, then the thinkers will put forth a number of possible solutions for His consideration. The negotiation process will involve an elaborate system of trade-offs in an attempt to avoid making a change.

In a perpetual attempt to figure God out, the thinker will end up in a state of confusion and anxiety. This condition that has been purposefully designed by the Holy Spirit to cause the thinkers to realize that "His thoughts are Higher than our thoughts." (Isaiah 55:9) When the thinkers arise out of confusion, they arrive at a place where they learn not to depend upon their own intelligence and knowledge. The thinkers become spiritually empowered when they are able to submit every thought and imagination to the test of whether or not their ideas and opinions are compatible with the will of Jesus Christ.

The leaders not only offer solutions, but will demand that their course of action be followed. Struggling to have their way, the Holy Spirit will set up roadblocks to frustrate them. The leaders will find that in spite of their every effort to lead, to succeed and to prosper, they end up in the midst of failure. They will be brought to a low estate. Normally high in self esteem, the leaders will begin to examine and question themselves. The Lord's goal for leaders is that they become less dependent upon themselves and more dependent upon Him. They must learn to trust in Him. They must master how to be comfortable at "the back of the line," instead of always having to be up front. They must learn how to be content not always having to speak "the last word." They must realize that others have as much or more to offer than they do. They must also realize that serving others is the mark of true leadership.

The workers also must be broken to the concept of serving and working. The Holy Spirit will bring them into situations where they realize that through Him alone, can they do all things. They must discover that they are not self sufficient. They must learn that they need others to complete God's will and therefore, they will be placed into situations that require collaboration and cooperation. As the hand is not more important than the foot, they must learn that one form of work is not better than another. The Lord will also confront the workers so that they can become more patient, less stubborn, more tolerant, and less judgmental and critical. Very often, workers are broken by being placed in situations where they are constrained to submit to authority. Ultimately, incarceration is conducive to growth in this area. The worker must also learn how not to be distracted by his own purposes in order to put the work of Jesus Christ first and foremost. In such cases, the Lord will confront personal ambition, the meaning of success and the love of money. Life experiences might include unemployment and even poverty.

Much effort can be saved and spiritual growth can be obtained if we give up the struggle and submit ourselves to the breaking. I can recall a significant example from my own experience, which will serve as a prelude to the next lesson. I myself tend to fall under all four (4) categories and therefore have had to endure more breaking than the average person. However, my breaking as a worker is a good example of the persistency of the Holy Ghost.

In the early years of my career in state government, I was extremely ambitious. Even though my nature was not conducive to the requirements of politics, my goal was to one day become a director or a commissioner. It took me three periods of unemployment for it to finally dawn on me that this was not the Lord's purpose for my life. As soon as I would gain some stature at my place of employment, I would be laid off from excellent jobs with career potential: first for six (6) months, then for another six (6) months, then for nine (9) months, and finally for fourteen (14) months! While unemployed, I learned how to trust Jesus Christ in times of want as opposed to trusting in my own abilities. I also learned how to yield to authority. It is interesting to note that once the necessary lessons of trust and humility had been mastered, I have continued to be employed at that particular job for seventeen (17) years. However, the series of experiences that I have learned over time have provided information concerning my overall purpose in life.

In matters of relationship, the Holy Spirit will often use our experiences with significant others, particularly with the opposite sex to break us in several areas. Three outstanding personality traits that require the Lord's breaking include: esteem, pride and vanity. The breaking of these three characteristics is very important because a life of self confrontation is an open door to CURSING THE ROOT!

ESTEEM, PRIDE AND VANITY

Breaking is not a process for cowards or for wimps. As a hitman in the underworld is contracted to bring someone to the death, the surrender of ourselves to the Christ is like the surrender of a "mark" to a hitman. There are easy deaths and there are hard deaths. Some marks may struggle and put up "a fight to the death" battle. Others may beg for their lives and try to reason with Him. However, in spite of the pleadings, battles and defenses, the ultimate term of the "hitman's" contract is death to the mark. A famous expression of the hitman is "this is not personal, its only business."

What are the characteristic of the hitman? First of all, he is a relentless stalker. He diligently studies his mark's habits and ways. He also selects the environment and chooses his weapons. Since stalking is a steady, laborious and gradual process, the hitman is thorough, meticulous and purposeful. However, once he has set his timetable, he strikes suddenly.

In these respects, God operates like a "Hitman." He knows us down to the number of hairs on our heads. In fact, before we were conceived in the womb, He knew us and had already established a grand design or purpose for each and every individual life. Therefore, we can throw Him no curves and no surprises. The Lord's blueprint for our spiritual development has been strategically plotted. Toward accomplishing His purposes in us, He carefully places various seemingly difficult experiences in our path to develop us according to His own timetable. Much of His breaking of us is gradual while some breaking is sudden, resulting in immediate inner change. Similar to the worldly hitman, the Lord offers us easy deaths, but sometimes, like a battery, we choose to "die hard."

However, God's contract is not just business, but it is highly personal. His intent is to develop and use each and every one of us for His own personal pleasure and satisfaction. Therefore, He sets out to remove the stumblingblock or hindrances to the completion of His contract by putting to death three personality traits that are endemic to all of us, namely; esteem, pride and vanity. These three traits are powerful hindrances because they pull us in the opposite direction from the will and the work of the Holy Spirit. Once the Holy Spirit is either quenched or grieved, our spirits become blocked from God's revelation about our future and from His power to cause us to be successful. As pride goeth before destruction, failure will be imminent. (Proverbs 16:18)

When we consider esteem, pride and vanity as a triune entity, we find that their commonality is that all three forces involve our relationship to how we are perceived by others. To be esteemed is to be in high regard in the thoughts, opinions, beliefs and feelings of others, while self esteem is a high regard for selfhood, as defined by how we are received by others. As pride is excessive self esteem while vanity is excessive pride. Therefore, I classify them in a trinity.

That which may be highly esteemed among our family, peers, friends and our social setting may be an abomination to God. We insult Him when esteem causes us to seek the support and approval of others and to adopt their ways, when their ways are contradictory to His. Esteem has some additional negative qualities:

1. it is outraged when others think that they are superior;

2. it causes us to defend and justify ourselves;

3. it causes us to tear down others in order to build up ourselves; and

4. it causes us to hunger for prestige by seeking the praise and approval of others.

Motivated by our longing to be validated by others, esteem will lead to pride. Pride is deceptive because it misrepresents our thoughts and feelings in order to put forth a façade or an act. Pride is also easily hurt or injured because it is always insecure. Other facets of pride is that it:

1. will block us from experiencing genuine feelings of love and commitment; in fact pride will cause us to deny our feelings;

2. will lead us to "front" before our enemies in our efforts to appear to be in control;

3. will cause us to over compensate and be over-confident, hindering us from success;

4. will prevent us from admitting that we need help and therefore block us from crucial resources;

5. will bring us into danger because we can't abide an insult or a slight. (Don't dis ME!!!)

It is foolish to lie to ourselves. As vanity is excessive pride, a vain person's conceit will bring about self deception. Self deception is a doorway to failure. Others will recognize our weakness and flatter us to our disadvantage. Vanity is foolish because it anchors itself in features of the flesh that are fragile, impermanent and transient. It causes us to live in the past, by placing value on that which is empty and fleeting. In matters of the heart, a vain man or woman will take such pleasure in his or her physical attributes, that he or she will be blinded to what is truly valuable to maintaining a lasting relationship with a significant partner.

When we enter into a meaningful relationship with another person, the Holy Spirit will take advantage of every opportunity to use the relationship to break or put to death esteem, pride and vanity. Until we receive the breaking, we will repeat the same mistakes in relationships. Take for example a woman who continues to select mates who eventually mistreat her in the same way. What seems to hold her in such relationships? A deeper inquiry will uncover that it was not the sex. It was not a need for companionship or intimacy. It was that each man flattered her vanity regarding her sex appeal, causing her to live in an empty image of a "femme fatale" that men just can't live without. Her vanity has blinded her spirit from a relationship with the Lord. Therefore, He will use people and circumstances as a refiner's tool to chisel vanity from her spirit.

In spite of the Holy Spirit's pulling up of our weeds from their very roots, weeding does not nullify His consolation, His comfort and His restoration. Unlike the worldly "Hitman"'s contract of death, our death or breaking is followed by life and empowerment. Once we decide to humbly receive the results of His breaking, His Spirit will be able to flow through us unhindered, and we will be able to accomplish all things through relying on His power. By losing all confidence in our own self esteem, we will gain His esteem. We will not be tossed to and fro by pride and vanity because He will cause us to be unmovable, unshakable trees that are rooted and grounded in

Him. His act of consolation will serve as a confirmation that He can be trusted in every crisis, every temptation and trial. Then He will fulfill a general purpose that He has for ALL of us: THAT WE BECOME CONSOLERS OF OTHERS THAT ARE LIVING THROUGH THE VERY THINGS THAT THE LORD HAS HIMSELF DELIVERED US FROM!

THE BREAKING OF AFFECTION

All of us are aware of the Ten Commandments. I would draw your attention to the Almighty's strong command that we have no other gods before Him. Who are these "other gods?" A simple definition would be "any person, place or thing." He requires of us that we yield our affection to Him totally and to allow Him to rule over our affections. In AA steps #1-3[4], we yield and surrender ourselves to the Higher Power because we have found out that we are out of control, and we seek Him to bring sanity into our lives and restore us. We turn over our will and our lives over to His care, primarily because all others have forsaken us. However, by the time we get to this point of complete surrender, we have probably lost our families, friends and loved ones, and we have no one else to turn to, but the Lord.

In such instances, we have yielded to the Him in fear and trembling, yet we still hold on to our affections. We made drugs, alcohol, sex and riotous living our "lover" or "god", while the Almighty was relegated to last place in our affections. When our lower "god" forsook us,--- stole our health, strength, sanity and freedom,---we crawled to the Lord for protection, recovery and safety. If He were like us, He would look at such a one and say, "so, you come running to Me, now that your former lover has abused you and you expect Me to take you in!! Ha!! " Insult is added to injury, in that the Higher Power knows that we would run back to our former lover, knowing how badly we were treated. Why? Because we are still compelled by them. Therefore, the Lord Jesus Christ requires those who are His to reject what we ourselves cling to because it divides our affections. He demands complete and total love from us. He demands that we love Him with all aspects of our being, spirit, soul and body. We cannot even reserve a tiny bit of affection that we ourselves direct. As a jealous God, He calls for ALL. He cannot tolerate any competition. Our ALL must be given to Him.

It is important that we understand that our loved ones can hinder our spiritual growth. If we are to experience God's power manifesting itself through our spirits, we cannot harbor a secret love outside of His approval and permission. As we continue to love that which is outside of His will, we will find that God will gradually lose significance for us. Surrender to Jesus Christ is what I refer to as the thirteen step to spiritual empowerment. For me, the term "thirteenth step" symbolizes any enlargement of or divergence from the Twelve Steps of AA. If we want to be spiritually empowered, there are three (3) things we must not do:

1. <u>We should not love Jesus Christ for the sake of our loved ones.</u> In such cases, the loved one has the power to rule our decisions. Today our loved one may agree with our Higher Power. However, one day that same loved one will cause us to abandon Him.

2. <u>We should not allow our loved ones to so excite our emotions that we develop an anxious or disquieted spirit.</u> If this occurs, we will find ourselves striving to obtain their attention by impressing them. A "fatal attraction" will kill our spirit by diminishing our desire to draw near to the Lord.

3. <u>We should not seek from another human being what only Jesus Christ can provide.</u>

There is an emptiness in every person that can only be filled by the Lord Jesus Christ. That emptiness is our longing to know the purpose and meaning of our existence. No human being can give you a lifetime purpose.

So, what then? Am I saying that the Lord does not want us to love other human beings? Of course not! However, He wants us to allow Him to manage and control our love for others. Consider Adam and Eve. In making my point, it is not necessary that you believe that mankind originated from these two persons. Whether truth or allegory, I use these two as examples to drive home the point that God wants to manage our emotions. Eve was given for Adam's pleasure. They were told to "go forth, be fruitful and multiply." In other words, romantic and sexual love was ordained by God. However, the first two humans were to serve as a check and balance to each other. Their love was not to be within their own control, surpassing the love that each one of them had for their Creator. So when one of them made a mistake by yielding to temptation, the other should have chosen to love God by being obedient to His word. When Eve was deceived into disobedience, it was up to Adam to renounce her for the sake of his love for His Creator. However, Adam esteemed Eve more than he love God. Adam should have realized that an almighty, omnipotent God could have created yet another mate for him.

Inherent within sexual and romantic love is the capacity to be so drawn to the will of the partner, that we are led by our affections to chose the wrong path, even when we are fully aware that the path we have chosen is not within God's will. In such cases, we choose our loved ones over our love for Him. Therefore, to be spiritually empowered, we must be able and willing to chose God rather than man or woman. When the Holy Spirit is in control of our affections, then we will love what He loves. God does not want us to love others because it pleases us, and therefore, we love others for what they bring to our lives. No! Our natural affections---our likes and dislikes---do not play a part. Jesus Christ will maintain control over our affections because we have allowed Him to rule over us. Then when He wishes us to love someone, we flow with His wishes, finding ourselves loving someone that we formerly would have found unattractive. Furthermore, when He desires that we terminate our relationship with someone, we can do this also.

How do we come to a place where we love for the Lord's sake alone? As the Gardener of our souls, the Holy Spirit will begin to break us through the weeding process. He may strip us of that which we hold dear. This may happen in various ways. Very often, God the Spirit will cause our loved ones to change their affections toward us, making it impossible for us to love them. Under the overall supervision of the triune God, the angels of Lord will set up obstacles in our everyday experience. For example, our loved ones may move away or even die. Regardless of the particular set of circumstances, sometimes the triune God will deprive us of every human relationship so that He can be the only One left for us to turn to.

I have had several such experiences in my life. I grew up not being a very popular person. I was used to not being loved by large numbers of people. However, once I became a young woman, I had one central affection. I desperately wanted to find my soul mate. It was an affection which I later found out that stood between me and God. This affection clouded my judgment and caused me to be blind to God's purpose for my life. Once I became partially aware of my purpose for my life, I attempted to combine my goals with His goals. In this regard, when I found out that I was called to be a minister, I decided that my purpose could only be fulfilled as a minister's wife. I could not perceive my own life separate from a mate. An erroneous assumption can be a stumblingblock to spiritual growth. It was not until I surrendered my affection to Jesus Christ, first and foremost, that I became empowered within my spirit. In her book "War on the Saints" written almost a century ago, Jessie Penn Lewis provides a sober warning on how demons can masquerade a divine counterfeit within a believer's affections:

The false personality caused by evil spirits can also be in a beautiful form, in order to attract or mislead others in various ways, all unwitting to the person or to the victim. This is sometimes described as 'unaccountable infatuation,' but if it was recognized as the work of evil spirits, refused and resisted, the 'infatuation' would pass away. It is so wholly apart from the action of the will in the persons concerned that the work of evil spirits is clearly to be recognized, especially when the supposed 'infatuation' follows supernatural experiences. (Penn-Lewis, pg. 1 29)

THE BREAKING OF DESIRE

We are traveling toward our purpose. However, we have become accustomed to trave ling alone, without a map. We have been walking for a long time when we come to a crossroad. Now we must make a decision. Our usual pattern is to select the road based upon our desires. Desire will be strongly influenced by our feelings and emotions. In the meanwhile, the Holy Spirit has a rather detailed travel plan and map. He knows exactly the road that needs to be taken if we are to find our life purpose. However, we are used to traveling independently. Therefore, desire and the emotions will form an alliance to oppose the will of God. We cannot be spiritually empowered until the Holy Spirit has performed His deeper work and our desire has been broken.

Every trip that we venture is a mission or a voyage to find our life purpose. However, the natural or human desire of our souls can cause us to live and die and never discover the hidden meaning of our lives. This natural desire stems from a love of self. Even when we desire something for someone else, our desire is self motivated in that we are usually expecting an outcome that will somehow benefit "US"! A simple example would be a sister who strongly desires that her older sister get married. Her desire seems to be motivated toward the happiness of her sister. However, deep down within is a desire to have the sister's room once she has moved out of the parent's home. Very often, we are not even aware that our desire, even for others, is so self interested. This same sister in our example is probably unconscious of her rather self centered motivation that has cloaked her hidden desire for self. In short, all of our aspirations, regardless of how apparently noble they are, cannot escape the influence of self.

Desire gives power to self esteem, pride and vanity. We desire a position or a place for ourselves so that others will think we "have the juice." I watch people who are name droppers, and those who boast about not only who they know, but about such assets as their education, heritage, abilities, and good looks. They love to display themselves, both to see and to be seen. These people always strive to be up front. Others have to notice them. Their desire for adoration, appreciation and self respect is what motivates and inflates them. You can observe these people by the way they walk. They are usually late to everything because they want to make an entrance. However, the words they say out of their mouths always gives them away. Generally, they will say something that is unnecessary to the general overtone or theme to the conversation. For example, when they leave your presence or hang up the phone, all that is necessary is to say, "I've got to go" or some such closing. But they are so moved by their desire to impress you with their self importance that they will add some additional, yet irrelevant information that will tell you that they "are somebody." For example, they might say something like, "gotta go. My housekeeper lost the key to the house and she won't be able to clean for me tomorrow until I get her a new key."

The more we become spiritually empowered, the more real we will become before others because we will have lost the need to impress them. Once we have been united with the Christ, we will find ourselves at rest. No longer will we be concerned about what others think. However, this lack of concern for public opinion is neither anti-social or rebellious. Having removed all pretense, life becomes relatively simple. Within my "thirteenth step" to spiritual empowerment is the mastery over our desires. To have no expectations, no requests, no ambitions other than to submit our desires to the Lord's will is the easy yoke. Jesus calls us to come unto Him, "all ye that labor and are heavy laden and I will give you rest. Lay your yoke upon me for I am meek and lowly of heart."(Matthew 11:28) Once we surrender to the Lord our cumbersome and arduous attempts to impress others with our self importance, we will appropriate His peace into our lives.

When the desire of our soul is broken, we find ourselves standing in the center of a satisfied life. If we cherish nothing but the Lord's will, our attitudes will be directed by Him. I find that I am so filled with satisfaction, that I have no personal requests to make before God. When I was ambitious, I had no rest. I was constantly discontent. I'd take a certain road, thinking that my desires would be fulfilled. However, shortly thereafter, I found myself wondering about the "road not taken", wondering "what if" this, and "what if" that. Yet, when I'd return to the other road, I'd find myself equally dissatisfied. In this regard, someone might think that I have neither ambition nor desire, and therefore, that I have become complacent and dispassionate. That would be further from the truth. I am still very ambitious and my desires are very strong. Notwithstanding, I have found all of my needs are fully met in Jesus Christ. I passionately and ambitiously desire WHAT HE DESIRES FOR ME!!! The Lord's desires for me are far above my ability to conceive within even the wildness of my own imagination.

How did I get to this point, having been an extremely ambitious, stressful, impatient, dissatisfied, self seeking woman? I believe that my desires gradually became renewed once the Holy Spirit began to give me snapshot glimpses of my future, primarily through dreams. Gradually, I became even more consumed with His desires for me than for those desires that I had for myself. Flashes like TV commercials began to parade themselves before me. As a result, my focus began to shift. Like a fisherman, the Holy Spirit casts the bait. We watch the bait, then salivate. We try to concentrate on some other thing, but then our attention is drawn back to the bait. Once we grab for the bait, the fisherman reels us in, and we are His. In this example, the bait is His will for our lives, or our purpose for living. Through the leadership and guidance of the Spirit of truth, God's will for my future is continually revealed to me.(John 16:13) As a person who is constantly being renewed, I believe the primary reason why I can change so readily is because the Lord continues to send me dreams in the middle of the night that change my desires in the morning!

Desire is very important because it is the power that energizes us to accomplish our goals. Just as a man without desire for a woman cannot conceive a child with her if he is impotent, we too are incapable of conceiving our purpose without desire. In order to renew our desire, very often, the Lord will lead us through frustrating circumstances. He will break us by causing us to be unaccepted by the people we are trying to impress. He arranges things so that we won't fit in with the crowd. However, once conception takes place, then our desire is directed toward nurturing the pregnancy. Once labor begins, our desire must be such that we can withstand the pain of childbirth and deliver the baby. Just as it takes physical power to deliver a baby, it takes spiritual power to seek after our purpose. Once our purpose is revealed to us, this discovery brings with it the power necessary for us to labor through to experience delivery. The natural delivery during childbirth is symbolic of the manifestation of our purpose.

Planting seed is another good illustration of the process of finding our purpose. Before a seed can become a fruit bearing tree, it goes through a time of preparation that includes both nurturing and upheaval. Much of the upheaval we experience is induced by those people around us who desire that we remain the same. People will try to distract us with their own desires. Our desire to discover our divine purpose has to be stronger than the desire of "our crowd" to hold us back. In these circumstances, natural desire will fight against spiritual desire. We manufacture an enormous amount of physical power to develop our relationships---a power that has the ability to destroy our peace, our joy and our relationship with Jesus

Christ. Therefore, our desire must stay fixed and focused so that we become empowered to fulfill the overall plan of God.

THE BREAKING OF FEELING

When we feel hungry, we realize that we should eat. When we feel cold, we know that we should put on a coat or find shelter in a warm place. Therefore, the feelings of our senses point to needs and conditions by directing us toward solutions. Just as we become adapted to the meaning of our physical senses or feelings, we must also be aware of our feelings in the spiritual realm. In the same manner, we must come to attach the correct meaning to the feelings that emanate from our spirits in order to learn how to guard ourselves. There is a proverb that says, "he that can rule his spirit is better than he that can take a city." (Proverbs 16:32)

Crucial to controlling our spirits is the ability to understand the way that our spirit habitually operates. Some of us function almost totally in the realm of natural feeling or sensations. For example, in a quest for masculinity, men have lost touch with their feelings while women have wasted their feelings in a cycle of emotional self-indulgence. Moreover, people who are in recovery have experienced the pendulum sway of moods and feelings during the consistent cycle of seeking pleasure and avoiding pain. The real "power" in empowerment evolves from being able to face our weaknesses so that we can find our real strengths. However, this process is blocked if we attempt to avoid the pain that plowing and weeding brings. No real growth and self understanding comes without pain.

If we are to function in the spiritual realm of feelings which I have called "spiritual sensitivity", we must overcome sensations that emanate from the soul and the flesh. Feelings of rejection, loneliness, unforgiveness and unresolved anger can lead to depression and negative attitudes. Ambivalence of this kind will attack our spirits and do it great harm and damage. At times, these sensations will feel like a heavy weight or an overshadowing dark cloud. As a heavy weight, negative feelings are an albatross around our necks, pulling us down each and every time. As a dark cloud, feelings can blocks us from the truth about ourselves, blinding us to those areas of our lives that work together to bring about our defeat. They can also give us false messages about people and situations. The more our natural feelings are broken, wisdom and discernment will increase, wherein spiritual sensitivity will encompass the cooperation of our natural feelings and emotions with God's purpose. Since natural feelings are both transitory and preferential. The Lord Jesus Christ's goal for our feelings is threefold:

1. that we choose to act beyond the original level of our natural feelings and emotions, by doing what is RIGHT, in spite of how we FEEL;

2. that we are able to discern the "real" condition of others; and

3. that we are moved to care for others as He cares for them.

Moreover, the Holy Spirit will use adversity to move us beyond the power of our natural feelings into the dimension of spiritual sensitivity. As a case in point, the emotional trauma of abusive relationships can destroy our feelings and block their accuracy. God's goal is that we learn to find comfort and rest in the midst of trials and tribulations. At times, He will keep us in situations that are impoverished, humiliating, and disappointing. Why? So that we who are broke, busted and disgusted will rise up to victory. Self indulgent "woe is me" pity parties will continue until we submit to the Lord's instruction on how to develop emotional strength in the midst of adversity and unpleasant circumstances. The Holy Spirit will exercise our innermost resources within us so that we will grow stronger and stronger with each failure, with each rejection and with each mistake. Consequently, we will learn how to be victorious in the midst of every situation.

An important element of spiritual sensitivity is the capacity to not only assess our own condition, but to spiritually discern the needs of others. For example, the Holy Spirit has gifted me to be able to place my hands upon a person, and feel within my own spirit those hidden feelings of the person touched. If my own natural feelings were not under control, I would not be able to distinguish my own feelings from those of the person in question. I have also acquired the ability to touch the Lord's heart and know how He feels about a particular matter, and in so doing, find that my own natural feelings have been dramatically changed.

I can still vividly recall the first time that my feelings were transformed. Shortly after Christ became my Lord and Savior in 1977, I had a supernatural experience of forgiveness and cleansing that is difficult to describe. In 1977, I counted several people as my enemies. Strong anger and bitterness were my soul's constant companions, and up until that time, I relished my hatred and my intense desire for vindication against my adversaries. But early one morning as I moved from sleep to consciousness, I felt like I was literally levitating about a few feet above the top of my bed. One by one, the faces of each of my enemies supernaturally travelled toward me on an invisible panoramic screen. As each face approached me, I could hear words which emanated from deep within my gut cry out, "I forgive you." My subsequent actions were totally incongruent with my former feelings of hatred, bitterness and vindictiveness. With an exhilaration that was beyond my normal state of being, I entered into a state of joy that motivated me to visit my worst enemy,---a woman that had seduced my first husband from me. The woman stared at me as though I was crazy. She knew the extent of my former rage because my husband had rejected my daughter for her two (2) sons. This experience taught me that the Lord can transform us from being a victim of abuse to an empowered survivor and overcomer.

Spiritual sensitivity is accurately defined in "Living in the Presence" by Tilden Edwards:

"The purest discernment is the simplest. Sometimes we are such open channels of grace that we spontaneously say or do something for others that is completely uncalculated. It is only afterward that we realize by the fruit of our actions that it was just what seemed called for. It may have been so uncalculated, so missing in any kind of self-image mediation, so self-forgetful, that we were not even aware that we had said or done anything of particular significance."(Tilden, 1994,p 99)

Sixteenth century Spanish mystic, St. John of the Cross poetically illustrates the renewal of feelings and emotions in his work entitled "Dark Night of the Soul", translated by E. Allison Peers:

> In poverty, and without protection or support in all apprehensions of my soul---that is, in the darkness of my understanding and the constraint of my will, in affliction and anguish with respect to memory, remaining in the dark in pure faith, which is dark night for the said NATURAL faculties, the will alone being touched by grief and afflictions and yearnings for the love of God---I went forth myself---that is, from my low manner of understanding, from my weak mode of loving and from my poor and limited manner of experiencing God, without being hindered therein by sensuality or the devil. THIS WAS A GREAT HAPPINESS AND A GOOD CHANCE FOR ME; for when the faculties had been perfectly annihilated and calmed, together with the passions, desires and affections of my soul, wherewith I had experienced and tasted God after a lowly manner, I went forth from my human dealings and operations to THE OPERATIONS AND DEALINGS OF GOD. (E.A. Peers, 1990)

Clearly, sixteenth century thought embraced as a truth the devil's obstructive role in the emotional and sensual realm. Demonic evil was not a mere archetypal image or a light fantasy of our present day Halloween, but a fundamental premise---a natural concept, firmly rooted in reality. The negative forces of demonic activity as hindrances to spiritual empowerment and recovery are referenced throughout this book. Where the emotions are concerned, It is obvious that negative feelings are conducive to demonic oppression. Such emotions can lead to addictive behavior, and other self-destructive acts. The mystery of the power of a negative emotion like hatred upon others is alluded to in the scriptures, for "whosoever hateth his brother is a murderer..." I John 3:15. A profound account of how a person's spirit can be used to harm another person without his conscious awareness is found in the book "He came to Set the Captives Free", by Dr. Rebecca Brown:

Hatred is a conscious sin. As such, it gives Satan legal ground in our lives if we permit it to dwell in our hearts. If you hate someone, Satan can step in and use your spirit body to attack the person you hate. Such an attack can produce all sorts of illness, accidents, emotional problems, and even physical death. The person doing the hating usually is never aware that Satan is using his spirit body. The person being hated usually has no idea where his trouble is really coming from. That is why we must be so careful to ask Jesus to cleanse and keep pure all three parts, body soul, and spirit. That is why the Lord Jesus gave us so many commands to forgive one another. Forgiveness puts a stop to hatred. We Christians should ask the Lord regularly to clean out our hearts of any sin. (Brown, pg, 177)

I can personally attest to the power of my own hatred. The supernatural forgiveness that I received from the Holy Spirit toward the woman previously mentioned who had seduced my first husband may have delivered me from being a spiritual murderer. However, two years before my spirit was cleansed and made new by the blood of Christ, I was probably a spiritual arsonist. For five long years, my hatred of this woman caused me to imagine her destruction by fire. Countless times I would repeat the same deadly image in my mind. I'd watch myself walk up her stairs with a vessel filled with gasoline in my hand.

Methodically I would see myself pouring the gasoline along her steps and under her door. I'd light the match. I'd drop the match. Finally, I'd wait with anticipation for the screams. Upon this deadly vision, I meditated almost day and night for five years.

During that fifth year, I was living in Hempstead New York and my enemy was in Springfield Massachusetts when I learned that she her house caught on fire, and she barely escaped with her life, while I was physically 200 miles away. As soon as I heard the news, I shouted with victory, "I DID IT!" Jumping from her window to safety, my enemy broke all the bones in her feet ---a condition requiring several operations, from which she still suffers even twenty years later. I believe that my hatred of this woman was so powerful that hatred gave Satan the authority to use my spirit body to attack her.

Notwithstanding, emotions and feelings come in a variety of expressions that are not always negative. Emotions can be both frustrating and exhilarating, bringing us from the mountain top to the valley in a quick, unexpected leap. At these times, there is a temptation to live by our feelings rather than by our spirit. When our emotions continually vacillate between positive and negative extremes, an open door is provided to the evil one to equip our sensory organs with physical sensations that counterfeit the true spiritual sensitivity that emanates in and through our spirits from God. In such cases, the devil will offer us sensual pleasures that cause us to lose control. If a believer remains ignorant of demonic devices and strategies, he may fall victim to a compulsive euphoria or similar elation and become deceived by false visions, dreams and revelations. These supernatural experiences will appear to be from the Holy Ghost but after the passing of time. will subsequently be proven to have been sent by the enemy. Satan's goal in this instance is to cause sincere believers to sink into a dark, gloomy depression, believing that their own lack of discernment is proof that they do not have the capacity to know the voice of the Lord.

In spite of Satan's deception, there are seven (7) kinds of feelings in our spirits that we will be able to recognize when we become spiritually sensitive. They include: heaviness, blockage, zeal, hardness, urgency, joy and peace. It is apparent from this list that like natural feeling, spiritual feelings are not always joyous or jubilant, but can also be mournful or sorrowful. The Sermon on the Mount provides enlightenment on this subject. Blessed are those that mourn, for they shall be comforted, declared Jesus the Christ. (Matthew 5:4) Inherent in spiritual sensitivity are the blessings that come from the Lord when we sacrifice our emotions for the sake of those who are emotionally oppressed. In all cases, spiritual feelings have a divine purpose. In order to arouse our spiritually sensitivity, the Holy Spirit will break our natural feelings by using people and situations in our environment. His overall purpose is to keep our spirits continuously free and untrampled.

PART THREE: SOWING

CHAPTER #4:
THE SEED AND THE SPIRIT

SPIRIT FOOD

Once the ground of our spirits has been prepared, we must consider the seed. As the body is fed with meats, fruits and vegetables, the spirit is fed with words. The expression from childhood which affirms that "though sticks and stones may break my bones, words will never harm me" is a fallacy. Our very nature, character, personality and behavior have been strongly influenced by words. Words provide the necessary nourishment to our spirits to grow and increase in strength. As our spirits grow stronger, we will discover that our intuition, conscience and discernment will be aroused. Furthermore, we will be able to withstand attacks to our spirits and resist the stimulation of our souls without shaking.

As the sensation of hunger communicates to us that we should eat, we should be able to interpret the sensations of the spirit. If words are to produce their desired affect, three essential conditions must be met: the ground must be prepared, the words must be powerful, and the words must be planted. The ground of our spirits is prepared by the interaction of faith, hope, and patience. The scriptures define faith as " the substance of things hoped for, the evidence of things not seen," while hope is a positive expectation that is invariably connected to the future. Our ability to believe in something that does not yet physically exist is itself the proof that we have received our future in the present moment AND that the spiritual reality has already conceived what will be birthed into the natural environment in due season. To walk by faith and not by sight is to be touched in a positive manner by our future in the here and now! (Hebrews 11:1) With our faith, we receive our future in the present. Without hope, faith could not withstand the fiery darts of Satan, for hope equips us to expect and receive God's vision by trusting in His word. in spite of our present circumstances.

Unlike an idle fantasy, faith and patience are both visionary and practical. Without faith, it is impossible to please God. (Hebrews 11:6) This is because our faith attests to whether or not we trust Him. God's word is so powerful that it will accomplish whatever He wills. (Isaiah 55:11) In the realm of the spirit where the God dwells, finite time of past, present and future does not exist sequentially but simultaneously. Therefore, He can speak life into the non-existent, and create something out of nothing. Briefly put, He calls those things that be not, as though they were, and then "they are." (Romans 4:17) Created in His image, we too create with our words. (Genesis 1:27) We bring into existence our own hopes or expectations by speaking forth a strong and powerful word to which we activate our faith, whether positive or negative.

Patience is a spiritual force that strengthens and supports both faith and hope during that period where there is no physical evidence of the vision that has been created in our spirits by the Holy Spirit. There will undoubtedly appear many physical signs and reasonings that will defy a vision's spiritual birth. By example, you may have envisioned receiving a particular job. However, unemployment is rampant and there are so many around you who are being laid off. Patience needs to come to our aid as we struggle with doubt and unbelief. As we continue to live at a lower level of our expectations--- perhaps eating beans and rice--- patience will cause us to appreciate the beans and rice, while we wait on the steak that the new job will provide in the future.

The difference between faith and fantasy is that the idea created by faith comes directly from the Holy Spirit while fantasy is a product of the imagination of the soul. A person who is not inclined to fully surrender His will over to God will generally mistake fantasy for faith. The way to distinguish the two is to observe how the vision appeals to the mind, emotions and will of the soul. By nature, the soul will resist the Lord, even though lip service has been given to commitment, obedience and surrender. This is only natural because the nature of the soul is to be contrary to the things of God and to operate independently. Usually, the things we want for ourselves are not the things that the Lord wants for us. His ways are not our ways. His thoughts are not our thoughts. (Isaiah 55:8)

Therefore, if you are in the beginning of your walk with Jesus Christ and if you discover that the vision is very pleasing to your thoughts and emotions, it is probably a fantasy that has been created by your soul and therefore is not from the spirit. For the most part, the thing that contradicts our minds, desires and emotions is the very thing that emanates from our spirits. However, once we become "practiced" in the ways of the spirit, true faith will overshadow fantasy. As we learn more about God's ways, our minds and emotions will be renewed and we will be better able to discern between the will of God, the will of man and the will of the devil. Those who have matured in Christ have been broken and restored through trials, tribulations, and trouble. However, even maturity is not in itself a guarantee against demonic deception where seeking after the will of God is concerned. For example, one of the ways that mature Christians can be deceived is by falsely assuming that obeying the Spirit means "to make the Holy Ghost the center of worship, a place that He Himself will never usurp from Jesus Christ." Therefore, the birthing of a vision is completely dependent upon whether or not the original seed emanated from the Holy Ghost. Premature assumptions can lead a believer away from the true will of God.

BIRTHING A VISION

As previously considered, the process of receiving God's will for our lives in the form of a vision or picture is very similar to planting seed and to childbirth. Spiritual harvesting begins with the Holy Spirit sending forth "a word seed" that is planted in our spirits. When seeds are planted into the ground, at first they are buried by the soil. If the ground is hard packed, the birds will eat the scattered seed. If the soil is filled with stones, the seeds will not develop a root and the sun will scorch them. If planted in the midst of weeds, the seeds will be choked. Similarly, Webster defines sperm as "seed to sow." Out of countless microscopic seed that travel up the females birth canal, only one sperm fertilizes her egg. These comparisons also apply in the realm of the spirit. The Holy Spirit may send forth several words that our spirits do not receive, having been hardened through denial, self pity, willfulness and disobedience. We have spiritual ears that cannot hear and spiritual eyes that cannot see.If our spiritual ears have heard from God and "word seed" has been successfully planted into our spirits, though imperceptible,--- nonetheless, the germination or conception process has begun.

The stages of childbirth, including conception, pregnancy, labor, and delivery are comparable to receiving a vision is received from the Lord. [5] The conception stage is characterized by potency and desire. A man must be potent and not impotent. If he is potent yet has no desire for the woman, coitus is not possible. If he is impotent, desire is a handicap because it leads to frustration and disappointment when the lack of potency leads to his failure in sexual performance. Therefore, conception requires power and desire. In spiritual matters, as we delight in the Lord, He will send forth a word-seed in the form of an idea, an intuition, a dream or a vision. (Psalm 37:4) Along with that word, He will supply the desire and the power to conceive it. Since the process will begin in the spirit, the mind and emotions will have to be convinced. Curiosity will stimulate interest while interest will lead to intensity and commitment.

I can use myself as an example. How did an agnostic become a minister? The path that I am now traveling was emphatically not on my own personal itinerary for my life. However, my mind and emotions were periodically and sequentially brought into agreement with God's plans and purposes. The overall vision for my life was conceived through dreams, spiritual discernment and prophesies received in 1983, less than two years after I entered the ministry. In the early stages of the vision's conception, my thoughts and feelings seemed utterly outrageous and ridiculous and I wondered if perhaps I was on a ego trip with delusions of grandeur. However, given the magnitude and the overflowing nature of God's glory, His presentation of my future seemed impossible to my natural reasoning, requiring at least three more lifetimes or generations.

I have discovered through personal experience with Jesus Christ that He protects each vision that He gives us, committing Himself to bring it to the birth, if we trust in Him and walk by faith. In order not to abort a vision in its early stage of conception, the Lord will supply His own dynamism and power to our spirits, that His will and purposes might not be swallowed up by the multiplicity of worldly experience. In this regard, similar to the energy of human coitus and conception, a word-seed or message conceived in our spirits by the Holy Spirit is an intense emotional awakening that is exhilarating, dynamic and compelling. Accordingly, God will excite our brains and our emotions so that we might hold the conception and move on to the next stage which is pregnancy.

Spiritual pregnancy is a time of preparation and expectancy. While in the natural, pregnancy is generally a nine month experience, in the spirit, waiting and preparing can be from a few days to years and even stretch beyond our own lives into future generations. During the first tri-mester of natural birth, the fetus is extremely small and there are few signs that an actual conception has taken place. This is the period of questions and reasonings. As the mother may ask herself, "am I really pregnant?," we ask ourselves, "did I really hear from the Lord?" Moreover, as pregnancy is uncomfortable in the natural, the stage of spiritual pregnancy can be equally awkward . The tensions of physical pregnancy are earmarked by changes in bodily functions and size of the expectant mother. In the spirit, it is a time when we confess before God, "I would have fainted unless I had believed in your goodness in the land of the living. I've got to wait on you and be of good courage and you will strengthen my spirit." (Psalm 27:13-27) Though I walk through the valley of the shadow of death, you are with me and I'll not fear the devil for my cup runs over with the blessing of your vision that is safely hidden within me. (Psalm 23)

During the period of waiting, strength comes in the mind and emotions of the mother to believe that what was conceived shall be delivered. She begins to picture or envision in her mind the sex of the child and begins early in the pregnancy to pick out names. She may even begin to buy baby clothes or to decorate a room with infant wallpaper and furniture. Similiarly in the spirit, we must keep the vision ever before us in our imaginations. We stand on this: "If the Holy Spirit said it, He shall perform it, because His word is truth and not lie. He will empower me to bring to the birth the vision that He Himself has implanted in my spirit. I shall not be moved. I shall not abort the vision. I don't care what people say, or what the present circumstances suggest. His purpose and plan for my life shall be accomplished. I will finish this assignment and bring it to completion." (J. Myers: The Birth of a Vision, seminal cassettes.)

Pregnancy is also a period of spiritual development where the Holy Spirit has sufficiently broken us so that we become trained and equipped to accomplish His purposes and bring forth His vision, which is now "our" vision. In my case, my twenty four year wait has been well spent in being prepared to minister in these end times, not by my own power and devices but by the power of the Holy Spirit. The birthing of my ministry has taught me that if I simply commit my ways to the Lord by trusting Him, that He will bring His vision conceived in my spirit through the spiritual labor and delivery stage to fruition. (Psalm 37:4-7) In the natural, labor is a time of travail, work, struggle and pain. For some women, labor is brief, lasting only an hour, but most women average about eight (8) to twelve (12) hours, with some labor lasting as long as 36 hours. A spiritual truth to highlight is that as physical labor pains immediately precede the birth of the child, similarly in the spirit, trials, troubles, tribulations and stress very often preludes the birth of a vision or a purpose.

As light is at the end of the tunnel, as the dawn follows the darkness of night, the fruition of the vision is on the horizon of an apparent defeat. During labor, the doctor does not encourage the expectant mother to lay back and relax. He tells her to push. We too must push in the spirit by pressing forward in spite of adversity. For joy is coming in the morning. In the light of the Holy Spirit, we shall see light. Though we walk through a dark place, we don't fear negative consequences, because we have faith that Jesus Christ is bringing us through our ordeals and trials. (Psalm 23:4) Once the child is delivered, the memory of the pain of childbirth is so diminished in the mind of the woman that she will consider having yet another child. We too will accept another vision. Multiple births, though possible, are not the rule in human pregnancy. However, in the spirit, we can have more than one vision or purpose, where one birth will either precede another or come forth simultaneously.

Consequently, spiritual empowerment is the regaining of surrendered territory or ground by periodically and

To Curse The Root

methodically pulling up the weeds, and re-planting good seed, according to God's precepts. As psychiatrist M. Scott Peck has written:

> "To develop a broader vision, we must be willing to to forsake, to kill, our narrower vision. In the short run it is more comfortable not to do this-- to stay where we are, to keep using the same microcosmic map to avoid suffering the death of cherished notions. The road of spiritual growth, however, lies in the opposite direction. We begin by distrusting what we already believe, by actively seeking the threatening and unfamiliar, by deliberately challenging the validity of what we have previously been taught and hold dear. The path to holiness lies through QUESTIONING EVERYTHING. (Peck, 1978, pg 193)

THE PERSISTENCE OF SEED

I received another revelation from observing my backyard. As previously mentioned, once a garbage dump, weeds seem to remember their former estate and they remain there tenaciously. Early one spring, my lawn mower was in need of repair. As a result, the grass and the weeds grew wildly. By mid-May, three foot weeds covered the entire length of the side of my house. Once the lawnmower was repaired, I hired someone to mow the lawn on a day that I was at work. To my amazement, I observed that once all the weeds were cut down, what remained were two rose plants and a strong bush of tulips with bulbs about to flower. Two summers before, I had hired a landscaper to plant flower beds but after a dispute over the terms of the contract, she stopped working, and told me that she had dug up everything that she had planted. Evidently, she overlooked the tulips and the roses.

This apparently insignificant life experience suggests to me some deep spiritual truths. First of all, seed is seed, and both good and bad seed can grow together. Secondly, bad seed tends to hide the good seed. Thirdly, bad seed cannot stop good seed from growing. Finally, care must be taken when pulling up the weeds not to pull up good fruit or plants. With the grass cut and the weeds chopped down, the beauty of the tulips and the roses are outstanding. This is the process of spiritual growth. "Word-seed" is planted into our spirits and begins to develop our characters and life experiences. As evil seed brings forth evil fruit, negative words bring forth negative results.

That summer, big, beautiful tropical flowers grew along the other side of my fence which connected my yard to my neighbor's. When I first moved into that house, my neighbor who is now deceased, was an avid gardener. For many years, she cultivated her rather wild, tropical looking garden, where colorful flowers grew larger than grapefruits, all over her entire yard. The grass was barely visible amidst her tropical paradise. At times, the flowers would even hide my neighbor from view. However, soon after she died, those who inherited the property cut down every flower, until only grass could be seen. Yet, the laborious work of my neighbor would not be destroyed. Apparently, the seeds that she planted were not dug up from the root. Pink, red and orange flowers boldly grew on large stems about seven feet high, crossed the fence and graced my yard with their presence.

Once more, spiritual truths were revealed to me. My "effortless garden" suggests to me that good seed planted in good soil that has been properly nurtured will continue to produce fruit, even when the obstacles of life may appear to have destroyed any possibility for continued growth and success. In other words, "you can't keep a good flower down!" Moreover, to be spiritually empowered sometimes requires us to cross the fences of life and regroup in a backyard that is more conducive to our growth, where we are appreciated. Although my neighbor's original intent was to create a garden for her own pleasure and enjoyment, the Lord caused me to benefit from her long labor of love. While I was preparing to hire a professional landscaper, the Holy Spirit had already arranged to beautify my former "garbage dump" of a backyard. Positive seed had already been planted. When we submit to His will and direction, spiritual empowerment seems almost effortless, where spiritual and material blessings seem to overtake us. Some may plant, and still others may water, but it is the Lord who provides the increase. (ICorinthians 3:7)

DEVELOPING OBJECTIVITY

Once the excitement of the conception of a vision has diminished, we must be balanced enough to try the spirits, to see if they be of God, particularly of all supernatural manifestations. Trying the spirits involves developing objectivity in the soul. Webster's dictionary defines objectivity as expressing or involving the use of facts without distortion by personal feelings and or prejudices. The opposite of OBJECTIVITY IS SUBJECTIVITY. To be subjective is to have "self" at the center of every act of discernment or judgment. This is because a subjective person cannot move beyond his or her own opinions, perceptions and point of view. Demons take advantage of subjective people by using their personal feelings and prejudices to distort the truth. Pride is a spiritual cancer that is a manifestation of our sinful, carnal nature. Objectivity is a way to resist pride where we move beyond looking at everything from a personal level.

In Chapter 1, the symbolic language of dreams was presented. Why does it seem that throughout the Bible, God speaks to His people in symbols? I believe that among the reasons why He speaks in symbols is because of our lack of objectivity. Very often the truth is hidden from us, because our subjectivity wil cause us to misunderstand a set of facts. Although some symbols are subjective, most symbols have universal meaning. Once the meaning of the symbol is revealed, the Lord will use it to overpower our subjective point of view.

A related quality to objectivity is tolerance. Tolerance is the capacity to endure pain or hardship. Tolerance is also a spiritual strength that will produce stamina in the face of unfavorable environmental factors. I am not looking at this term from a worldly perspective, where a person who is tolerant is indulgent of false beliefs and practices that are in direct contradiction to the gospel of Jesus Christ. Rather, a tolerant believer is one who does not allow his own subjectivity to hinder his ability to respect the will of others. A tolerant person will esteem others more highly than he esteems himself. In this regard, he will be equipped to place into spiritual perspective and understanding his own particular situation, recognizing what is from God, the devil, and his own soul.

Uncovering demonic deceptions requires a flexibility of mind that can go beyond subjectivity to uncover an objective presentation of the truth. True empathy is the ability to go beyond one's own subjective reality toward embracing the feelings, ideas and experience of the client, without keeping the demonic residue of the experience. A person who is objective will be free to be magnanimous. A magnanimous spirit is flexible, forgiving and generous. In other words, to be magnanimous is to be filled with the abundant life of the glory of God. A magnanimous person is also hopeful. As long as the client agrees to forsake sin, unforgiveness, and to stay true to the word of God, nothing is impossible to him that believes. In order to be magnanimous, you need to be delivered from the importance of your own personal "I am." You can't be full of God's glory if you are full of yourself. The reality is that every time you try to rid a brother or sister of demonic infestation, you are personally risking contamination yourself. Therefore, we must not only be aware of our own subjective weaknesses but also confident that in spite of our particular vulnerability, our desire to be set free is stronger than our own susceptibility to "a brush with evil." Simply put, magnanimous Christians believe that God's grace is sufficient, and as we humble ourselves before the Lord, we will be protected.

Each one of us has our own particular weaknesses of soul and body. For example, I recognize that I am particularly vulnerable to the spirit of rejection. From the time I was a child, I experienced rejection. Since I refused to compromise, as a consequence, I experienced a great deal of rejection from parents, peers and the world, just for being different. Once I became born again, and thereafter a preacher of righteousness, I experienced even more rejection within the church. Spiritual abuse, one of the outgrowths of rejection in the church, can create or magnify a spiritual vulnerability. A few years ago, I experienced the residue of rejection within hours after I cast this demonic spirit from a client. Almost immediately, yet rather covertly, the spirit of rejection tried to find a doorway. It was very subtle. Very sneaky.

It began with a phone call wherein I thought someone with whom I had enjoyed friendship and intimacy for a long time was now nonchalant and uninterested in what I had to say. Then someone made a remark that I took as a put down based upon age. I internalized a harmless comment that was not intended to suggest that I was too old to relate to the needs of a younger generation. I started to feel mildly depressed, which is very unlike my persona. It did not take me long to realize what had happened. The spirit of rejection that I had recently expelled from someone else perceived my own weakness in this area and attempted to enter into me. Within three days, I recognized this demon by an OBJECTIVE observation of my own behavior. I examined each incident one by one and took my "I AM" out of center stage. Immediately and outloud, I commanded the demon of rejection to go from me and it left, not to return. I resisted the devil with OBJECTIVITY, and he fled from me, as James said that he would. I humbled myself by resisting subjectivity, the root of pride.

POWER-PACKED WORDS

Most people are aware of the biblical account of creation. God said, "let there be light, and there was light." (Genesis 1:3) However, before HE SPOKE, the earth was dark, without form and void. Yet as His words proceeded from His lips, light came into being, and overpowered the darkness. With the words of His mouth, God has the ability to create something out of nothing---the visible from the invisible, the material from the spiritual. Creation comes from inside out as opposed to from outside in.

Since the Almighty has shared His creative power with us on a material level through the biological processes of our reproductive systems, it would logically follow that He has also shared with us His capacity to create with words. There are three points to consider that, if believed, will enlighten our understanding of the process of creating with words:

1. God has absolute faith in His own words;

2. Words spoken in faith produce results; and

3. Darkness cannot survive when His light appears.

This account demonstrates how a vision is birthed. Conception in the spirit is manifested through the speaking forth of power-packed words with the mouth, so that our spirits can HEAR THEM. Our spirits need to HEAR the words, so that our faith will be increased. Faith is required to strengthen us during the period of pregnancy, our time of preparation and development. During this stage, we live in expectation and patience, learning how to cope with difficulties and to adjust to change. In this case, my colleague learned to be abased through facing the possibility of unemployment, to adjusting to demotion, to promotion to his former position, to "RUNNING THE AGENCY!" Labor and delivery, though quick and relatively painless, were the aftermath of a very difficult period of pregnancy.

When we speak forth power-packed words that have been inspired by God, point three (3) affirms that darkness cannot survive under the power of light. God IS light, and in Him there is no darkness, AT ALL! (IJohn 1:5) Once He applies His own faith and power to our words to bring forth results or fruits, negative power-packed words that develop into weeds-----wither and die. However, power-packed words will remain mere possibilities if they are not believed. At times, God's will may overshadow our lack of faith, and results will occur in spite of us. Notwithstanding, the key to their fruition is that once power-packed words are spoken, both the hearer and the speaker must believe and receive their possibilities "right now." As the Holy Spirit has absolute faith in His words, we must have absolute faith in the words that He inspires within us to speak forth.

Power packed words fall in two categories: blessings and curses. In biblical times, sages would gather their families and communities together and speak forth power-packed words into each person's future. A blessing is a power-packed word of prosperity, abundance and goodwill while a curse is a word of power that seeks poverty, affliction and misfortune. An idle word lacks power because:

1. it did not originate in the spirit;

2. it was not inspired by God; and

3. it was not believed when it was spoken.

As blessings are inspired by the Holy Spirit, curses are inspired by His opposing power, the devil. Previously unmentionable and unbelievable in our society, for centuries we have been rejecting the old symbols, names and metaphors that personify evil. However today we are living in a generation that is beginning to include in its a worldview such spiritual entities as angels, demons, powers, gods, Satan and other spiritual forces. With the longstanding repression of spirituality for so many years and the constant denial of what has been considered "superstition", in our time society has begun to search for wisdom in the ancient cultures of the past, where evil was personified. The following causative factors are reflected in a quotation found in the introduction of the book entitled "Unmasking the Powers:

> "More intimately, a reassessment of these Powers---angels, demons, gods, elements, the devil---allows us to reclaim, name, and comprehend types of experiences

that materialism renders mute and inexpressible. We have the experiences but miss their meaning. Unable to name our experiences of these intermediate powers of existence, we are simply constrained by them compulsively. They are never more powerful than when they are unconscious. Their capacities to bless us are thwarted, their capacities to possess us augmented. Unmasking these Powers can mean for us initiation into a dimension of reality 'not known, because not looked for,' in T. S. Eliot's words." (Wink, 1986)

To continue, power-packed words inspired by evil forces in the realm of the spirit combine with the negative faith within the evil hearts of man to bring forth evil results that I have named and identified as "weeds." The process of sending forth a curse is exactly equal to sending forth a blessing. Like a blessing, a curse originates in the spirit, is spoken forth in faith, is believed by the hearer, and will materialize in the future.

CONFESSION CAN BRING RECOVERY

Public confession during the process of recovery is a forthright utterance to a group of like-situated people that reveals the weaknesses and faults of the "I AM." Group confession can be empowering because it is based upon the scriptural principle which states "confess your faults one to the other, that you might be healed." (James 5:16) The key to the power of confession lies in three fundamental spiritual truths:

1. the words that come out of our lips reflect our spiritual condition;

2. once our spiritual condition is revealed openly, the content of our lives becomes accessible to us; and

3. the confessions of others can edify and strengthen us as we seek to overcome similar tests and trials.

Unless we have the power of discernment to hear hidden truths in our own words as well as in the words of others, like the blind leading the blind, we will be the deaf leading the deaf. It is necessary that we cultivate our spiritual ears so that we might hear truth in the spirit. Therefore, it is important to develop listening skills, not only in hearing others, but in hearing the words that proceed from our own mouths. Listening to ourselves is important because our words present a picture of our inner condition. Listening skills supply us with the ability to feel the essence of the life of the one who speaks, including his or her concerns. We can even learn about ourselves and others by listening to how we habitually phrase our questions. For example, questions can be phrased from the affirmative or from the negative cases. Does the person generally ask questions that begin with "can" or do they begin with "can't." Furthermore, a "spiritual ear" will pay attention to the ordering of words and phrases, noticing whether or not the words are focused or scattered, logical or irrational, argumentative or persuasive.

Discernment through listening can also tell us what is important to the one who is speaking. Equally true to the adage which states that "as a man thinketh, so is he," are the Saviour's words: "out of the abundance of the spirit, the mouth speaks." (Matthew 12:34) Our words reflect our attitude about life, what we believe about our personal destiny: whether it be positive or negative, uplifting or discouraging, fearful or secure, clear or confusing, strong or weak. Our words also can have a profound affect upon our emotions. I can remember a time when my emotions were calm. Yet as I sat down and wrote a very sad, melancholy letter, I began to feel discontent and frustration. This experience caused me to realize that we DO make ourselves happy, sad, stressful or frustrated by the words that we either speak or write.

Whether the contents of our own lives are revealed to us by the words of our own mouths or by the open confessions of others, such utterances have a way of directing us toward a time in our past or our immediate circumstances that holds the key to our future progress and growth. In this regard, the Lord will often provide us with the answers that we need out of the confessions of our own mouths. Listening not only involves hearing others but also hearing the communications that come from our own spirits. Many answers come to me as I listen to myself either talk to myself or to God in prayer. I can remember those times when I have heard myself confess things that reveal that I am too pre-occupied with myself and not with "the other guy", whoever that person might be. I have listened to my own frustrating words and received a revelation from the Lord, as He has counselled me to put all of my care on Him and to shut my mouth.

Consider people who use words with sexual connotations such as "the F word", expressions and gestures that direct people to their genitals, tell dirty jokes, put other people down with gender or racially biased name calling, speak words of spite, envy or jealousy, and who are constantly screaming or yelling at their children. We must ask ourselves the nature of the unhealthy condition of their spirits. If we really listen to and examine words such as these when they proceed from within ourselves, we may find the root cause of our problems. In such cases, we need to surrender our lips to God for cleansing. Our reaction to such words coming from others can also serve as a clue to our own spiritual condition. For example, does off-colored humor make us laugh or do we feel sick to our stomachs?

The secret to victory not only from drugs and alcohol but also from "loose lips" is to develop a close, intimate relationship with God. Drawing near to Him will reveal what is wrong with us. Recovery through confession is threefold. Confession before others and to ourselves is strengthened by confession to the Lord. Such confession will go into the spirit and cleanse it. If we ask Him to put conviction in us each time we start to say something that is either careless, uncaring or unkind, the Holy Spirit will empower our listening skills. Conviction is a feeling of the spirit, that is often referred to as a check. It is a twisting, sinking feeling, deep in your gut. Conviction will stop us in the middle of a "bad confession" and put a zip to our lips.

Confession also provides spiritual empowerment when we listen to the weaknesses, trials and victories of others in three ways: First of all, the Holy Spirit comforts us during our sufferings so that we may be able to comfort and console others who are enduring the same trials in their own lives. A person who has overcome many trials and tribulations is qualified to enhance the recovering of others who are still seeking victory. One who has been tempted to give in to loneliness, rejection, sorrow and pain and yet trusted in the Lord and came forth strong and powerful is a true "professional." Such people have an influence that they could not have obtained any other way than through learning how to endure suffering. Secondly, the confessions of a victorious professional directs others to trust solely in God. When someone comes before us and says "I tried everything. I was pressed on every side. I was at my wit's end. Every one forsook me. I lost everything. I was in an impossible situation. I could not rescue myself. I had no where to turn but to the Lord Jesus Christ. But I would not have had it any other way. Through the Lord, I have "come a long way, baby!"

Such a confession brings life to those who find themselves trying to work out their own problems independent of God. Finally, confession stirs up faith in the hearers by providing confirmation that the Lord has the capacity and the inclination to deliver us. We have a tendency to revel in self pity, considering that our own crisis is unique and therefore, outside of any human or divine intervention. Notwithstanding, when we hear that He has delivered someone who we might consider to have been in a worst predicament than ourselves, our self-righteous hold on our right to self pity is so attacked that we are pressured to relinquish it. Ultimately, even negative thinking will strive toward a positive reality by saying, "How could the Lord deliver such a one as that bum and NOT consider me!" Moreover, when we hear ourselves speak forth how we were delivered in the past, the sound of our own words reinforces our faith to believe that if God delivered me in the past, then He can bring me through this present ordeal. The Lord wants us to build our faith on all of His past deliverance. He wants us to come to such a place in our faith that we consistently and totally trust Him in every circumstance, facing the future with confidence.

Even though confession can be liberating to the soul, it is important to warn the Christian in recovery that those groups you choose to confess in front of must be people who care for you---people that you can trust, but most of all, people who love Jesus. Since the spirit of the Anti-Christ is in the world, and since the devil is the god of this world, if Jesus Christ is your Lord and Savior, people who are lost will be driven by invisible demonic forces to hate you, simply because the demons that lead them also hate Jesus. Jesus informed His disciples to prepared to receive rejection and even hatred from those who are still in the grip of the unseen demonic forces. Since the rooms in 12 Steps meetings are filled with Jesus haters, the Christian in recovery must be both vigilant and wise. I do not believe that you should share your heart's innermost secrets and intimacies with people who hate your Savior and consequently, hate you for loving Him. The adversary walks around from place to place, and most definitely from "room to room", seeking whom he may devour. So be careful not to give the enemy an open door to use an unwise confession to condemn and persecute you. Your Christian pearls of faith should not be cast to swine.

CHAPTER #5:
THE SEED AND OTHER SPIRITS

THE DEVIL MADE ME DO IT!

Just as faith in our spirits is cultivated by words received from the Holy Spirit and from our own self-talk, doubt and fear are the consequence of words that have been planted in our spirits and souls by the Lower Power. As indicated by the subtitle of this book, there is a dimension which I have referred to as "a thirteenth step" in recovery that is mandatory to a victorious deliverance from the bondage of addiction, namely, the existence of a "lower power" and his agents, referred to in the Bible as "Satan", "demons" or "evil spirits." Just as the Lord and his angels have access to us, it is crucial that we not be ignorant to Satanic deception, for the demons have access to us as well. Therefore, it is imperative that we learn how to tell the difference between both spiritual influences. An obedient surrender of our will to Jesus Christ is a major step toward overcoming evil---as outlined in AA's first three (3) steps. The self-examination process as defined in step four (4) is also important. Self-knowledge equips us to be able to discern thoughts and feelings that are alien to our own characters and personalities. However, more is required. We must also know the will and the ways of our enemy. We should know our enemy so that we will never mistake his words God's words.

Clearly, there are destructive people, systems and circumstances in the world that produce full grown weeds with blatantly negative calling cards--- obviously evil in motives, methods and results. Moreover, the Lower Power is a destroyer who leaves a conspicuous trail of destructive evidence behind him. Even so, we still tend to blame the Lord for acts of senseless loss, mayhem and violence as "an act of God." False accusations of this kind point to clear evidence that we do not possess an intimate knowledge of the Holy Spirit. If we do not know God's thoughts and ways, we remain ill equipped to recognize Satan's influence. Another facet of spiritual empowerment is to know the wiles, schemes and plots of the "evil one" and to receive power from God to be victorious in each maneuver that the demons will inevitably attempt against us.

Satan's greatest advantage is to be allowed to work in our lives without being recognized. In his masquerade as God, he skillfully uses the same words of his apparent opposition to fully attack and disavow himself. This kind of "counter espionage" is a trick, where the spy brings back information about the enemy, solely for the purpose of deceiving the agency or persons who have employed him. Satan's goal is to win our confidence by virtually attacking himself through those who appear to be his enemies, but who, in fact are either his avowed, or uninitiated friends and servants. Many professed believers in Jesus Christ fall under this category. They verbally attack demon forces yet a closer scrutiny will uncover extremes and excesses---either a repressive, judgmental morality or an opposing tolerance of man's sinful nature that borders on moral weakness, disguised as mercy, grace and love. Within BOTH ethical extremes, though anonymous and disguised, Satan and his demons maintain a vital continuum of power and control.

Our human struggle with the evil side of the spirit world is a daily event. With a well known biblical prayer, we ask the Lord not only to give us our DAILY bread, but we ask Him to deliver us each day from evil or "the evil one." (Matthew 6:11) Therefore, we must be take heed to the scriptural advice of the Apostle Simon Peter:

> Be sober, be vigilant; because your adversary the devil walks about like a roaring lion, seeking whom he may devour. Resist him, steadfast in the faith, knowing that the same sufferings are experienced by our brotherhood in the world. **(PETER 5:8,9)**

To be sober is to take demonic influences seriously and realistically, without exaggerating or under-estimating their power. In this sense, sobriety is marked by a sound and stable mind that is neither seduced by excesses of emotion, habit or opinion nor pushed or hurried by cognitive or emotional extremes. We who are sober will not allow our thoughts, emotions or feelings to motivate us to form an unhealthy opinion that will ultimately lead to "giving Satan place" to operate in our lives. For recovering people, the term "sober" or "sobriety" used in this biblical context should signify that the state of being drunk or otherwise intoxicated is an open door to Satanic intervention.

Within this framework, vigilance is more than just being watchful or cautious, for the hallmark of vigilance is self examination and self knowledge. We must know ourselves down to our patterns, habits and motives. As the treatment of a disease begins with an assessment and a diagnosis, vigilance is operationalized by opening ourselves to the Higher Power for scrutiny and by our willingness to come to terms with his assessment and His correction, without defending or minimizing our weaknesses. Watchman Nee, a Chinese Christian philosopher puts it this way:

> "Should the child of God desire freedom, his folly must be removed. In other words, he must know the truth. He

needs to appreciate the real nature of affairs. Satanic lies bind, but God's truth unshackles. Naturally the knowledge of truth is going to be costly, for it will shatter the vainglory one has assumed due to his past experiences. He looks upon himself as far more advanced than others, as being spiritual and infallible. How hard hit he will be if he confesses the possibility of his being invaded or if he is shown to have been so invaded! Unless God's child sincerely adheres to all the truth of God, it becomes very rough for him to accept this kind of painful and humiliating truth. One encounters no difficulty in accepting that truth which is agreeable; but it is not easy at all to take in a truth which blasts one's ego. To acknowledge himself as liable to deception is relatively easy; whereas to confess that he is entrenched by the enemy already is most difficult. May God be gracious, for even after a person has known the truth he may yet resist it. The acceptance of truth is thus the first step to salvation. The child of God must be willing to know all the truth concerning himself. This requires humility and sincerity. Therefore let him who vehemently opposes such truth beware lest unknowingly he actually be enslaved. (Nee, p 128, 1968)

The spoils of the "invasion" to which Watchman Nee refers is the ground or territory of our souls that has been surrendered to the Lower Power---territory that this book is devoted to ensuring that we reclaim. Demonic influence has many styles of deception. Where addictive behavior is concerned, demons revel in depression, oppression and vexation of spirit because these three (3) emotional conditions are open doors to relapse during the recovery process. Depression is spiritually nurtured by a poor sense of esteem, dissatisfaction, and alienation---each rooted in a lack of patience. Evil spirits thrive on the three "d"s of doubt, disappointment and despair to lower our physical energy and vitality. Their method is to entangle weeds of negative thoughts, emotions and attitudes into a stronghold or spiritual underground root system that develops into a solid fortress or base of operation from which demons can function unhindered. Condemnation and accusations are central to the guilt experienced by the depressed.

Oppression brings a sense of being smothered or weighed down with the burdens of a troubled, problematic life. In such cases, demonic oppression will be like a "monkey on our backs", hovering around and pressing us down with a persistent attack, until our spiritual backs break and we relapse. At times sudden and shocking, demns will apply a steady and relentless attack with persecution and disarming calamities of all sorts. Vexation of spirit takes several forms. Restlessness can lead to a feeling of annoyance or irritability. In this regard, evil spirits will employ sequentially ordered petty harassments to cause worry and a disquieted state, akin to mild or even acute stages of paranoia. In the mental realm, vexation also brings confusion and disorientation. The weapon of choice is fear and intimidation. He will use others close to us to create situations that incite our emotions. The agitation we feel may become so intense that we may literally "lose it" and physically assault somebody.

Satan's goal is to take advantage of our guilt and condemnation for past and present failures, coupled with the worry and fear over the consequences we may face for our actions. Then Satan will maneuver these circumstances to motivate a relapse. When we are ignorant to Satanic devices, the enemy can repetitively and consistently employ the same strategies to defeat us simply because we are ignorant to the fact that indeed "the devil made us do it.!" In fact, I have found that the entire cycle of addiction incorporates demonic activity within the flesh, mind, emotions and habits of those so afflicted. Although both my ministerial and social work colleagues may disagree, my spiritual experience within Satan's domain of addiction, coupled with scriptural confirmation, attest to my freedom in using personified terms such as "demons" and "angels" as an acceptable and ordinary part of my vocabulary.

When and how did I first discover demons? As discussed in Chapter #1, this question takes me back to 1974 when the head of a demon manifested itself at my first seance. At the time, I did not know that the appearance of a foggy, V-shaped, bearded man's head, with the ascot around its neck was a demon. I thought that it was a ghost, or a human spirit of a deceased man. I believed it to be a human spirit because it lied to me through the Ouija Board and spirit writings. It was only until I began to seek my Heavenly Father through His Son, Jesus Christ that I learned about demons. Through scripture study, trial and error and revelations of the Holy Spirit, I was taught to discern the difference between spirits. After twenty-two (22) years, I am still learning.

ALCOHOL--A SPIRIT OR---A SPIRIT!

My first revelation of the influence of demonic activity upon the addictions occurred in the summer of 1983, when an acquaintance brought a very sad, but drunk Christian woman to my door. As I watched Laura being helped up the stairs of my house, I remember thinking, "I don't think I've ever seen any one so apparently unhappy about being drunk!" Her chin was dropped down to her chest and her thin frame was as limp as a dishrag. When she got to the top of my stairs, she dropped to her knees and prostrated herself across my carpet. While Laura laid there, her escort whispered to me, "I think she has a demon." The escort advised me that Laura was a full gospel Christian, a former heroin addict---a nurse by profession. She was a recent convert to Jesus Christ and was an active church member. Then I realized why Laura was so sad. She was experiencing condemnation for relapsing.

I sat down on the floor beside her and began to talk to her. However, the demon answered me by saying from Laura's lips with conviction and in the first person, "I am not coming out!" At that time, I didn't know if it was really a demon or if Laura was in some kind of catatonic state, where she was simply escaping into herself. Perhaps she was just so intoxicated that she was merely babbling. Time would tell. A few weeks passed from our first meeting, when I began to have foreboding dreams about Laura. When I dreamt that she was going to commit suicide, I decided to take immediate action, and I hurried to her home. I arrived at Laura's basement apartment around midday, only to find that it was almost completely dark inside. The place smelled like a brewery. Once my eyes became accustomed to the dark, the trail of the smell became apparent. Throughout the entire flat were large garbage bags filled with empty beer cans! There were several in every room, including the closets. Her young five year old son was whimpering in the bedroom, when Laura said, "he's my problem. He's the reason why I am suffering so." Then it hit me. The devil was telling Laura to kill her son and then herself. I called a friend to babysit for her son and I practically carried Laura to my house---she was so drunk.

Once there, I really didn't know what to do with her. I had never conducted a deliverance before but I believed God's word so I began by rebuking the spirit and commanding it with a loud voice to come out of her in the Name of Jesus Christ of Nazareth. My daughter, fourteen years old at the time, began to join me in the command. I don't know how long this went on, perhaps thirty (30) minutes. From the moment I began, Laura started to cough and vomit up a greenish fluid, which I thought was bile. We got her a pail, as she continued to heave and retch. Then, like the wisping sound of wind, an unearthly, guttural, rasping gasp issued forth from deep in Laura's throat. At that chilling moment, my daughter Zonnita began to roll around on the floor. With clenched fists, Zonnita looked as though she was wrestling with an invisible person or thing. The fervency of my command increased as this strange fight proceeded. In the meanwhile, frightened into sobriety, Laura leaped up from the couch, ran into my bathroom and locked the door. All of a sudden, my daughter started to laugh uproariously, and I joined her. The battle was over. We had won!

Laura was not so convinced. Once coaxed from trembling in the bathroom, she expressed concern that since she was completely sober and had severe stomach pains, that she might be in withdrawal. As a nurse, she was well aware of the danger of convulsions that accompany delirium tremens(the DT's), so

Laura begged me to take her to the emergency room. However, once at the hospital, doctors could not find anything medically wrong with her and she was sent home. Although physically addicted to alcohol prior to this deliverance, Laura did not have to be medically detoxed. When the demon spirit left her soul and her body, she was supernaturally detoxed.

Since that day, Laura has been sober for twelve 22 years, with only a few minor relapses that lasted just a few days. The relapse occurred because Satan began to intimidate her with a past sin, threatening to expose her sin to her husband. She called on me once more, and this time all that was required was a counseling session. Laura confronted the problem by immediately revealing her secret to her husband, thereby effectively resisting and disarming the devil. The key to Laura's recovery is that once delivered from evil spirits of alcohol addiction and a suicide spirit, Laura made a decision to change her patterns of thinking, feeling and responding. Laura destroyed the root of Satan's hold on her and therefore has not relapsed in twelve (12) years, without ever entering a twelve (12) step program.

In presenting this particular case, I do not mean to suggest that physical manifestations will always occur or that deliverance sessions will be as dramatic. In fact, since this first encounter, I have experienced deliverances where no observable physical manifestation had transpired. Since every human being is unique, each case of deliverance is a new experience. However, the case of Laura was particularly significant for me because it opened my eyes to seriously acknowledge the impact of demonic activity on addiction.

THE SEVEN WALLS: FINDING MY PURPOSE

The case of Laura is significant on several levels. First of all, even though the war was won that eventful day in my livingroom, demons would continue to wage numerous battles in her mind and emotions. The key to Laura's enduring deliverance was that she persistently and steadfastly immersed the empty space left by the demon that had tortured her soul with the infilling of the Spirit of God, His word and with prayer. As Jesus warned, when a spirit comes out of a person, he wanders around in the dry places of the earth, seeking a place or person to inhabit. When he is unsuccessful, the demon with team up with seven (7) others, and together they return to the first demon's original habitation. If they find that the persons's soul is empty, then the original demon and its new companions join together, and re-enter the person. (Matthew 12:43-35)

Likewise with the addictions, a person's physical, mental and emotional condition will experience regression to a worst state with each ensuing relapse. Detoxification is where the first battle is waged. The unclean spirit is medicated when the addicted is detoxed and his or her flesh has been cleansed of the physical addiction. However, the possession has always been in the mind and emotions of the soul and it is there that the battle takes place. The inner craving for the substance is a major obstacle to victory. The way to victory is to accept responsibility for the physical and mental pains of withdrawal. They don't last forever. In Jesus Christ, deliverance may be instantaneous but it is more likely to be progressive. It takes about 30 days to be rid of habitual, repetitive behaviors of most kinds. However, the mind must be renewed by the word of God.

Just a few months after Laura's deliverance from the spirit of substance addiction, the Holy Spirit brought forth a prophetic message from her lips---a message that revealed God's purpose for my life. Laura was among a small band of women who met at my house to seek the Lord together in prayer. On one particular evening, the Spirit fell upon Laura in a powerful way, when she began to prophesy to me in the fall of 1983, thirteen years ago:

The Seed And Other Spirits

"You will use my name, my blood, my word and the power of My Spirit to contend with the seven walls that hold my people captive: These are the seven walls:

1. alcohol and drugs

2. homosexuality

3. prostitution

4. religious spirit (false teachings)

5. witchcraft

6. prejudice

7. poverty

I will teach you how to be victorious over these principalities and powers, the rulers of the darkness of this world, and spiritual wickedness in the heavens."

It is not by chance or coincidence that the first three walls are the major ways that the AIDS virus is transmitted: drugs, anal and oral sex, and vaginal sex. Though already in the earth and not yet named, HIV infection and AIDS was totally unknown to me in 1983. Yet God was already preparing His people to spiritually combat it.

Laura's deliverance illustrates some key points about some of the strategies and methods of the Holy Spirit:

1. <u>He will turn a vessel of dishonor into a vessel of honor!</u>

    If we realize that apart from Christ we are nothing and we can do nothing---if we define our self worth only by who and what we are in Christ, then we will be able to draw on His understanding and His power as opposed to our own. Both Laura, Zonnita and myself were vessels of dishonor. Yet He gave me His knowledge and His wisdom through dreams that revealed the demonic plans to destroy Laura. He empowered my daughter to boldly wrestle with a demon without fear. As He used both of us to cast it out, He then anointed Laura with His Spirit to send me the most important message that I have received from Him thus far--a message that holds His will and purpose for giving me life.

2. <u>He will accomplish several purposes in us once we submit ourselves to Him and step out in faith and obedience.</u>

One of the most liberating and victory inducing empowerment principles is that we can become aware of our own destinies according to the will of God, if we remain in Christ. If Christ is in us and we are in Him, then all wisdom and knowledge that is in Him is also in us. I believe that if I had not challenged and confronted that alcohol demon in Laura's soul, that the alcohol spirit and the suicide spirit would have joined together to kill Laura and her son. Furthermore, I would have missed the will of God for my life.

As I recall the trials, tribulations and teachings of the last twenty-two years since the prophecy, God's plan has become ever increasingly clear. Today, my daughter Zonnita contends daily, without fear, with demonic forces as a psychiatric social worker. She is also my assistant pastor in Healing Waters. Laura joined me briefly in ministry in 1996, assisting me with a jail setting where demon forces were rampant. She is now also an evangelist, who has a secular job as an addiction counselor. Personally, I have found that my own growth in self empowerment has caused me to draw my experiences and challenges into focus as God continues to prepare and empower me with His Spirit to combat the forces of darkness as originally outlined in Laura's prophecy concerning the seven walls.

AN ENEMY HAS DONE THIS!.

In one of his parables, the Lord announces that in the midst of His planting wheat in His field, an enemy came along and planted imitation wheat or in other words "weeds." As a result, toward the end of the age, there would come a point in time when the imitation wheat and the true wheat would look identical. Therefore, I believe that an important point to emphasize regarding the process of weeding is that no one should attempt to separate the saved from the unsaved because the Lord warns us that we might endanger or even damage some of His true wheat in the process.Therefore, in cases where salvation is not obvious, we must proceed with caution.

Sometimes the saved looks like the sinner and sometimes the sinner looks like the saved. The one who is in most danger of course is the sinner who looks like the saved. If demons are cast out under the assumption that the sinner is already saved, then you can expect that the demons will return and the captive will be bound even tighter. Prayer is definitely the answer in such cases. As a personal case in point, although the witchcraft demon lost the power to use me as a medium when I got born again, I was still confused. The confusion centered in the fact that I believed that the occult practices that were still a significant part of my spirituality were the reason why I got saved. In other words, how could "communicating with the spirits be so bad when it drew me to the Lord?" I did not understand that it was "in spite of" those practices that I became born again. Either an angel or the Holy Spirit Himself reached into the occult world and practically "pulled me out." My confusion remained for about 4 years due to my very limited knowledge of the word of God that I had at the time. Those in the Christian community who had contact with me were also not grounded in the word.

Even so, I was a true believer who looked like the lost. Most of those who claimed to know the word among my Christian associates at the time could not recognize that I was a believer, and I was considered by them to still be a witch. However, there was one wise man whose bible study I faithfully attended twice a week who could discern that I was a child of God. Although he admitted that he was afraid of me, this man prayed for me, "that the Lord would send someone in my life whom I would receive to rightly divide truth to me." His prayers were answered within a week.

Then there are those who are not saved who appear to be saved. In my third book "Faces of the Religious Demon," I have presented a case study of Millie. For now, I will summarize that Millie was born a catholic and believed that she was "born again" as a charismatic. In the course of her deliverance, she was completely "taken over" in a trance and the demon railed at us that he owned Millie because she had been given to him by her grandmother. Her grandmother remains a practitioner of Santeria, a form of witchcraft practiced by Hispanics. Santeria is a combination of African voodoo with Catholicism.

Witchcraft is the practice of cursing and controlling with a counterfeit spiritual authority and power. Therefore, weeding will seek to uncover what caused the captive to become subject to witchcraft and its various forms. The captive's victory from deception and bondage is attainable if he is guided or counseled to be enabled to see the Lord clearly and serve and respect Him obediently. It is not the purpose of weeding to study darkness in any great detail. For example, you do not need to study all of the rituals, false doctrines and practices to realize that witchcraft and or the religious demon is involved.

A case in point. Recently a woman who I will call "Irene" wrote to me and sought prayer for her 10 year old son who was diagnosed with a rare form of cancer a year ago. Since she believed that this cancer was "demonically inspired" and might be caused by an ancestral curse, I asked her to complete a form called "The Deliverance Assessment Form", the DAF. Irene appeared to be a committed, dedicated believer. However, the DAF revealed occult involvement. The most outstanding

The Seed And Other Spirits

insight into the problem was the fact that Irene and particularly her husband belonged to a religion that I have never heard of called "the Coptic" faith. To make a long story short, I did not have to study the Coptics to know immediately that this was a false "Christian" religion. As soon as I learned that it originated in Egypt and that it uplifts black people as a "superior" race and glorifies the elders of the church by calling them queens, kings, princesses, etc., I did not have to go any further into a deeper study of this darkness.

In the course of the initial interview, Irene revealed that during a special prayer and fasting vigil that her Coptic church had for her son, hundreds of mice broke forth throughout the church. People ran screaming from the building as you could hear the splashing sounds of mice being crushed underfoot. NEEDLESS TO SAY, THIS WAS NOT A GOOD SIGN. Mice in the old testament are symbolic of tumors or in other words, cancer. A knowledge of the symbolic language of the scriptures as well as the scriptural reference in Galatians that declares that there are no distinctions in Christ---He is no respector of persons—caused me to discern immediately that Irene and her entire family were under the influence of a witchcraft spirit.

Once again, a review of the DAF opened the door to stimulate the client to reveal additional information. Early in our interaction, I became convinced that Irene's son's cancer was connected to his parents' attachment to a witchcraft demon that rules the Coptics. As an aside, although Irene did not deny the assessment, she indicated that for her to pull herself and her son out of the Coptic Church would be devastating on all aspects of her life, particularly because her pastor was her brother in-law, her husband's brother. Such a step would bring about a family discord that Irene stated she was not prepared to contend with.

As her counselor, I sympathized with her, not underrating or trivializing the impact of her decision not to leave the Coptic Church, even though she had deep reservations about it prior to contacting me for prayer. Unfortunately, I was placed in a position to have to refuse to participate in her case any further. All I could do was to ask the Lord to continue to reveal and expose this idolatry to Irene, her husband and the rest of the family. I have learned from experience that I would have put myself in jeopardy when those with knowledge refuse to obey the Lord. As Jesus said in Matthew 10: I DID NOT COME TO BRING PEACE, BUT A SWORD! IF YOU LOVE BROTHER-IN-LAW MORE THAN YOU LOVE ME, THEN YOU ARE NOT WORTHY OF ME!! Some may disagree, but since Irene knows the truth yet refuses to obey, she is not worthy to stand with me in the gap for her son to receive his healing. In addition, I would be risking myself to a counterattack.

Rather than attempt to study darkness in detail, my contact with false religions and the like is to study the overall strategies and devices of darkness as they relate to the captive's personality traits and qualities of the soul that cause him to be vulnerable. Since light will overpower darkness when light is "turned on", so too both the counselor and the captive should not just study the light but practice walking in the light. Since we can never really know with absolute certainty that the captive is saved, one of the most effective weeding strategies built into the DAF is to assess the captives understanding about salvation.

THE THREE "R'S": REPENTANCE, RESURRECTION, AND REBIRTH

Let us consider the words of the Lord as recorded in John Ch. 3. Jesus declared that "that which is flesh is flesh, and that which is spirit is spirit." Put another way, the Lord is saying that there are natural laws and there are spiritual laws. There is a material world and there is a spirit world. There is a gulf or an invisible separation between the supernatural and the natural. The Lord Jesus Christ can understand us because He created us. However, until we become "saved" or "born again", we can't understand Him. Jesus said it this way. Unless you are born again you can "see" or "perceive/understand the kingdom of God. Also, you must be born again to enter the kingdom of God. I interpret this to mean that no one can become saved unless he understands the basic elements of salvation: repentance, rebirth, and resurrection.

These 3 "R"s must be understood in order to be saved. Therefore the DAF asks the captive to define these crucial elements of salvation to assess whether or not the captive understands these basic truths. The DAF is not looking for a memorized, intellectual statement that is learned in church, but an understanding that comes from the heart and demonstrates not only a mindset, but faith in the heart. Faith in the heart is addressed through a question that asks the captive to describe in detail his salvation experience.

REPENTANCE

Where these 3 doctrines are concerned, I look for evidence of understanding rather than evidence of doctrinal or scriptural competence. In order to assess whether or not the captive understands repentance, the keyword is "godly" sorrow, as opposed to human sadness. Repentance will often be accompanied by tears, but everyone who goes to a church altar with tears running down their faces has not necessarily repented. Tears may be motivated by human sorrow: loss, disappointment, anger, regrets, etc. Godly sorrow is when a person recognizes that within the core of his nature that he is a sinner and as such, has hurt God. Beware of sorrow that is no more than self abasement that is ashamed of not being perfect. The sorrow that is felt should be directed toward the Lord Jesus Christ and the cross.

I have found that tears for Jesus's suffering at the cross can also be deceptive. For example, when a child watches a cartoon friend on TV be hit over the head by another cartoon villain, the child will feel the sorrow of that situation and cry. This example is to suggest that human beings will feel sorry for the suffering that other human beings go through. Disasters that are reported on newscasts will provoke tears. Such sorrow is not godly sorrow. To be saved is not to focus on the Lord's suffering alone. The focus of repentance is that God Himself died for ME because of the wretch of who I myself am. This is godly sorrow that will produce the fruit of salvation---a repentance that will translate us from the kingdom of darkness into the kingdom of light. Baptism is an important weapon in deliverance because its symbolism is a message to the demons that the captive has left the kingdom of darkness and therefore, the demons no longer have any legal rights to him.

REBIRTH or "regeneration" should be understood as an escape from the wrath that is to come because of sin. The wages of sin is death but the gift of God is eternal life. The captive needs to understand that his salvation is an unearned gift that is a result of the fact that he has been called and chosen by God Himself to be saved. One of the major doctrines of false religions is that the salvation that is preached is often either subtly or blatantly connected to a works doctrine. What the captive should understand regarding his salvation is that he is not born "of blood, nor of the will of the flesh, nor of the will of man, but of God." Generally you will be able to tell if a person is not saved, if asked directly 'are you saved?' Those who do not understand the "3 R's" might respond in any of the following manners: "I've been in church since I was a child" or "I've never known a time when I didn't believe in God" or "my father is a pastor" or "I've read the bible from Genesis to revelation", or "I don't smoke, drink cause I was raised in a good Christian home." Such answers suggest that the captive does not really understand salvation and is therefore not saved.

RESURRECTION must also be clearly understood, for it is essential to salvation. You would be surprised to know how many people are in church who believe that resurrection means "to die and become a spirit." Even when they have a knowledge of the meaning of mortality and immortality, they still do not understand that Jesus visited His followers after His resurrection in a material body of human substance. Nor do they understand that the dead, both those in Christ, and unbelievers will one day materialize in a physical yet immortal body. When a captive does not understand the true meaning of the Resurrection, it will be clear that this client is not saved. Why? Because Paul wrote to the Corinthians that "if Christ is not risen then your faith is vain and you are still in your sins." Therefore, if the captive does not have a clear understanding of what it means "to be risen", then he is not saved.

FALSE RELIGION AND 12 STEPS

Since 12 Steps programs are "religious", they can be grouped with other religious cults who have a form of godliness but who deny the power of Jesus Christ as the Almighty God. They deny Him, the One who declares that He is the only way to the Father, by teaching that there are several ways "to the Higher Power." As such, there are two religious groups within traditional recovery programs: those who claim to love Jesus but who also love the world in subtle and often deceptive ways, and those who hate Jesus outright. The unseen forces behind both strategies are the withcraft demon and the religious spirit. Both of these demons are very clever. While the religious demon will pretend to the end that the captive/addict is a faithful follower of the Lord Jesus Christ, the witchcraft demon, the spirit of the anti-christ will never do it. In the unseen world, the witchcraft demon is in charge of addiction for two reasons: the elements of sorcery or phamacology and the fact that addicts tend to be extremely rebellious. As the bible says, "rebellion is as the sin of witchcraft." ( )

Once the witchcraft demon has been exposed, it will use the captive to scream obscenities with Jesus's name, and the demon will speak out and openly confess Satan and deny that Jesus is Lord. Where the witchcraft demon is concerned, you must realize that you must walk in the power of God, or you will be defeated. Where the conflict between the kingdom of God and the religious demon focuses on truth and error, the conflict between The Lord's followers and the witchcraft demon is a struggle between counterfeit power and the supernatural power of the Holy Spirit. In these last days, everyone should be prepared for the challenges of living in a supernatural age. To overcome the increasing power of the enemy, particularly the witchcraft demon, you must earnestly seek knowledge, discernment and wisdom.

A true and a living faith is demonstrated by a Christian who not only preaches, teaches and counsels, but who also demonstrates the power of God. If you do not have the faith to walk the supernatural walk, then you ought not challenge this demon. If you are going to be a "half steppin" Christian, your sobriety will be in danger and therefore, you should hold on to 12 steps and not venture into the recovery option of the seven keys as presented in Part VI. Once you have decided to walk by faith, you should also be very patient, deliberate and careful.In truth, where unbelievers are concerned, no demon should be cast out until that person becomes saved. I myself am personally an example of a person who had a witchcraft demon: a spirit of divination, that the Holy Spirit sovereignly cast from me at the moment of rebirth. Once I was saved, demons could no longer enter my soul and speak through my larynx according to their own will.

Twenty eight years have passed and I have not had one such occultic experience ever again, wherein it was a constant occurrence prior to my salvation. Nevertheless, my experience has shown that this is not really the way the Lord chooses to contend with this or any other demon. Where the witchcraft demon is concerned, the Lord is seeking "a Moses" with a rod in his hand to set his people free. The witchcraft demon in the sorcerer was able to turn a rod into a snake. However, Moses' snake devoured the sorcerer's snake. As Elijah challenged and defeated the supernatural power of Baal with the power of the Holy Spirit, believers in the Lord Jesus Christ are called to do the same.

Therefore, in order to stand against the demon of addiction who is under the command of the spirit of witchcraft, these demons must respect the fact that you are anointed to cast them out and that your faith in the name of Jesus is greater than their faith in the name of Satan. Without this respect, you will not be victorious because the witchcraft demon is the strongest fighter in the enemy's army. Even so, it is easier to cast out a spirit of witchcraft than a religious demon because of one thing: the freewill of the captive. Because of the repeated cycle of torment characterized by the witchcraft demon in general and the demon of addiction in particular, the addict who has reached his bottom is more prone to participate in the struggle to be set free. On the other hand, the religious demon will cleverly use certain so called Christian captives to continually demonstrate within the institutional church and the 12 Steps community that the power of Jesus Name to deliver them is not as strong as the power of 12 Steps. These captives are those who religiously show up every Sunday for church but who consistently fail to remain clean and sober thereby proving that the rooms of NA/AA are superior to "going to church."

: TILLING**

CHAPTER #6:
THE LABOR AND THE REST

THE SPIRITUAL RECIVIDIST

As the gardener of the ground of our own souls, tilling involves our cultivation of the seed through study, care and labor. While the weeding process involves the uncovering of those attitudes, thoughts and habits that have been hurtful or have hindered our growth, the tilling stage ensures our freedom from being ensnared by the same traps that caused our original defeat. Weeding is to self examination as tilling is to self determination. As we examine our weeds, we strive to know ourselves better than the demonic world knows us. Coupled with weeding, tilling produces a steadfast determination never to yield to any person, place, thing or circumstance that originally caused our defeat. In a manner of speaking, tilling is a form of weed control geared toward avoiding relapse, which I refer to as spiritual recidivism or backsliding. While weeding kills or breaks, tilling builds or strengthens. Both processes occur simultaneously and continually throughout life. God ever tears down in order to rebuild and restore.

"And I will restore to you the years that the locust hath eaten, the cankerworm, and the caterpillar, and the palmerworm, MY GREAT ARMY WHICH I SENT AMONG YOU." (Joel 2:25)

In the natural realm, a recidivist is one who gives up by relapsing into a previous condition or mode of behavior---a term most often used to describe the failure of rehabilitation and a return to a life of crime. In this context, rehabilitation is restoration to a former capacity that is socially acceptable. Similarly, the old testament used the term "backslider" to describe one who falls away from a life of faith and returns to a life of unrighteousness or sin. However, in the new testament, the concept of regeneration transcends rehabilitation and the term "backslider" is not mentioned. On the contrary, in Christ, rehabilitation is impossible because the work of the cross is to symbolically "kill" the life of the soul so that from the spirit will spring forth newness of life wherein the soul will be renewed daily. As Paul declared to the believers in Galatia, "I am crucified with Christ, nevertheless, I live; yet not I, but Christ liveth in me. And the life I now live in the flesh I live by faith of the Son of God, who loved me, and gave Himself for me." (Galatians 2:20). Therefore, regeneration or "rebirth" involves the death of the soul life and the infilling of new life, which is God Himself.

Tilling is an ongoing process that involves a permanent surrender to this significant spiritual truth---WE MUST DIE DAILY! We are to "work out" the salvation of the soul with fear and trembling, "for it is God which worketh in us both to will and to do His good pleasure." (Philippians 2:12,13) We labor in vain when we attempt to rehabilitate or revive what Jesus Christ compels to die! It is God's good pleasure to crucify the soul life, because the carnal human mind is His enemy, having been molded by the world. (Romans 8:7 and James 4:4). Death and rebirth are well described by Dr. M. Scott Peck in "The Road Less Traveled:"

The pain of giving up is the pain of death, but death of the old is birth of the new. The pain of death is the pain of birth, and the pain of birth is the pain of death. For us to develop a new and better idea, concept, theory or understanding means that an old idea, concept, theory or understanding must die. (Peck, p. 74)

The downfall of the spiritual recidivist is a belief in man's capacity to change himself. Consistent and intense tilling will ultimately bring us to the revelation that without the divine essence of God working within us, we cannot affect a lasting self change. Even strong will power and discipline are no match for the desires and appetites of the human flesh.

Furthermore, as we till, we discover that the Lord will very often create the best out of the worst. Within every relapse is the seed of a breakthrough if we learn how to understand the symbolic language of the spirit. Through study, care and labor that is guided by the Holy Spirit, we can become empowered to find the strength to resist temptation, to overcome persecution and to triumph over challenging circumstances. In order to strengthen our spirits, The Lord will use various "spiritual" fertilizers. A natural fertilizer is an earthly substance applied to the soil by a farmer or a gardener to enrich the soil's productivity so that it might bare fruit in an abundance. By comparison, within the field of human productivity, fertilization is the process of enhanced impregnation. Consider that as manure is a fertilizer to earthly ground,---faith---a spiritual substance--- is God's fertilizer for the human spirit. Faith enriches the spirit's ability to bare fruit in a barren land where past failures and defeats have depleted our source of hope, trust and courage.

GIANTS IN THE LAND!

Recorded in the old testament book of Numbers,--- the symbolically speaking "THIRTEENTH" chapter--- and summarized in the third chapter of the book of Hebrews beginning with the "THIRTEENTH" verse---is an account of the Israelite's reaction to the giants in Canaan. At God's command, Moses sent 12 men to spy out the land which God promised to give to the Israelites. At the end of forty days, the twelve spies returned to the people, ten with a negative report, and two with a positive report. The negative report was quite clear. Ten spies declared: "Look here, Moses! We came to the land to which you sent us; it flows with milk and honey, and this is its fruit. Yet the people who dwell in the land are strong. The bottom line is that there are giants in the land, and we are like grasshoppers in our own sight." By contrast, Joshua and Caleb spoke power packed words: "Let's go up at once and occupy Canaan, <u>FOR WE ARE WELL ABLE TO OVERCOME IT.</u> Do not rebel against the Lord and do not fear the giants because they are bread for us; The Lord is with us. <u>DO NOT FEAR THE GIANTS!</u>" (Numbers Ch 13)

The writer of the book of Hebrews further explains why the Israelites did not enter into the Lord's rest for four reasons: they hardened their hearts, they did not know God's ways, they were rebellious, and they did not believe. As a result, they wandered about in the wilderness for forty years until each person died, except for Joshua and Caleb. Less than a day's trip took forty years because God removed His guidance and direction, and the people remained ineffectual and confused. The Lord revealed to me that the cycle of addiction is akin to the Israelites wandering around in circles, never reaching the land of promise because they are fixated on faulty beliefs about Him. Challenging an addict's myths that have multigenerational roots is a formidable task, even for God. For example, the quest for unwavering self control is a time consuming giant that can only result in harmful preoccupation and bondage. The fact that substance abuse can be controlled for years and then suddenly and elusively re-appear is a perplexing paradox within the addictive cycle that fosters overconfidence on the one hand, and shame, doubt and depression as the aftermath of a relapse. This "gigantic" dilemma keeps the addict's life unmanageable, as the abyss between victory and defeat deepens and becomes hell on earth.

Addicts arrive at the doorstep of a 12 Step program as though it were the land of Canaan, seeking solutions, only to hear familiar testimonies of vulnerability that confirm the tenacity of the addictive cycle, namely, that there are "giants in the land." As a part of the recovery process, they develop a network of associates, --- the ten spies--- each of whom are bound to the same cycle of victory and defeat---each anxiously counting days of sobriety---sporting their number of days clean as a tangible badge of their momentary self worth and for each relapse, having to recount from day one. I believe that the Lord Jesus Christ's prophetic word to the addict is a word of warning and rebuke:" You do not know me. You are in disobedience and rebellion for by my stripes you are healed. Not only are you healed physically, but I have even bore your anxiety, shame and frustration on Calvary's cross. Yet, in your rebellion, you refuse me as your Higher Power. I have asked you to come unto me, all of you who are heavy laden with this addictive cycle, yet you refuse. My yoke is easy. My burden is light. In me, you will find freedom. In me, you will enter into rest. Yet, you have hardened your heart with doubt and unbelief. You refuse to give me my proper place as God. AA is your God and not Me! Therefore, YOU SHALL NOT ENTER INTO MY REST! You will wander about in your self created wilderness, and Satan will continue to make it a living hell for you."

Consider Gertrude. While still caught in this hellish addictive cycle coupled with HIV infection, Gertrude became born again, receiving Jesus Christ as her Lord and Savior. With her conversion, she received faith to believe the prophecy of Isaiah[6]--- that Jesus Christ had already healed her of HIV/AIDS two thousand years ago at his bloody cross. Gertrude has remained asymptomatic for several years. Without any fear of the blood disease and in spite of her faith in healing, she has continued to struggle with episodic drinking. How could Gertrude believe for the physical healing of a deadly disease for which there is no man-made cure, and yet not believe for healing from alcohol? The life of God is in her, and this life continues to issue forth to believe for one kind of healing, yet this same life is blocked from passing through her spirit to reinforce her sobriety. Confused and bewildered, Gertrude stands with one foot in Canaan and one foot in the wilderness.

I suspect that the blockage is threefold. First of all, it is easier to believe God when there are no giants in the land. For five years, Gertrude has known that she was HIV positive, and thus far, she has been as healthy as the next person. Her T-cell count has remained normal, her body weight consistent, and her immune system triumphant over the common cold and other infections. However, the test of her belief that she is healed will be challenged if an early sign of the disease were to appear. If or when the giants rear their ugly heads, Gertrude's trust in the healing power of Jesus Christ will be confronted. Secondly, it is easier to believe God when mankind has failed to discover a cure. When, like the Israelites, our backs are up against the Red Sea and the enemy surrounds us on every side, we have no place to turn for deliverance and rescue except to God. This is the reality of the first step in AA. Once we admitted to our powerlessness, then we considered turning ourselves over to a god who is more powerful than we. However, as soon as we gain a few days of sobriety and find a semblance of self control, we begin to put our trust in "the Program" and not in God. Even though we at first admitted that our lives were unmanageable and that we needed Him, now we begin to define our recovery in our own terms.

Once established in recovery, addicts trust in meetings more than in God. They trust sponsors more than God. In fact, they become possessed by "working" the Program, and not by trusting God! The cost of this kind of recovery is that they surrender their rest and their peace by investing overwhelming effort, time and energy into works, as opposed to leaning on God's grace. As they steadily count the number of meetings they attend each week, with forked tongue, non-Christian sponsors warn Christians in recovery that spending too much time in church is a crutch! Nonetheless, very few churches offer more than two services a week in comparison to the availability of city wide, round the clock AA meetings.

Attempting to control the addiction with human will power is an exhausting struggle against life that Satan will ultimately win. However, not by (human) might and not by (human) power, but by My Spirit saith the Lord!(Zechariah 4:6) Greater is He that is within us than He that is in the world.(IJohn4:4) That same resurrection power that raised Jesus Christ from the dead is within us.(Ephesians 1:20) That same power is the Holy Spirit within us that works IN us exceedingly abundantly more than we could ask or think! (Ephesians 3:20) Therefore, we can do ALL things through Christ who strengthens us. (Philippians 4:13) Moreover, the things that are impossible with men are possible with God. (Luke 18:12) The victory lies in the operation of the spirit of life in Christ Jesus, who has made us free from the law of sin and death.(Roman8:2)

Finally, Christ-centered counseling revealed that the root that sustains Gertrude's giant of addiction is her deep feelings of guilt and shame. As a by-product of her addiction, Gertrude never felt accepted by other people. Consequently, she developed a root of perfectionism in order to avoid rejection. To illustrate, Gertrude recently admitted to her sponsor of a slip, wherein she drank a couple of beers. Expecting to find encouragement and understanding, the sponsor criticized and reprimanded her. "You have lost all of your previous days of sobriety. Now you have to start all over again." Looking for acceptance of her less than perfect behavior, Gertrude then turned to her pastor for counsel and advice, where she was surprised to find an aloof disinterest or lack of expertise. Her pastor declared,"I cannot advise you on these matters." So Gertrude's slip turned into a relapse. However, not yet physically addicted and with eight days of sobriety to her credit, Gertrude admitted herself into a 30 day residential detox program. Why? Well, in her own words, "I needed to be assured of having at least thirty days sobriety under my belt. I needed to be able to tell my sponsor that I've been clean for thirty days."

It is clear that persons who are shame-filled and discouraged are much more likely to relapse at the thought of losing the very thing that has sustained their self respect. A gentle and sensitive person, Gertrude continues to struggle with slips and relapses because she has not been able to appropriate the liberty that is in Christ Jesus. All too familiar with the shame and humiliation of the wilderness of addiction, Gertrude could easily surrender to the Lord Jesus Christ as a sinner and believe Him for healing from AIDS. However, she did not allow the power of His forgiveness to cleanse her from the condemnation and guilt of her past. Besides, she had grown to think of herself as an addict. In her mind, an addict is a defective person. Therefore, each day of sobriety represented ever increasing tangible proof that she was worthy of approval and acceptance from others. Therefore, her record of recovery became too crucial to her survival.

Once Gertrude's soul absorbs the reality of her new birth in Christ Jesus---that she has been made the righteousness of God in Christ---that there is no guilt or condemnation to those who are in Christ Jesus---that in God's eyes she has no past--- and that each day is a fresh start with God, she will become spiritually empowered. When she internalizes the truth,--- the truth---, who is Jesus Christ, will set her free. The whole truth is that once we have confessed and repented of our daily wrongdoing, He is faithful and just to forgive us and to cleanse us. (I John 1:7-9) The power of this truth is that once planted in the ground of Gertrude's soul and spirit, it will curse her root of shame and guilt! This truth further suggests the insignificance of 30 days or even thirty years of sobriety in the annals of eternal time in the spirit.

The Labor And The Rest

ENTERING THE PROMISE LAND

The promise land of the old testament children of God was the literal place of Canaan. However, the promise land for post-Calvary believers is a spiritual place which Jesus Christ has named "the kingdom of God" or the "kingdom of heaven." Although in the spiritual world there is an actual place beyond outer space called "heaven", the spiritual location of heaven is within the reborn, recreated spirit of every believer in the Lord Jesus Christ. Inexplicable and mysterious, this spiritual kingdom is the seat of all spiritual empowerment and recovery. If we can "enter in", we will find joy unspeakable, full of glory. (IPeter 1:8) For eye has not seen, nor has ear heard, neither have "entered in" to the heart or spirit of man, the things which God has prepared for them that love Him. (ICorinthians 2:9)

Jesus said that no one could either see or enter this kingdom unless his or her spirit becomes born again. Although rebirth is necessary for entering heaven after death , I propose that Jesus was not necessarily emphasizing the physical place called heaven. I believe that to "see the kingdom" is to be spiritually enlightened to understand God's will and His ways. For according to Paul the Apostle:

> ...Even so, the things of God knoweth no man, but the Spirit of God. Now we have received, not the spirit of the world, but the spirit which is of God; that we might know the things that are freely given to us of God. Which things also we speak, not in the words which man's wisdom teacheth, but which the Holy Ghost teacheth; comparing spiritual things with spiritual. BUT THE NATURAL MAN RECEIVETH NOT THE THINGS OF THE SPIRIT OF GOD; FOR THEY ARE FOOLISHNESS UNTO HIM; NEITHER CAN HE KNOW THEM BECAUSE THEY ARE SPIRITUALLY DISCERNED. (ICorinthians 2:11-15)

Since the Lord's ways are not our ways and His thoughts are not our thoughts, we need a newly created spirit to be able to discern spiritual truths. Yet once our spirits have been so transformed, we also need to learn how to enter into His blessings, grace and power so that we might take the land that is ours. Once we receive Jesus Christ as Lord and Savior over our lives, we inherit the blessings that are His and we enter into heaven while we are yet on earth. Within this context, "heaven" for a person in recovery is being able to walk in the spirit and not surrender to the lust or cravings.

Through the tilling process, the Holy Spirit trains us to walk in victory on earth, as though we were already in the literal place called heaven! In order to live a victorious spiritual life, we must be fit to "take the land" because we realize that our God is able. For according to Paul, within His resurrection is our entrance into a heavenly seat which we take at the moment of our conversion. For rich in mercy and love, God has resurrected our dead spirits and saved our souls. Every believer in Christ is positionally seated with Christ in heavenly places while we are yet on earth. (Galatians 5,6) Although He is literally seated at the right hand of God the Father, we are spiritually with Him. This spiritual position is activated when, by faith, we use His name. For Jesus said that whatever we bind on earth is bound in heaven and whatever we loose on earth is loosed in heaven. Simply stated, God and His angelic kingdom in heaven will back us up when we stand our ground and trust in Him to help us take the land from Satan and his cohorts.

Within this framework, to be spiritually empowered for a person in recovery is to first of all realize that an addict is the devil's prey or captive whom Jesus Christ came to set free. However, Satan's captivity of all so-called addicts is unlawful because Jesus has inherited the heathen. From the prophetic utterances of David, this truth is revealed:

> Why do the heathen rage, and the people imagine a vain thing? The kings of the earth set themselves, and the rulers take counsel together, against the Lord, and against his anointed, saying, Let us break their bands

asunder, and cast away their cords from us. He that sitteth in the heavens shall laugh: the Lord shall have them in derision. Then shall He speak unto them in His wrath, and vex them in His sore displeasure. Yet have I set my king upon my holy hill of Zion. I will declare the decree: the Lord has said unto me, Thou art my Son; this day have I begotten thee. Ask of me, and I shall give thee the heathen for thine inheritance: and the uttermost parts of the earth for thy possession. (Psalm 2:1-7)

This prophecy of David indicates that once the Holy Spirit had raised Jesus from the dead, the Father gave the Son permission to ask for the heathen of the earth for His inheritance. We can safely infer that Jesus asked for and received ALL of His inheritance. Webster's dictionary defines a heathen as one who doe not acknowledge the God of the Bible. In keeping with this definition, I further presume that recovering addicts without Christ as Lord could be categorized as "heathen". Therefore, whether an "addict" likes it or not, he is a part of the Lord's inheritance, and Satan has no legal right to his life. As joint heirs with Christ, we too inherit. We inherit the kingdom. (Galatians 4:7, James 2:5, Hebrews 6:17) Coupled with every inheritance is a legal document or a will. In the bible, the old and new testaments contain the terms of our will and is called a covenant.

A covenant is a contract or an agreement that requires all parties involved in it to give all of themselves to the partnership or friendship. In western countries, contracts or covenants are sealed and validated by written signatures. However, in ages past, African, Indian and Semitic tribes authorized a covenant by the shedding and mixing of blood. Blood covenant between two tribes was an act of strong friendship and brotherhood, where all goods and services were mutually available, one tribe to another. The penalty for trucebreaking was death. By comparison, today blood has been replaced by ink and written contracts or covenants are often broken. Nonetheless, the blood covenant of Jesus Christ is everlasting because the blood shed at His death established the covenant in this age and in all ages to come. When we consider the blood covenant of Jesus of Nazareth, it becomes clear why Paul tells us that presenting our bodies as a living sacrifice as our part of the contract is a reasonable service. With the shedding of His blood at the cross, we are brought into an inheritance that requires us to give our all to Him as He has given His all to us. We receive within the terms of our contract or covenant all that is His to give---salvation, righteousness, faith, healing, justification, forgiveness, deliverance, abundant blessings. In exchange, the life we live on earth belongs to Him. Our contribution to the contract is more than reasonable since our lives are not worthless when we consider that a sentence of death was placed upon us at birth, for all have sinned and come short of the glory of God. (Romans 3:23)

Nevertheless, to God, we are valuable. He has a work to do in us. He has His own expectations of each and every one of us. Since the Christ gave all, He expects all. No one would even die for a righteous man much less for a sinner. The blood of Jesus buys us from Satan. We were chained to the devil's slave block, sold to the highest bidder. Jesus is the highest bidder. He buys us and puts His seal on us in the same way that a rancher brands his cattle. We are His sheep, and as a good shepherd, Jesus brands us as His own and becomes our Master. Once purchased and branded, He then transforms us into His equals. What a Master! He is our Master yet He refers to Himself as our Servant. We are transformed from servants or slaves to friends. We are washed and clothed in the fine spiritual linen of righteousness and caused to:

1. sit in heavenly places with Christ Jesus;

2. walk in the spirit; and

3. stand our ground against the fiery darts of Satan.

There are many born again believers, both in and out of recovery, still positioned in the wilderness and have not entered into God's rest. They have seen the kingdom but they have not enter it. Moreover, they have an inheritance that they have not claimed as their own by faith. Such people sit in worldly places, walk according to the vanity of their minds and cannot stand their ground against the trials and tribulations of the wicked one. Once the reality of who they are in Christ becomes sealed in their spirits and renewed in their minds, they will become spiritually empowered. The tilling experience of the Holy Spirit is a developmental process where the ground of the soul is prepared to transform its conceptual position into an actual spiritual reality.

CHAPTER #7: WATERING THE SEED

A THIRST FOR RIGHTEOUSNESS

In the natural environment, watering the seed bed can be a very delicate matter. For example, too much rain can flood the seed while a lack of rain can dry up the seed and produce famine. However, in the spiritual realm, even though we may be spiritually starved and parched, the seed can never be destroyed by an overabundance of water, because the water is God Himself in the personality of the Holy Spirit. Jesus pronounced that the Holy Spirit shall flow out of our inner fountain, as recorded in the gospel of John: If any man is thirsty, let him come to me and drink! He who believes in Me {who cleaves to and trusts in and relies on Me} as the Scripture has said, From his innermost being shall flow {continuously} springs and rivers of living water. But He was speaking here of the Spirit, Whom those who believed (trusted, had faith) in Him were afterward to receive.) (John 7:37-39 The Amplified Bible.)

In order for seed to grow and to develop into the spiritual fruit of love, joy, peace, patience, meekness, gentleness, goodness, faith, and self control, we must experience a spiritual hunger and a thirst. This spiritual truth is recorded in the Beatitudes of Jesus Christ:

"Blessed are those who hunger and thirst after righteousness, for they shall be filled." (Matthew 5:6)

The blessing is the result of the well of living water of the Holy Spirit within, an outgrowth of the born again experience. Located deep within our spirits is a fountain of tap water that is activated by our thirst for righteousness and motivated by our desire to know the truth. (John 4:14) The blessing that we seek is spiritual empowerment and recovery. I believe that as we thirst for righteousness, we shall be filled and satisfied with self control and victory over the addictions. In this context, the righteousness that we seek is not based upon our conduct of self achievement or good works ---not upon the number of recovery meetings we attend a week. Our righteousness is not even based upon the length of our sobriety. However, as we obtain a right relationship with our God, ---a relationship of intimacy based upon our knowing Him through His word and through a personal closeness with His Son--- the righteousness of God will activate the inner fountain of His Very Self within us. As we ever seek to please Him by knowing Jesus, our inner fountain will begin to water the word-seed within. This inner watering will create the condition for fruits of righteousness to grow. An essential fruit within recovery is to discover that we are empowered from within to remain sober. The need for meetings should be replaced by a desire for group worship and fellowship with those who love the same Lord.

The personal and spiritual power of the well within is recorded by The Apostle John in regards to the Lord's message to the woman at the well. (John 4) Once the inner well has been transformed into an overflowing river, the goal of the watering process is not only for personal nourishment, but also for group enhancement. Therefore, I suggest that if we can unleash the outpouring of the well within, we will not

.y be able to supply ourselves but we have the capacity to be a vital source for the nourishment of others. The well and the river are symbolic of both the in-dwelling and the overflowing power of the Holy Spirit within our spirits. He equips us to be outpouring witnesses of the Lord 's eternal immortality as He leads us to demonstrate the power of the risen Lord in our very own lives. However, we cannot be witnesses unless we have a testimony. John wrote in his letter that we have an unction from the Holy One and we know ALL things. (IJohn 2:20-27) Rephrased and amplified, this scripture suggests that deep in our fountain within is the source of all knowledge and wisdom, both generic and specific, both general and personal. This unction is a special anointing or endowment given by the Holy Ghost. It is God's supernatural ability applied to man's natural insufficiency.

RECEIVING THE TRUTH

Jesus said that those of us who worship Him, must worship Him in spirit and in truth. (John 4:14) It is the role of the Holy Spirit to enlighten us. "Howbeit when he, the Spirit of truth, is come, he shall lead us into all truth." (John 16:13) Truth is the spiritual essence of a person, situation or circumstance, without deception or confusion. Spiritual truth is God's revelation and understanding applied to a host of outward facts. To know the truth and to deny it is to lie, while to believe a lie is to be deceived, a condition that can lead to obsession. There are those who welcome obsession because it can be the soul's easiest defense mechanism toward avoiding the hurt and pain that real truth often brings. Therefore, in our desire to find solutions, we create our own superficial doctrines and teachings. However, only in the light of God can we know what God knows and see what God sees.

In his book entitled *"Spiritual Reality or Obsession"*, Watchman Nee reveals how we can avoid obsession:

"Those who know themselves in the light of God know their own selves indeed. If we are not in God's light we may sin without being conscious of how wicked our sin is, we may fall without being fully aware of how shameful our fall is. ... Our judgement is undependable, our thought is undependable, our action is undependable. We are subject to error. What we judge as right may not necessarily be right; what we judge as wrong may not be wrong at all. That which we consider to be sweet may actually be bitter, and vice versa. That which we take as light may not be light after all, and that which we take as darkness may turn out not to be darkness. We must not substitute for the light of God the firebrands which we ourselves kindle. We should receive light from God." (Nee, pg. 62-63)

To worship the Christ in spirit, we need to respond to His invitation to come unto Him and drink! Once we flood our spirits and quench our thirst with the presence of the Christ, we will lose our desire for drinking and drugging, for a clean and an unclean spirit cannot drink from the same fountain. (James 3:12) However, we cannot drink of Him if we come to Him with preconceived notions about addiction that hinder the outpouring of the Holy Spirit. If we submit to the truth of God's word, the Holy Spirit within us will wash away misconceptions, confusion and false teaching. We must ask the Lord to reveal the truth to us about addiction.

DISEASE OR SIN?!

Likewise, one of the most inconsistent teachings within the 12 Steps of recovery to the concept of the righteousness of God is the perpetuation of the disease model. Although sin and disease are closely linked, other than for mental illness, a disease is a physical impairment or sickness of the body that may or may not be the result of personal or generational sin. It is true that repetitive acts of unrighteousness can bring about disease. By illustration, sexual immorality can open the door to HIV infection and other sexually transmitted diseases. Fornication can also lead to a compulsive sexual addiction. However, there is a difference between those who acquire a disease as a result of their own debauchery than of the guiltlessly infirmed paralytic or the chronically ill. It is unfortunate that the eyes of secular treatment have been blinded by the human intellect, will and emotions. The basic truths of the scriptures have been replaced with therapeutic jargon that denies the existence of the spirit world and the power of God. According to God's word, drunkenness is a progressive infirmity that originates as sin comparable to idolatry, crime, and sexual immorality and not to diseases such as cancer or multiple sclerosis.

"Do you not know that the unrighteous and the wrongdoers will not inherit or have any share in the kingdom of God? Do not be deceived (misled): neither the impure and immoral, nor idolaters, nor adulterers, nor those who participate in homosexuality, nor cheats (swindlers and thieves), nor greedy graspers, NOR DRUNKARDS, nor foulmouthed revilers and slanderers, nor extortioners and robbers will inherit the kingdom of God. And such some of you were (once). But you were WASHED clean (purified by a complete atonement for sin and made free from the guilt of sin), and you were consecrated, (set apart, hallowed), and you were justified (pronounced righteous,) by trusting in the name of the Lord Jesus Christ and in the Holy Spirit of our God." (lCorinthians 6:9-11)

This scripture unmistakenly links drunkenness to unrighteousness, wrongdoing and immorality and not with disease. The opposite of righteousness is sin, rebellion and disobedience. Therefore, to those who uphold the disease model, we could rephrase by its polarity the Lord's teaching in the Beatitudes (Matthew 5: in this manner:

"Cursed is the man who hungers and thirsts after sin, for he shall be empty and dissatisfied."

It is truly a curse to hunger and thirst after euphoric substances that perpetuate the very things that God hates. It is also pitiful to be in such rebellion toward God that He is only acknowledged out of desperation as a brief sanctuary of protection and safety from the afflictions of an uncontrollable life. Is it not the way of the one who has achieved sobriety to hide in his unfaithful heart a love of his former lascivious life, where God is only a temporary substitute for the lusts of the flesh that lead to death?

Furthermore, to indulge one's flesh is sin. The wages of sin is both physical and spiritual death. Once the flesh has become habituated to the substance, repentance is almost impossible. Without true repentance, there can be no forgiveness. How can one be sincerely sorry for partaking of the very substance that he craves! This is why Paul warns the believers at the church in Corinth that drunkards cannot inherit the kingdom of God.

Although an extreme example of a lust for intoxication of all kinds--- Blanche was an example of an addict who was fully anesthetized to the desperation of being out of control. From heroin, to methadone, to alcohol and finally to crack addiction, Blanche was never overwhelmed by any of the repercussions of living on the edge. Countless detoxifications were endured as a means to gain enough strength to continue drinking and drugging. However, the most profound aspect of this case is that Blanche's love of darkness was so strong, that she would argue tenaciously when her concept of God was confronted. Bound with all sorts of false religious teachings, Blanche would do almost anything to avoid the truth about Jesus Christ, choosing any other conceivable explanation for God except Jesus.

A year after my own conversion, we met in 1978 at a substance abuse treatment program where I was employed as her counselor for about a year. A closeness developed between us and I continued to counsel Blanche long after I left that job. In fact, Blanche was a faithful friend of mine for years. When I was unemployed, she used to put a few dollars in my hand by calling me to drive her places, instead of paying for a cab. A faithful friend, Blanche was at the church when I preached my first sermon in 1981 and for the next ten years, I continued to witness to Blanche about the Lord. Our friendship was not onesided. I was the one who took Blanche to the hospital when she went into acute alcohol and methadone withdrawal. A novice in matters of demon possession, I cast several demons from her. Once she even poured her alcohol down the kitchen sink, only to purchase another bottle fifteen minutes later. Finally, she said to me, "enough is enough. Leave me alone, Sis. I'm just not ready. I'll call you when I'm ready." She never called me. However, in 1995, God spoke to me in an audible voice about Blanche. He said these words. "BLANCHE IS DEAD!"

Since God often declares those things that are about to happen in the present tense, I believed that there still might be enough time for the Lord to save her. Consequently, I telephoned various people about Blanche until I found someone who knew where she lived and I went to see her. In April of 1995, Blanche was in the final stages of AIDS. She weighed 70 pounds and was addicted to crack. Even so, she refused to believe that she was dying. Still hopeful, she talked of getting detoxed so that she could gain some weight. Blanche was as attentive as her physical condition would allow, considering that every few minutes she would fall asleep on her feet, ironing the clothes that she was packing for her next hospital detox in the morning. I began to witness to her from Genesis to Revelation and for the first time in our relationship of 18 years, Blanche was interested and attentive, in spite of her physical limitations. I had to read each scripture to her several times because her eyesight was now impaired. However, I watched the light come into her eyes and upon her face as all of her religious confusion disappeared. What she had not understood about Christ all of those years had finally been revealed to her.

I felt in my spirit that Blanche's salvation was very close at hand. With diligence and care, I softly spoke these words: "Blanche, all you have to do is confess that Jesus is Lord, believe that He was raised from the dead and receive his shed blood for the forgiveness of your sins." Blanche looked me in the eye and said "is that All that I have to do? That is too simple. NO. I won't accept Him. Jesus is not black. I don't want Jesus. I want Allah. I want the black Muslim God." At that moment, Blanche's procrastination became clear. Years of addiction were rooted in sin that ultimately took on the symptoms of a disease. Like several alcoholics I have counseled, a root cause of drunkenness is very often rebellion and an unwillingness to submit to authority of any kind. Whatever substance that induces a euphoric state becomes itself a god. In a flash, I realized that her confusion about Christ was a purposeful form of self- deception aimed at justifying her abnormal love of intoxication. Therefore, when she finally understood the truth, she had to protect her own version of the truth by rejecting Him.

I sat quietly for a minute, watching the iron that was in her hand. I whispered, "Blanche, do you know why I am here? Do you know what the Lord said to me about you, that led me to find you?" I noticed her hand grip that hot iron. With quiet anger and with fear, Blanche warned me. "Sis, I don't want to hear no bad news. Don't tell me about none of your dreams. It won't be fair. I am going to detox in the morning to get this crack out of my system so I can get my strength back and gain 20 pounds or so. Don't bring me no bad news."

I was well aware of Blanche's history of violence. In her stronger days, she had stabbed her share of male and female adversaries. Before she could muster the strength of her 70 pound frame to swing that iron and bash me in the head with it, the spirit of the Lord revealed that Blanche was bracing herself by clutching that iron in order to attack me. I leaped from my chair in a dancing swirl. Smiling I declared, "Blanche, I didn't come to bring you bad news. I came representing a God who wants to save you and to heal you. So, I'll be moving on. See if Allah will save you." And I left, never to look back again. A year passed and I didn't hear any news about Blanche. However, recently I dreamt that she rose up from her grave in hell to try to coerce me to go before Jesus and plead her case. Running from her grasping hands, I woke up thinking that her death must be imminent if she had not already passed. A month later, the news came. The Lord's word was fulfilled. Blanche is now dead.

It should be noted that Blanche was never sober long enough to ever experience any stability, for never once did she ever attempt to submit herself to a higher power. However, those whose sobriety eventually produces fruits of balance and security will reach a stage where the sense of their former desperation has been anesthetized. Their self deception will be disguised in yet another form. Convinced that they have surrendered to a higher power, they are unaware of the true nature of their so called submission. Since their relationship with God is one of convenience and not of genuine love, it is inevitable that they will begin to postulate that "one drink won't hurt, "---a first step toward relapse. When knowing God out of our love for Him becomes our one and only thirst, the lust for substances will be quenched, where addiction is cursed at its root.

THE WASHING AND THE CLEANSING

As depicted in Paul's letter to the Corinthians, the drunkard is included with a group of former sinners who have been washed and cleansed of unrighteousness- - - the thief, the homosexual, the adulterer, the troublemaker, the worshipper of false gods AND the drunkard have been declared righteous by God Himself. This righteousness is manifested in a spiritual renewal that has transformed them from sinners into the righteousness of God.

> But after that the kindness and love of God our Savior toward man appeared, not by works of righteousness which we have done, but according to his mercy he saved us, by the washing of regeneration, and renewing of the

Holy Ghost; which he shed on us abundantly through Jesus Christ our Savior; (Titus 3:4-6)

As the nature of the former thief is to steal no more, he is no longer a thief. As the nature of the former adulterer is to cheat no more and to be faithful to his wife, he is no longer an adulterer. In keeping with this comparison, as the nature of the drunkard is to drink no more, he is no longer a drunkard or an alcoholic. Consequently, when a drunkard declares before his peers that he is an alcoholic and as such, is afflicted with an incurable disease, not only are his thoughts, emotions and spirit negatively affected by the faith that he has in his own words, but he is also denying the power of God to cure and to heal. Crucial to recovery is to have our conscience washed and cleansed from evil thoughts and the memory of the addiction removed from the cells of the flesh by the Holy Spirit:

> Let us draw near with a true heart in full assurance of faith, having our hearts sprinkled from an evil conscience, and our bodies washed with pure water. (Hebrews 10:22)

Jesus provides a comprehensive deliverance of spirit, soul and body. Once an addict has been restored, Jesus no long views him or her as an alcoholic or a drug addict. A believer should not use such negative labels to define himself, once he or she has been set free. To even call oneself a "recovering" addict is to remain captive to the lust and hunger of the flesh for intoxicants. Complete deliverance is available in Christ Jesus wherein the captive is completely set free from the lust or hunger for drug or drink.

THE ATONEMENT OF BLOOD

A straightforward definition of atonement is an effort of making amends for one's wrongdoing, the subject of AA's step number eight. When we attempt to make amends toward each other, we put forth our best efforts to compensate those

we have injured or abused by providing them with some form of satisfaction, conciliation or balance. Furthermore, we hope that through our efforts, the injured parties will forgive us.
However, what about the Higher Power? How do we make amends toward Him? The human soul is a natural enemy to God because we have been alienated from Him. (Romans 8:7, Colossians 1:21,22) This alienation takes the form of spiritual blindness. We simply cannot comprehend the truth about the Lord. God is light and there is no darkness at all in Him, yet our humanity has a natural affinity for darkness. (John 3:19) To compensate for the contamination of man's soul, God Himself provided His own solution:

For the life of the flesh is in the blood: and I have given it to you upon the altar to make an atonement for your souls: for it is the blood that maketh an atonement for the soul. (Leviticus 17:11)

And almost all things are by the law purged with blood; and without shedding of blood is no remission. (Hebrews 9:22)

How much more shall the blood of Christ, who through the eternal Spirit offered himself without spot to God, purge your conscience from dead works to serve the living God? (Hebrews 9:14)

Giving thanks unto the Father, which hath made us meet to be partakers of the inheritance of the saints in light;

Who hath delivered us from the power of darkness, and hath translated us into the kingdom of his dear Son: In whom we have redemption through his blood, even the forgiveness of sins: (Colossians 1:12-14)

To summarize these four passages of scripture, God has declared in His word that the purging or cleansing of the soul-- --the mind, emotions, willpower and personality of man--- can only be obtained through shed blood. In reading the old and new testament, various scriptures suggest that blood, both animal and human, has the capacity to speak when it falls to the ground. In some supernatural way, the Father God can hear a voice cry out to Him from the ground and He is compelled to respond. (Genesis 4:10) To Cain in the first book of old testament, God declared that the voice of his brother Abel's blood cried out to Him for justice. Consistent with this explanation is a scripture in the last book of the new testament which indicates that the blood of the martyrs continually cries out to God for vindication. (Revelation 6:10). Therefore, I suggest that human blood spilt to the ground has a compelling voice.

This would explain why the Israelites would continually offer blood sacrifices of lambs, bulls and turtledoves at the altar of God. The blood of innocent, non-violent animals such as lambs, bullocks, goats and turtledoves voiced a temporary atonement. Similar to the eighth step in recovery, the Israelites were required by law to make amends for their wrongdoing on an ongoing basis. However, the blood offering of God Himself through His Son is a remarkable provision. The blood of Jesus speaks better things than the blood of Abel. (Hebrews 12:24) For within the dispensation of God's grace, we can obtain an extraordinary atonement by the blood of Jesus the Redeemer. Redemption is an eternal atonement that sets us free from the bondage of our tainted souls. Oh, to be set free from the bondage of addiction! Yet it seems too simple a process for the addict to believe by faith in the blood atonement of the Christ. He can understand punishment, suffering and penance, but he cannot fathom the grace of God. Human nature compels the addict to cling to his personal testimonies of the shame, guilt and disgrace of drunkenness.

Some prefer to relive the sordid debauchery of their addiction, hoping that the remembrance of the past will somehow prevent them from repeating it. Yet, continued public sharing of past excess and indulgence only energizes the ravenous hunger of the flesh for more alcohol or drugs. The best examples to support this premise are the many confessions I have heard from recovering addicts who have revealed to me that their cravings for substances invariably has increased after an AA meeting, where the memories of the past were revived as a result of hearing the testimonies of other addicts. The revealed truth of God's word is that the blood of Jesus cleanses our conscience from the dead works of the past. This truth is not for the mind to understand. It is for the spirit to receive the Lord's grace and for the soul to believe His word. We shall overcome by the blood of the Lamb and the word of our testimony. (Revelation 12:11) The testimony is that it is impossible to make amends for even a tenth of our wrongdoing, for even a tenth would be insurmountable. The Lord is looking for those in recovery who can testify that when they received the shed blood of Jesus at the cross for the atonement of their own souls, their conscience was cleansed from the dead works of their past wrongdoing. (Hebrews 9:14) Who could possibly make amends, without the blood of Jesus?

Likewise, to strive to make amends by the efforts of our own flesh is to refuse the grace of God provided in His Son's sacrifice. Grace is not only God's unmerited favor but it is also the power of the Holy Spirit to do a work in us for His own glory. God offers us grace because he knows that it is impossible for any of us, particularly those who have lived lecherously, to make amends for each and every mistake. It is true that the former addict does not deserve such mercy, but this is the meaning of God's grace. It is beyond our human reasoning and understanding. We are saved by faith through grace and not of ourselves, for it is a gift from God.(Ephesians 2:8) That same grace that is capable of washing the spirit and renewing the mind, can also cleanse the soul from a lust for an unclean life of addiction.

Moreover, we cannot understand such mercy since we find it difficult to even forgive ourselves. How could God remove my affliction without me doing some form of penance? Therefore we feel more comfortable attempting to make amends in our own strength. Our rational mind does not conceive that such an easy way out is fair when we consider the extent of our wrongdoing. In "the People of the Lie", Peck suggests that some sinners suffer from self absorption or narcissism:

> "What distinguishes the evil, however, from the rest of us mentally ill sinners is the specific type of pain they are running away from. They are not pain avoiders or lazy people in general. To the contrary, they are likely to exert themselves more than most in their continuing effort to obtain and maintain an image of high respectability. They may willingly, even eagerly, undergo great hardships in their search for status. It is only one particular kind of pain they cannot tolerate: the pain of their own conscience, the pain of the realization of their own sinfulness and imperfection. (Peck, pg 77)

Nevertheless, it is the very pain of the addict's conscience that the blood of Jesus is capable not only of cleansing but of eradicating. Jesus blotted out the handwriting of ordinances that were against us, which were contrary to us. (Colossians 2:14).He took the pain of our conscience, the sting of our own self hatred. To actualize this truth is to be set free to forgive ourselves and to allow the Holy Spirit to impress and convict those we have wronged to eventually forgive us.

PART FIVE: FRUITBEARING

CHAPTER #8:
NURTURING THE INNER ROOT

WALKING IN THE BLESSINGS

According to Christ centered spiritual principles of recovery and empowerment, to be blessed is to be fruitful, successful or productive in spite of circumstances. In the book of Psalms, King David provided the framework for cultivating roots that will manifest empowerment and victory:

> "Blessed is the man (person) that walketh not in the counsel of the ungodly, nor standeth in the way of sinners, nor sitteth in the seat of the scornful. But his delight is in the law of the Lord; and in His law doth he meditate day and night. And he shall be like a TREE PLANTED by the rivers of water, that BRINGETH FORTH HIS FRUIT IN HIS SEASON; HIS LEAF ALSO SHALL NOT WITHER, AND WHATSOEVER HE DOETH SHALL PROSPER. The ungodly are not so; but are like the chaff which the wind driveth away." (Psalm 1:1-4)

Within this text, the psalmist addresses three main soil conditions for healthy roots:

1. a rej 1. rejection of worldly opinion

2. a love of God's word

3. meditation on God's word.

In order to achieve these three (3) soil conditions, the divine life of the regenerated spirit must be formed and perfected in us. When seed is first planted, the actual substance of the plant or fruit cannot be visibly seen for a period of time or "a season." Each season of productivity requires a period of time to allow the fruit to bud, blossom and flourish. Tilling is that period of cultivation that precedes a fruitful harvest.

REJECTING THE WORLD

In a similar vein, although the life of Christ within is perfect, our carnal weaknesses hinder His life from taking shape within us. We have been shaped by the world since birth, having grown accustomed to societal guidance and counsel. The world is not only society, "the system" and custom. The world is everything---opinion, lifestyle, family and other significant relationships---where Jesus Christ is not received as the Head. Although Jesus is the head of the church which is His spiritual body, there is a political or societal church "world" where Christ is not in authority. Paul warned the believers in Rome to resist the influence of the world:

> And be not conformed to this world: but be ye transformed by the renewing of your mind, that ye may prove what is that good, and acceptable, and perfect, will of God. (Romans 12:2)

According to Webster's dictionary, to be conformed is to be in harmony or agreement, to be similar or identical or to adapt oneself to the prevailing standards or customs. The implication is that one who conforms is one who submissively embraces the world's views. A conformist follows every fad or point of view that is in contradiction to or denies Jesus Christ.

Nurturing The Inner Root

As it is the devil who is referred to in scripture as the god of "this world", (2Corinthians 4:4) he is the one who frames the world's view of life. He is the one who blinds the minds of the ungodly, the sinners and the scornful. Satan trains these ungodly counselors to become the blind who lead the blind to misunderstand and reject the gospel of Jesus Christ.

As the natural enemy to God, Satan maximizes the world's influence over us to actualize his hatred of the Christ. These words of Jesus ring true:

If the world hate you, ye know that it hated me before it hated you. If ye were of the world, the world would love his own: but because ye are not of the world, but I have chosen you out of the world, therefore the world hated you. (John 15:18,19)

I have given them thy word; and the world hath hated them, because they are not of the world, even as I am not of the world. I pray not that thou shouldest take them out of the world, but that thou shouldest keep them from the evil. They are not of the world, even as I am not of the world. Sanctify them through thy truth: thy word is truth. (John 17:14-17)

In the measure that the Lord is being formed within our spirits by the Holy Ghost, in that same measure will we scrutinize the words of significant others and avoid unsavory friendships. For the born again Christian in recovery, to seek guidance from those who have not accepted Jesus as "Higher Power" is to heed counsel from those who hate Jesus and who therefore hate those who believe in Him.

I have met Christians in recovery who admire non-Christians because these unbelievers have demonstrated longstanding success in sobriety and gainful employment. Entrapped by esteem for such people, I have witnessed babes in Christ who selected non-Christians as spiritual advisors and sponsors--- people who have no concept of spirituality. According to Paul in the scriptures, there will come a time when people will not endure sound doctrine. Instead, in accordance with their own lust, they will heap to themselves teachers, having itching ears, who shall turn their ears away from the truth. (II Timothy 4:2) Moreover, the way to true spirituality is hidden from unbelievers because evil spirits have blinded their minds to understanding the reality of the resurrected Lord. (II Corinthians 4:13) As Jesus astutely declared, "can the blind lead the blind? Shall they not both fall into the ditch?" (Luke 6:39)Such a case comes to mind of a newly released Christian ex-offender in recovery who was advised by his sponsor that a church service was not as important to his recovery as an AA meeting, particularly when both meetings were held at the same time. The sponsor was esteemed because he had been released from prison for 10 years and had been sober for 15 years. The sponsor's words of wisdom were "you've got to do what you need to do as opposed to what you want to do. You want to go to church but an AA meeting is what you need to do!"

Such counsel clearly depicts the spiritual poverty of the sponsor. When we delight ourselves in the Lord, it is He Himself who infuses in our spirits a desire to worship Him. The burning desire in our hearts for God can only be satisfied with worship. A fervency to worship is in itself a sign that the Lord is abiding in our lives. When we pray and seek God with a fervent desire, much power is made available to our spirits. (James 5:16) Furthermore, believers in Christ have been given at rebirth an unction or a measure of the Holy Spirit, abiding within our spirits. (IJohn 2:20) This unction is sufficient to counsel us concerning the will or desire of God's own heart as well as to guide us in decisionmaking. The steps of the righteous are ordered of the Lord, and He delights in his way (Psalm 37:23) For this particular believer in recovery, his "want" and his "need" are synonymous, because his desire is the ultimate fulfillment of the inner need of his spirit for a closeness to God that can only be fulfilled by tasting the sweetness of the love of Christ through worship.

LOVING GODS WORD

In order that we might bare fruit, God sanctified us to be set apart for special service. Jesus Christ revealed that the Father's word and His truth are counterparts. As Jesus Himself is the truth, those who follow Him are set apart, protected and cleansed by His word. According to Paul the Apostle, God's word is also our spiritual offensive weapon against the lower power, figuratively called "the sword of the Spirit." (Ephesians 6:17) The author of the book of Hebrews wrote:

> For the word of God is quick (alive), and powerful, and sharper than any twoedged sword, piercing even to the dividing asunder of soul and spirit, and of the joints and marrow, and is a discerner of the thoughts and intents of the heart. (Hebrews 4:12)

To love God's word is to allow it to take precedence over worldly opinion and to change us. The more we love God's word, the more we will submit our souls to it. The word of God is the new seed that will cause fruits of righteousness, peace and joy to take root in us and grow. As we yield to the word of God, His word will consistently renew our souls, including our personalities, thoughts, emotions, affections, feelings, desires, perceptions, attitudes, behavior, and even our will power. At times, change is immediate. However, fruitbaring is usually as gradual in the spirit as it is in a natural garden. A spiritual harvest is proportionate to the extent that we are able to detach ourselves from the world.

Struggling with God word is hard work. There is no rest in such labor. When we discover that some aspect of ourselves is in conflict with God's word, a battle within will take place. Since the word of God is the food of the human recreated spirit, the more it is rejected, the weaker the spirit becomes. When the spirit is weak, the word will actually feel like a knife in the gut, as it begins to tear our spirit and our soul apart. If the soul wins the battle, then our love for God's word is weaker than our self love. Jesus declared that those who are unable to bare spiritual fruit are those that have no root in themselves. He declared that when the word of God is revealed, Satan and his demons immediately attempt to steal God's seed by applying four worldly pressures:

1. confusion and misunderstanding;

2. persecution and tribulation;

3. the cares or concerns of this world; and

4. the deceitfulness of riches. (Matthew 13:19-22)

Cultivated and nurtured by the world, the roots of every human being have become strong. This is why we must curse the root with God's word. We can curse worldly roots because God's word is alive and powerful. "So shall my word be that goeth forth out of mouth: it shall not return unto me void, but it shall accomplish that which I please and it shall prosper in the thing whereto I sent it. (Isaiah 55:11)

Consider my personal struggle with sexual sin. Once I was saved and born again, it took five long years to gain victory over fornication. I did not have a sexual addiction, as I could control my sexual drive. However, re-examining my struggle for empowerment in this area, the Holy Spirit revealed that the root of my problem was that I had rejected the word of God concerning ungodly sexual conduct. In fact, I not only felt that His word was in error, but I resented the Lord for restricting me from what I believed myself to be entitled to. After a year of sexual abstinence, I was moody and hostile. I believed it unfair that I would have to be so "righteous" when so many in the world and in the church were reveling in the freedom of sexual promiscuity and I believed I deserved that same freedom. It is not surprising that I relapsed. I continued to debate the issue of sexual freedom and to covet worldly pleasures. I also believed that I could not work for God in the ministry without having a husband. This false imagination caused me to be impatient and frustrated. I had no rest. Struggling against God's word was debilitating. Once I fell, I finally made a decision to simply obey

God's word without contending against it. At an age when the world expected me to be sexually active, I put on my chastity belt and stopped all flirtatious behavior. I took control of my mind, emotions and my will with these words to God: "I don't care if I'm 85 years old before you provide me with a husband. I WILL NOT sleep with another man as long as I live, unless I am married to him."

I stood by my word for the next five more years until I married. Since most of my adult sexual life has been in contradiction to God's will, I take no pride in what some might consider an accomplishment. Notwithstanding, once the word of God concerning fornication was rooted and grounded in my spirit and my soul, sexual sin lost its hold on me and I began to enjoy fruitfulness in areas of my life that had been barren. For example, I am no longer lonely, even when I am alone. I can cope with rejection without fear or despair. The resentment and anger that I have harbored against the male gender has been replaced with a spiritual love for men who are lost and a special calling to see unsaved men come to Christ. My soul has found rest and cleansing through obedience to God's word.
To the extent that we become rooted in our commitment to the Lord, will we find gratification in God's word and adore it. As Jesus declared, we demonstrate our love for Him by keeping His commandments. As a result of loving His word, Jesus promises that the Father God will love us and the triune godhead will live with us and in us. (John 14:21) God's abiding presence is the key to fruitfulness and productivity.

Similarly, where the addictions are concerned, relapse very often occurs because the word of God has been rejected and worldly opinion about drinking and drugging still prevails in the soul and the spirit. Besides, the one in recovery may harbor an inner thought or feeling that he or she is "entitled" to "being high." Furthermore, addictive patterns of behavior comprise the gratification or validation of the self with the substance. In addition, self glorification may result from his or her ability to consume large amounts of drugs. Even so, the scriptures admonish us to "be not drunk with wine, but to be filled with the Spirit of God." (Ephesians 5:18) When we are filled with the Holy Spirit, there is no room for substances. When all of our appetites and desires are satisfied in Christ, the struggle will subside. In Christ, the burden and the yoke of addiction becomes easy. Dying is hard work, but actual death is easy. If we resist change, we resist death. If we resist the death of our former carnality, we fight against our fruitfulness. Jesus revealed that to resist the death of the lower soulish life is like a grain of wheat, once planted, refusing to die, and thereby remaining alone or unfruitful. However, once it dies, it brings forth much fruit. (John 12:24) Consequently, we labor or struggle to keep our old ways, in order that we may enter the Lord's rest. Giving God's word first place in our lives will strengthen us to flow with ease into the death of the old way of life so that we can find rest and peace in the rebirth of the higher life of the spirit.

MEDITATING GOD'S WORD

A recent personal experience stands as a startling example of why meditating on God's word is crucial. I had just finished my laundry, folding and stacking various garments. The bras were neatly stacked together in their own pile in the laundry basket as were the rest of my intimate apparel. As I was putting the bras where they are always kept--- in the second drawer of my dresser---, my thoughts wandered to the fact that the panties were kept in the top drawer of my mirrored vanity might be confusing to anyone else but me. My mind spoke to itself, "the bras and the panties should be in different drawers of the same dresser. When you go into the hospital, remember to tell Zonnita that the bras are in the second drawer of the bureau and the underpants are in the right hand top drawer of the vanity. She'll need to know this when she comes to the house to pack your suitcase when she brings it to the hospital."

Such "self talk" would not be noteworthy if it were not for the fact that I am healthy, with no plans to enter a hospital. Although the medical profession could consider my age, weight, and race as risk factors for various diseases, my doctor has assured me that he is not particularly concerned about them. Yet, on a semi-conscious level, my mind was projecting upon myself a vague sickness that would cause me to be hospitalized. Even my genetics has been so blessed that I have never been at a sick bed in a hospital for any of my relatives, yet I had incorporated "my risk factors" for various and sundry diseases into my mind. In a split second, I stopped my thoughts and shouted out words of rebuke. "That's a lie! I will not be hospitalized. My God redeems my life from destruction. Her satisfies my mouth with good things. He heals ALL of my diseases. My youth is renewed like the eagle's." I began to ponder on the goodness and truth of His word, focusing on some of the verses in Psalm 103. At this writing, more than 10 years have gone by, and I have not been hospitalized.

This one instance of my own self talk is only one example of why I believe that we ourselves bring about much of our own future by the power of subliminal suggestion from others and from the thoughts of our minds. Similar to the workings of a computer, the soul saves in the backup file of the subconscious or the spirit diverse thoughts, feelings and emotions as possibilities and probabilities. Most of these potential realities are contradictory to God's plans and purposes for our lives. However, the word of God---which is God's truth and His will---is able to delete from this subconscious and invisible back-up file those impressions that are contradictory to God's guidance and direction. Once planted into the ground of our inner consciousness, God's word can produce fruits of recovery and empowerment when it is received by faith and believed. Unfortunately, to a greater extent, the ground of the human soul is more conducive to producing weeds of negativity than fruits of success. Jesus explained the nature of the soul to his disciples:

> For from <u>within,</u> out of the heart (soul) of men, proceed evil thoughts, adulteries, fornications, murders, thefts,

To Curse The Root

covetousness, wickedness, deceit, lasciviousness, an evil eye, blasphemy, pride, foolishness: ALL these evil things come from <u>within</u>, and defile him. (Mark 7:21,22)

Since lasciviousness is a form of lust or gluttony characteristic of addictive behavior, this scripture suggests that the thought life of an addict is not only as evil as that of the adulterer and the fornicator, but that it is also comparable to the thoughts of a murderer. The Lord associates addictive behavior with such weeds as sexual immorality, violence and greed, for they share a common root system; namely, a corrupted soul, with particular emphasis upon the mind. Evil thoughts generated in a negative inner life necessitate consistent meditation on God's word for cleansing, renewal and purging of the soul's thought and emotional life of the soul. Once we meditate on God's word, the cleansing power of the Holy Spirit will permeate all aspects of our being---spirit, soul and body. As the process of thinking is the function of the mind within the soul and the brain within the body, deeply pondering on God's word is the source of the spirit's nourishment. Once the spirit is nourished, the ground of our souls will be prepared to bring forth a fruitful harvest. Simply put, whatever we put our hands to perform will prosper.

Notwithstanding, God's word is not only in written form. It also includes the Lord's personal messages or words to our spirits in the form of intuitions and revelations which may manifest themselves in prophecies, visions and dreams. God's word is His will, His way, His plan and His works. As an illustration, God's will has been revealed to me in several different ways since the early '80's concerning my own personal work for Him. In 1982, I received a prophecy through my daughter's nine year old playmate, Linda. Linda was watching Saturday morning cartoons when suddenly she began to shake and speak forth this utterance:

"The waters of heaven shall flow down upon the house of the minister and the minister's daughter and HEAL

THE CITY. GREAT MIRACLES SHALL FLOW FROM THIS HOUSE."

I have since named this message the "Healing Waters Prophecy"and my ministry, Healing Waters. In searching the scriptures to find the meaning of this prophecy, I noticed the conversation between Jesus and John concerning those who were casting out devils in the name of Jesus (Mark 9:38,39). In the Lord's response to John's concerns, Jesus indicated that no one who performed a miracle in His name could speak lightly of Him. A logical deduction is that Jesus considered the casting out of demons to be a miracle. Moreover, as recorded in the gospels, (Luke 11:20, Matthew 12:28) Jesus stated that He Himself cast out demons by the finger of God---a metaphor for the Holy Spirit. In terms of the "healing waters" prophecy, I believe that the miracles that are referred to in the first prophecy of 1982 are from the captivity and bondage of the seven walls identified in the second prophecy of 1983, namely drugs and alcohol, homosexuality, prostitution, witchcraft, religious spirits, prejudice and poverty.

As I meditated on these texts, I remembered that the first miracle to flow from my house occurred about a year after Linda's "healing waters" prophecy, when my daughter was 14 years old. At that time, together we successfully fought the battle with Laura's demons of addiction. (See pgs.147-155) Shortly after Laura's deliverance, the Lord used her to bring forth His prophetic word to me through her message about the seven walls. The Lord continues to direct my steps with these two prophesies and other related dreams. For 22 years, I have meditated upon them almost day and night. As I continue to increase in the power and anointing of the Holy Spirit, the fruits of my ministry have multiplied.

BRINGING IN THE SHEAVES

The Lord's words remain true after 2000 years. The harvest is still plenteous. (Matthew 9:37) I have discovered that deliverance ministry is too vast for any one minister to attempt to accomplish singlehandedly. Jesus also said that the laborers were few. However today, though more in number than in the days of the early church, the laborers are poorly equipped and indiscriminately placed. By example, once associated with a church that was equipped with four ministers, I don't believe that four souls have been saved in that church in twenty years. Spiritual barrenness of this kind is related to several factors. In their book entitled "Pigs In The Parlor", Frank and Ida Mae Hammond point out that since Satan has ga special interest in the church, he does everything in his power to side-track, hinder and weaken the church's fruitfulness, which of course is the saving of souls.

This obstruction is accomplished in a number of ways. Through false doctrine, obsessive emphasis on one doctrine, denominationalism, sectarianism, worldliness and materialism, and relying on human talents and abilities rather than upon the power of the Holy Spirit, the church itself is in need of deliverance, for Satan has commandeered a high seat. "The listing goes on and on---formalism, ritualism, control by a pastor or group, complacency, indifference, pessimism, discouragement, obsession with problems without solutions, etc. etc. etc." (Hammond and Hammond, pg 15-17) By comparison, demons use similar strategies within the world system of the addictions. Although its principles are taken from the bible, the Twelve Steps have become a formal ritual that combine worldliness with spirituality, where the ritual itself seizes the place of the God, while the devil is allowed to remain in its home of addicted flesh, ever ready to "take over" as soon as its victim has fallen to worldly pressures and cravings that demons themselves have contrived to hinder deliverance.

CHAPTER #9:
THE WAY TO DELIVERANCE AND GROWTH

DYING TO LIVE

When the Christ walked on earth, He taught His disciples that to live for the self or the life of the soul is like a grain of wheat, once planted, refusing to die and thereby remaining alone. (John 12:24) However, if it dies, it will be extremely fruitful. In like manner, when we are bound too strongly to our minds, affection, emotions and our desires, we will hinder spiritual power and productivity. In order to operate exclusively by the power of God, Jesus Christ calls for death. However, within a spiritual context, death does not imply utter destruction. Rather, the death of our soul life is manifested in His crucifixion, where the human personality becomes transformed and renewed in the fruitfulness of His resurrection. As discussed in Chapter 2, God's weeding hand is His way of transforming our minds, emotions and our wills so that He can cause us to bare fruit, ...for if we become united with Him in The likeness of His death, we shall be also in the likeness of His resurrection." (Romans 6:5) Rather than becoming intellectually or emotionally deprived, a spiritually empowered personality is one that has been recreated by the hand of God for spiritual productivity.

Paul the Apostle is one of the best biblical examples of a spiritually fruitful person. Once filled with pride over his scholarly achievements and his cultural and religious background, Paul's soul and his spirit figuratively died on the road to Damascus, while his physical body was blinded and struck down by the glory of the Lord Jesus the Christ. (Acts Ch 9). Though zealous and committed to God as he perceived Him, Paul did not realize that he was barren and unfruitful in spite of all of his efforts to serve God. Paul describes his symbolic death in his letters to the Galatians and to the Corinthians. To the Galatians Paul writes "I was crucified with Christ but nevertheless I live, not I but Christ who lives in me. To the Corinthians he writes: "baring about in the body the dying of the Lord Jesus Christ that His life might be made manifest in our mortal flesh."

This kind of death is neither a forced or contrived breaking of the soul through sacrifice or penance. Rather it is that we were made dead through the death of Jesus. The secret of victory is never to consider ourselves apart from Christ. Since a dead person cannot relapse, God does not expect the corpse of a dead addict to struggle every waking moment in the abyss of sin and of the world in his mind and emotions, ever promising Him to "do better next time." He does not require a corpse to improve itself. He has no expectations of the dead, for the dead know nothing. Of course, we are to confess our faults and ask for forgiveness when we have failed. However, we must realize that the root of our failure is that we allowed the corpse to live. In other words, we ourselves resurrected the old nature outside of Christ and consequently, we fell.

The water baptism of the Christian faith is a holy and symbolic ritual of our death and resurrection in the Son of God. Its significance lies in its message of the burial of the soul and the flesh, followed by the rebirth of the spirit. Through His death and burial, Christ has redeemed us from the curse of the law and supplied us with God's grace in His resurrection. (Galatians 3:29, Ephesians 2:8) The curse of the law is the inborn weakness of our souls and our flesh to satisfy God's commandments, rules and demands. In short, we are habitual sinners without Christ. Nevertheless, when we symbolically rise out of the water of baptism, grace supplants the law and sin no longer has dominion over us. (Romans 6:14) Grace is both unmerited provision, anointing and power of the Holy Spirit within us, Who overshadows our weakness and frailty with His supernatural and divine ability. (II Corinthians 12:7)

It is a great discovery to experience a victory that transcends the soul and the body. Just as we once depended on our minds and our willpower to work the principles and practices of the 12 Steps, true deliverance and freedom is trusting in the 13th step: the resurrection life of Christ, the True Vine Who is the source of grace and power. The 13th step is a place of unexpected victory that is beyond the reasoning of the mind and the determination of the will. In matters of sobriety, victory is obtainable when Christ is the life or the Vine of recovery. Jesus declared Himself to be the true Vine of fruitfulness and productivity. To His disciples in recovery, Jesus declares that He is the true Vine. Without Him, we can do nothing. In order to be fruitful and successful, we must satisfy our inner craving and thirst by drinking from the true Vine. The life of the Vine is the Holy Spirit within our reborn spirits. His life produces victory by supplying us with the strength to be sober and clean without our conscious awareness. (John 15)

Jesus would agree with AA in its evaluation of addicted flesh, for addicted flesh is hopeless and it cannot change. After suffering many relapses and defeats, some persons ultimately stop all treatment. Others hate their defeat and with renewed determination remain sober for a time, only to fall once more. We cry out in despair:

For that which I do I know not: for not what I would, that do I practice; but what I hate, that I do. But if what I would not, that I do, I consent unto the law that it is good. So now it is no more that I do it, but sin which dwelleth in me. For I know that in me, that is, in my flesh, dwelleth no good thing: for to will is present with me, but to do that which is good is not. For the good which I would I do not: but the evil which I would not, that I practice. (Romans 7:15-19)

The source of victory is to abide in the Vine and believe that we were made dead to the law through the body of Christ, "that we should be joined to another, even to Him who was raised from the dead, that we might BRING FORTH FRUIT UNTO GOD." (Roman 7:4) When Jesus died, we died also. A dead person is neither fruitful nor barren, successful nor failing. Just as the Lord's resurrection followed His death, resurrection also follows our death. Just as Christ was raised by the glory of the Father Who is the Holy Spirit, we too are so raised, if we abide in the Son. In his book entitled "The Glory of His Life", Watchman Nee provides an excellent portrayal of this spiritual truth:

> "We who are resurrected in Christ will bring forth fruit to the glory of God. Since God has given the life of Christ to us, we hereafter are able to live out Christ's life. Whatever be the grain of wheat that is sown, there shall be the thirty, the sixty or the hundred grains which grow out of it. If a person plants barley he will not get wheat or squash. What is sown is that which grows. There can be no change. If what is sown is wheat, all which grows out will be wheat. How can we live like Christ and bear fruit to glorify God as Christ did? <u>In only one way: by letting Christ live in us and letting Him live out of us.</u> Consequently, Christ not only died for us on the cross but He also lives for us within us. Who can make us live like Christ? None except the One who gives the life of

Christ to us. As we have the life of Christ, we may bear fruit to the glory of God." (Nee, pg. 95)

Resurrection life is evident when we experience revelation, power, and discernment under the guidance and instruction of the Holy Spirit. Revelation is to receive God's own personal knowledge and wisdom about our lives. Power is God's supernatural ability applied to our human frailty. The Holy Spirit within us will also reveal how to discern between good fruits and harmful weeds as well as provide the power to bear fruit.

KNOW YOUR ENEMY!

Those who vehemently defend 12 steps wll do so by informing you that AA is adapted from the Bible. Let me warn you that every cult can make the same boast. The devil is famous for taking scripture out of context to suit his own purposes. Every false religion has distorted and misinterpreted scriptures taken out of context to uphold its tenets and doctrines. A careful study of scripture as recorded in the parables of Jesus Christ in the gospels of Matthew, Mark, Luke and John provide insight into the manipulative and deceptive methods of demon spirits whose ultimate goal is to kill, steal and destroy. (John 10:10) As previously mentioned, Jesus compare a field of wheat to the world. A farmer sowed good seed but while everyone slept, an ememy came and sowed weeds amohg the wheat. Jesus explained that this particular parable was presenting the entire history of mankind and what would happen at the close of the age, where the ground or field represents the world, the good seed or wheat are his followers and the bad seed or weeds are the followers of Satan.(Matthew 13:37-43)

In yet two other instances the metaphorical meaning of the words "fruit and weed" in His parables bestow a more personal focus. In the gospel of Matthew, Jesus spoke words which serve as the foundation of this book. He speaks of a farmer who went out to plant seed. While he was sowing, some seed fell by the wayside and the birds came and ate them. Other seed fell on stony places where they did not have much earth, and they immediately sprang up. Since these seed had "NO ROOT", the sun scorched them and they withered. Then some of the farmer's seed fell among thorns, and the thorns sprang up and choked them. But other seed fell on "GOOD GROUND" yielding a crop, some a hundredfold, some sixty, some thirty.(Matthew 13:3-9)

Later in this same chapter, Jesus enlightens his disciples to the spiritual reality of the parable's symbols. In this case, the seed is the word of God. Jesus explained that when the word of God goes forth, "by the wayside" people will not understand it because the "wicked one" snatches it from their hearts or spirits. Those "by the stony places" will receive the word, but the enemy brings persecution and oppression to cause them to fall because "they have no root in themselves." Those "by the thorns" are caught up in the love of money and the cares of this world while the "good ground" hearers are those who hear the word of God and UNDERSTANDS IT. Out of the spirits that are "good ground" will come forth a fruitful harvest. (Matthew 13:18-23) The meaning of "fruit" is linked to words in the gospel of Luke where Jesus compares some basic agricultural truths about the fruitbearing of good and bad trees. Simply put, a good tree does not bare bad fruit. So as with a tree, Jesus declared that a human being will bare fruit out of the good treasure of his or her heart or spirit, just as an evil heart will bring forth evil fruit or weeds. This fruit is the product of the words of his or her own mouth for " out of the abundance of the heart (spirit), THE MOUTH SPEAKS!" (Luke 6:43-45)

A collective review of the cited scriptures underscores the following important spiritual truths relative to the influence of evil forces upon the human spirit:

1. Both the Holy Spirit and Satan plant seed into our spirits with words; Furthermore, when God's word is

spoken to us, evil spirits are dedicated to preventing us from understanding it.

2. We empower evil spirits to snatch God's word out of our heart when we have "no root in ourselves" and when the desires of our soul---ESTEEM, PRIDE AND VANITY--- cause us to prioritize and conform to societal trappings of the Three "P"s of prestige, position and power;

3. Oppression, depression and vexation are Satanic tools for scorching or hindering God's word from becoming rooted in our spirits.

4. As alluded to in Chapter 4 in the Section called "Power Packed Words", human beings have a creative power to produce results with their words. The devil manipulates us by employing the words that he himself planted in us to come forth out of our mouths to harvest the weeds of our own self destruction.

The Holy Bible is the only textbook that has been written concerning the nature and operation of evil spirits. Moreover, Jesus Christ is the only Higher Power who has ever unequivocally confronted evil as well as comprehensively pronounced His authority and power over sin, sickness, disease, in short---"over all the power of the enemy." (Matthew 28:18, Luke 9:1, Luke 10:9, Acts 10:38, Colossians 2:5) Jesus also proclaimed that He has given His authority and power to command evil spirits to those who believed on Him and received Him as their Higher Power. In light of this finding, I am compelled to warn recovering readers who have not chosen Jesus as their Lord and Savior to realize that other than an invitation to convert, I cannot convey my own experience with Jesus and with the devil into terminology that will be compatible with your particular religious experience. Simply and boldly put, if Jesus is not your Lord and Savior, you have no power to control, command or exorcise evil spirits. YOU ARE DEFENSELESS! Essential to a complete recovery is not only to be convinced of the reality of the Satan and his demons, but also to become equipped to recognize and victoriously combat them. The weapons of spiritual warfare are not manmade but they are powerful through God in overpowering the devil. (IICorinthians 1:4) However, the effectiveness of these spiritual weapons is only compatible with a faith and a commitment to Jesus Christ as not the Higher Power, but the name that is above every name, to whom every knee shall bow and every tongue shall confess that He is Lord!

As both an ordained minister and a licensed social worker, I am not acquainted with a more masterful form of combat than what Jesus has provided. I had been employed in the social work field for nine years prior to my rebirth experience (see pages 23-26)---a period wherein I had experienced a modicum of success with substance abusers. Nevertheless, shortly after I became a disciple, Jesus revealed to me that although there are some basic truths relative to counseling and recovery within the body of knowledge, values and methods of my profession as a social worker, most of my education and training involved merely the treatment of the presenting problem or symptom. The Lord revealed that humanistic therapies are devoid of ultimate healing and a long-lived recovery because they deny the existence of the spirit world and the lordship of Jesus Christ.

It is unfortunate that the eyes of the secular therapeutic world has been blinded by human intellect. Yet, I admire psychiatrists like M. Scott Peck who have humbly submitted to God's spiritual truths by acknowledging the relationship between demonic combat and psychotherapy. In Peck's own words:

" being convinced of the reality of demonic possession, however rare, I am equally certain that clergy and psychotherapists and human-service institutions are seeing such cases, whether they know it or not. To help the victims of possession, they will need all the assistance they can get.... exorcism stands in relation to ordinary psychotherapy as radical surgery does to lancing a boil. Radical surgery can be not only healing but life-saving, and, in fact, may be THE ONLY WAY TO HEAL IN CERTAIN CASES UNRESPONSIVE TO MORE CONSERVATIVE THERAPY." (Peck, pg 184 and 187)

Jesus Christ professed that His power over evil forces came from the third person of the godhead---the Holy Spirit. The Holy Spirit's job is to promote and carry out the authority and power of Jesus Christ and toward this end, He will draw the unbeliever to Him. Once the believer has received Jesus as Lord and Savior, then the Holy Spirit will plant into his or her spirit seeds of recovery that will produce nine "fruit of the spirit" : love, joy, peace, longsuffering, kindness, goodness, faith or faithfulness, gentleness and SELF CONTROL! Linked to the new creation of the born again spirit, these seeds develop into fruits of character and integrity, wherein our soul is changed and renewed.

In agricultural terms, harvesting of fruit involves pruning or purging. As the nine fruit of the spirit develop and become rooted in the soul, the destructive roots of the past are put to death or pruned.(Galatians 5:22-23). Every branch that bares fruit is purged or cleansed so that it can bring forth more fruit. (John 15:2) Old things are passed away and all things have become new! (IICorinthians 5:17) For people in recovery, this is GOOD NEWS!

PREPARE FOR BATTLE

We cannot escape the fact that recovery is a difficult process because it is a kind of demonic oppression and obsession of the complete person, spirit, soul and body. Although the human spirit becomes the temple of the Holy Spirit immediately upon receiving Jesus Christ as Lord and Saviour, demons may have to be cast out of the soul. When the unclean spirit vacates the flesh as a result of medical detoxification, the addict will invariably enter into a supernatural power struggle with demon spirits over his or her soul. Demonic tactics will involve bombarding the addict or alcoholic with powerful inner cravings and lusts for intoxicants of all kinds. Even so, in Christ Jesus, complete deliverance is possible. In Christ, deliverance may be instantaneous but it is more likely to be progressive.

Moreover, the person who has been set free must learn how to draw on the supernatural power that is in the authority of the name of Jesus and in the power of His blood. The way to a victorious deliverance is to know yourself better than the enemy knows you, to obtain continual nourishment, healing and support through active fellowship with believers in the body of Christ, and to actively participate in your own deliverance. To summarize and conclude, the way to recovery and spiritual empowerment is to be prepared for battle. It is important to realize that once addicted, the body and the soul have become a temple for demon spirits that have been comfortable in "their home." They are difficult to evict, but in Jesus Name, all things are possible for the one who has been "born again" in his or her spirit.

The overall purpose of this book has been to arm, forewarn and equip those in recovery and those seeking spiritual growth to live victoriously. Victory and productivity are obtainable if we would heed Paul's recommendation to the Romans. It is a simple instruction. In short we are to present our bodies as a living sacrifice that is holy and acceptable to God. This sacrifice of our soul life is our reasonable service. Furthermore, we should not be conformed to this world. Rather, we can be transformed into the image of Christ if we allow the Holy Spirit to renew our minds. When our minds are renewed, we will discover God's will and purpose for our lives. (Romans 12:1,2) In review, these thirteen principles must be understood, believed and incorporated into daily living in order to curse the root of demonic weed systems of addiction:

1. <u>Just as we are three part beings but one person, God Himself is a three part being: God the Father, God the Son and God the Holy Spirit.</u> In other words, one, plus one, plus one equals ONE! When we approach God, we cannot decide to only address the Father and to leave out the Son. Jesus declared Himself to be the only way, and no man can come to the Father except by Him. He is either telling us the truth or He is a liar. If He is telling us the truth, then all other gods are false. If we are to be spiritually empowered and be delivered from the addictions, we can not be eclectic in the selection of our gods. Jesus does not share a position with any other godhead, other than in a divine trinity with the Father and the Holy Spirit.

2. <u>Surrender to God should be a continual and long lived consecration, not only because our lives have become unmanageable but because Jesus Christ has paid a blood price for us and we belong to Him.</u> When we enter covenant with the Lord, He expects us to pick up our cross and follow Him. Such a sacrifice is reasonable when we consider that we exchange our lower life of the soul and the flesh,---a life of struggle and defeat--- for the higher life of the spirit. When we present our entire beings to God as a living sacrifice, our thoughts, emotions, feelings, opinions, personality and all that represents the ego or the soul of man must be crucified daily.

3. <u>We must allow the Holy Spirit to take His inventory of our shortcomings and not we ourselves.</u> We do not know ourselves like God knows us simply because our thoughts are not God's thoughts and our ways are not God's ways. To illustrate, what we may consider a shortcoming, God may find pleasing and vice versa. He will reveal to us in a sequential and timely order those traits that need to be crucified.

True humility is to submit the "I AM" to the breaking of the Holy Spirit without contention, murmuring or complaining.

4. <u>Jesus desires us to obey Him out of love.</u> Although we belong to Him, He will not force us to serve Him. Jesus defines love as obedience to His word. In other words, If you love God, you will keep the terms of the covenant. (John 14:15, 15:12-20)

5. <u>If you are born again, then you are among the friends of Jesus.</u> There is no greater love than a man lay down his life for his friends. Friendship involves commitment. We can't be friends with God and follow the dictates of the world. As an example, sober dances do not belong in the church in general, nor should they be a source of entertainment for Christians. Furthermore, we cannot expect to live according to the world's loose moral standards and expect the blessings of God to be ours. Friendship also involves intimacy. As we hunger and thirst to know God through Christ, our hunger and thirst for drinking and drugging will be dissipated and ultimately swallowed up in victory.

6. <u>In reality, Jesus is not the Higher Power. He is the Highest Power.</u> He is the Almighty God. Technically, Satan could be called a higher power. He is the god of this world, the prince of the power of the air, the ruler of spiritual wickedness and the powers of darkness and lesser demons. However, all power has been given to Jesus both on earth and in the heavenlies. The higher principalities and powers and the lower dominions and demons recognize and fear the lordship of Jesus Christ. If we submit ourselves to God, the devil will flee from us. If we draw near to God, the Holy Spirit will draw near to

us. (James 4:7-8) However, if we are disobedient, proud and wilful, we give place to the devil.

7. <u>Addiction falls under the rulership and domain of Satan and his army.</u> Addicts and alcoholics are the prey of the mighty one who was once called Lucifer and who was renamed Satan or the devil. Demons are referred to as principalities and powers, the rulers of the darkness of this world and evil spirits. The so-called hallucinations of the alcoholic or the addict are not imaginary or unfounded. Rather, their spiritual eyes have been opened to see and experience the reality of the evil side of the spirit world that has kept them bound.

8. <u>Only the Highest Power can deliver an alcoholic or an addict from demon spirits.</u> There is no name under heaven that demons obey other than the name of Jesus Christ of Nazareth. In fact, no other god of any other religion has ever claimed to have power over Satan but Jesus Christ. During his earthly ministry, Jesus was anointed with the power and authority to cast out demons by the Holy Spirit. "He went about doing good and healing all of those that were oppressed of the devil because God was with Him." (Acts 10:38) Jesus transferred this power to those of his followers who believed on Him. Even though there are some of his disciples who specialize in demonic warfare, every believer in Jesus Christ has the power and the authority to resist the devil. If not from them all, demons must be cast out of most alcoholics and drug addicts by a person anointed to intercede for them and to cast them out. When demons of addiction are cast out, they can almost be visibly seen making there way up the back and through the throat of their victim.

9. <u>Addiction begins as a sin that may ultimately develop into a disease.</u> As a sin, it is self induced unbridled lust of the soul and the flesh for intoxicants. Addiction and gluttony are synonymous. Once the flesh has become habituated to a substance, repentance is not possible. Without true repentance, there can be no atonement, no forgiveness. How can we be heartily sorry for partaking of the very substance that we crave? Finally, without forgiveness and cleansing from sin there can be no salvation. Although the disease may hinder the addict or alcoholic from being able to stop the gluttony or, once sober, from relapsing, the Lord is searching for a heart and a will to be free. The addict must not only despise his lifestyle, but he must also renounce the euphoric pleasure and his flight from the pain of responsibility. He must not accuse the disease for his uncontrollable life. Rather, he must blame the lust of his own flesh that led him to sin not only against himself, but against God.

10. <u>Addiction is a weed and not a root.</u> In other words, it is an outward manifestation of the flesh that stems from a hidden problem within the soul and the spirit. One root cause of alcoholism is very often the sin of rebellion where the person is unwilling to submit to authority of any kind. Furthermore, The scriptures associates drunkardness to the sin of idolatry. The substance that induces a euphoric state becomes a god to the addicted person. As a god that induces worship and as the ruler of alcohol and drugs, addiction is a form of Satanic worship.

11. <u>Complete deliverance is obtainable in Christ Jesus where the person will no longer crave or lust for the substance.</u> When the demon is cast out, it must be replaced by the filling of the Holy Spirit. To remain free, those who were captive MUST receive Jesus as

Lord and Savior, meditate on God's word continually, devote themselves to God through prayer, worship and fellowship with other believers in the body of Christ.

12. <u>One whom Christ has set free is no longer an addict.</u> Whatever a man thinks in his heart, so is he. Therefore, we should not accept a negative label. A Christian in recovery is one of the redeemed of the Lord, a saint, a born again child of God. Once delivered, such a person should have a life changing testimony that tells the world that Jesus Christ is alive! We overcome the devil by the blood of the Lamb and the word of our testimony. The blood provides the 3 "P"S: pardon, purification and protection. In short, our sins are forgiven AND forgotten by God and our spirits are cleansed to receive the indwelling of the Holy Spirit. As our souls are renewed by the word of God, His blood protects us from being invaded by demons against our will.

The ultimate step or key to deliverance and recovery is that <u>spiritual empowerment is about restoring others with our testimony concerning our walk with Jesus Christ.</u> Jesus said that His followers are the salt of the earth. Spiritual growth is not self centered. In particular, those who have made AA their higher power need to hear the testimonies of Christians who have recovered and been fully restored by the power of God through the name of Jesus. The field of alcoholism and the addictions is ripe with fruit for Christ. As we remain steadfast and continue in the faith, we will visibly manifest the power of God both in our character and in our behavior . Let us not be plain or bland in our faith, because the world needs our flavor and our seasoning.

We must go forth and CURSE THE ROOT!

¤

PART SIX: RECOVERY IN CHRIST WORKBOOK

THE RIC PROGRAM

(Note: The RIC Program Workbook is the practical application of the principles in "To Curse the Root." You may notice that some direct quotes are taken from it. This is to assist you with your self study so that you do not have to flip back and forth to the referenced pages.")

Introduction

From the outset, it is important to emphasize that the RIC Program is for Christians in recovery. RIC has not been developed to replace AA for people who don't accept Jesus Christ as their "higher power" or who are either atheists or of a religious persuasion other than Christianity. I believe that AA and NA would be even more proficient relative to sobriety and addiction as an exclusively secular model if there were no mention of God or of a Higher Power within the 12 Steps. However, once God becomes an integral part of recovery and once a model boasts that it has been derived from the Bible, then it is open to scrutiny from the the Body of Christ. The separation of church and state must not be one sided and apply only to Christians meddling in secular business. Such separation should also apply to worldly influences into matters of the spirit. Even more than psycho-social treatment interventions, recovery through a "higher power" is most definitely a spiritual matter that comes under the authority of the holy scriptures and the church.

It is important to acknowledge that even if AA is not God's program, there are many addicts who have successfully maintained their sobriety through following its tenets. But as my recovery ministry and counseling center flourishes, I find myself preaching and teaching about the satisfied life. Why? Because I continue to meet sober, clean, yet confused and dissatisfied people who though sober, are headed for hell. I continue to meet people who have worked the 12 Steps in such a manner, whether they know it or not, that inevitably raises the question of idolatry and false religion. I continue to meet people who talk of a "higher power" whom they seem to know very little about.

Therefore, the overall purpose of the RIC Program is to train, arm, and equip those in recovery and those seeking spiritual growth to live victoriously. I also use the 7R's as keys to deliverance from not only addiction but from all aspe cts of deliverance from demonic oppression. Victory and productivity are obtainable if we would heed Paul the Apostle's recommendation to the Romans. It is a simple instruction. In short we are to present our bodies as a living sacrifice that is holy and acceptable to God. This sacrifice of our soul life is our reasonable service. Furthermore, we should not be conformed to this world. Rather, we can be transformed into the image of Christ if we allow the Holy Spirit to renew our minds. When our minds are renewed, we will discover God's will and purpose for our lives. (Romans 12:1,2)

Defining Addiction and Recovery from a Christ Centered View
A Portrait of an Addicted Person

A person is addicted when he or she has been brought under the power of something that would cause them to lose their God given self control. Even when drug free and not physically addicted, an addict is controlled by an obsessive and compulsive mind that will relive his addictive behavior in his thoughts, keeping alive the experience with the help of memory cells in his body that create physical and mental cravings. Satan and his demons are the unseen forces that send messages to an unsuspecting mind. The addicted person assumes that his thoughts and feelings are his own, since he or she experiences powerful urges in his or her flesh. Demons choose the weakest time and place to attack, and since an addict's impulsive and compulsive behavior is predictable, it is a simple matter for demons to attract, lure and trap a person into addictive behavior. The following moments, circumstances and or places of weakness may have acted as doorways to demonic influence that led to your addiction:

1. **A generational curse**---Within your family tree is a long line of substance abusers giving the appearance of a genetic predisposition. Social and cultural factors have been influenced by unseen demonic forces wherein you have developed a vulnerability to the

substance abuse demon. A review of Deuteronomy Ch. 27 points to the following as open doors to generational curses:

...idolatry or witchcraft ...oppression of the weak

...sodomy ...dishonoring of parents

...incest...theft

...injustice ...perjury

2. **A family background in the occult or false religions**---Someone in your family has practiced divination, sorcery, roots, santaria, or some form of witchcraft, ie. astrology, yoga, acupuncture, hypnosis, reincarnation and the use of a Ouija board. These practices have also been linked to religious idolatry or involvement in mediumship or psychic phenomena.

3. **Pressures in early childhood**-- When as a child you were denied basic emotional needs for love, safety and self esteem, you became vulnerable to demons.

4. **Emotional shock or sustained emotional pressure.** Traumatic events such as violence, incest or rape as well as a sudden and frightening accidents. These kind of episodes are breeding grounds for demonic activity. Intense fear can also lead to denial and escapism.

5. **Sinful acts or habits**---Demons have a right of access when you made a conscious decision to practice sin. Whoever practices sin over a prolonged period of time is actually imitating the devil's nature and character and cuts himself off from the power of God. In particular, demons are attracted to sins of

long duration such as sexual immorality, including not only fornication but sodomy or homosexuality.

6. **Negative emotions** ---Anger, hatred, unforgiveness, rejection, and self-pity can lead to rebellion. Rebellion is as "the sin of witchcraft."

7. **Character defects.** Unaware of the impact of unseen forces on your personality, demons have been empowered to develop your mind, emotions, feelings, and will. Your personality has become a mixture of your own soul under the influence of demons.

Adapted from "They Shall Expel Demons" by Derek Prince, Chosen Books 1998, pgs. 103-112

The goal of the RIC Program is to help you to recognize hidden battlegrounds in your own life so that you can find victory in the blood of Jesus. The blood of Jesus breaks all curses.

A PORTRAIT OF A RECOVERED PERSON

A person is recovered when he or she has taken back control of his own soul. Although Satan will do everything in his power to regain his control, a recovered person is sober not only as a drug or alcohol-free person, but he or she is vigilant, watchful and wise,--- prepared for the demon's counterattack. Although a recovered person is no longer an addict but a child of God, he or she is aware that there is a weakness in his or her flesh that has a predisposition to relapse. Therefore, a recovered person has a relapse prevention plan that includes but is not limited to:

1. **living by God's word**---the person begins to live the reality of the cleansing power of the blood of Jesus

Christ---that before he or she believed on Christ, he was anaddict, but as a born again believer, he or she is washed, or in other words "clean"by faith in His word. (I Corinthians 6;9-11)

2. **delighting in the Lord**---the person has pursued the fruit of joy and peace, by an active commitment to lifestyle of prayer, praise and thanksgiving. His offering of praise to the Lord operates as a cover of clothing that protects him or her from the return of the "addiction demon." (Isaiah 6:3)

3. **submitting to the cross**---the person has found out the root cause of his or her addiction by allowing his flesh to be crucified. Whether or not addiction was linked to the sin of rebellion, selfishness, self-centeredness or pleasure seeking, he is committed to obey God's word. The most important area of discipline is that a recovered person has learned to control his tongue. The control of the tongue is the key to spiritual empowerment and recovery, because "if anyone does not stumble in word, he or she is a perfect man, able to bridle or control his own body, including his predisposition to addiction." (James 3:2)

4. **seeking right fellowship**---the person has learned that to love the world is to be an enemy towards God. Therefore, he or she chooses his relationships not by the desires of his flesh, but by the spirit. He or she will not seek counsel from the ungodly, nor stand in the way of sinners, or sit in the seat of the scornful. He or she has learned how to live among unbelievers without becoming "one" with them. He has learned how to overcome the pain of separating oneself from people of unhealthy influences and to do it with the wisdom, mercy and grace of God.

5. **connecting with believers**---He does not neglect the active assembling of himself with his brothers and sisters in Christ. Committed to his spiritual leader and to other Christians, he comes together with the brethren to intensively explore his own character defects. As led by the Holy Spirit, he examines and confesses his own faults to find healing and recovery. He is also a tither, giving 10% of his income to the work of the Lord (Hebrews 10-24,25, Psalm 1, 2Corinthians 6:14, James 5:16)

6. **embracing the vision** --- He views himself as an important member of the body of Christ, sharing in the overall mission of the faith in general, and with a particular ministry. He is an important member of the larger body with a Spirit inspired vision, mission and goal. Armed with the courage of his own convictions, he is not easily discouraged, walking by faith and not by sight. Faithful and committed to the few things, he supports his pastor and uses his spiritual gifts to be an instrument for church growth and development.

7. **walking in the witness of the Spirit**---the person is blessed with a thirst for the Lord and **His** righteousness that has replaced his or her thirst for craving for the thing or substance that formerly had him or her bound and captive. As the scripture says: Be not drunk with wine but be filled with the Spirit of God. As demonstrated by the words of the mouth and the selection of priorities, he or she has grown from having addiction or being clean and sober as the center of his life. As a result, He has overcome Satan by the word of his testimony. His testimony is a personal witness to the healing power of the Holy Spirit. His witness is capable of drawing others to the Lord.

THE SEVEN KEYS TO RECOVERY

As a Christ-centered alternative to the 12 Steps Model, the RIC Program,--- Recovery In Christ---, is based upon 7 Keys as derived from the words of our Lord and Savior Jesus the Christ in Matthew 16:16-19. In this text, Jesus declared that Peter's revelation that He was the Christ earned for Peter and the church the keys to the kingdom. These spiritual keys have the capacity to unlock the knowledge, wisdom and power of the kingdom. The kingdom is the realm of the spirit. Since Jesus has built His church upon Peter's revelation of His Lordship, these same keys are available to everyone who believes on Peter's affirmation to Jesus: "You are the Messiah, the Son of the living God." In the language of recovery, in order to defeat the cycle of addiction with a complete victory of absolute restoration, Christ must be not only your "Highest Power" but your "Only Power". Jesus of Nazareth must be the one to whom not only all knees BOW and all tongues CONFESS that He is Lord, but that He is YOUR Lord!

Throughout the Bible, particularly the New Testament and the letters of Paul the Apostle, all things consist or hold together IN CHRIST! (Colossians 1:17) What this means is that all doctrine, knowledge, wisdom and power center in the person and the work of Jesus Christ. This also includes all precepts and methods of "spirituality." For example, the doctrine of salvation centers in Christ the Savior; the doctrine of sanctification centers in Christ the Sanctifier, the doctrine of intercession centers in Christ the Intercessor, the doctrine of deliverance centers in Christ the Deliverer; the doctrine of healing centers in Christ the Healer; and so following, the doctrine of recovery centers in Christ the Recoverer! As Jesus Christ is given his rightful position as Highest Power in recovery, those who suffer from the bondage of addiction will be set free by His anointing.

Anointing is the supernatural power of Christ. Jesus of Nazareth declared that He is anointed to break yokes and bring recovery to those who are in bondage by setting free those who have been bruised. (Luke 4:18) With His anointing, Jesus "went about doing good and healing all that were oppressed of the devil, for God---in the person of the Holy Ghost was with Him." (Acts 10:38) Since Jesus said that the kingdom of God is within the spirit of man, an initial foundational premise of recovery through the anointing of Jesus Christ is that once His anointing within our spirits is activated, we have access to complete recovery and restoration. In order for His anointing that is within you to teach you concerning everything, (including addiction and recovery), you must abide in HIM!

Another major recovery principle is that His anointing is triggered by our profession or affirmations of faith. In this regard, the anointing for recovery is activated by faith-filled words emanating from our spirits through our mouth, lips and tongue. For as Jesus said, once you have possessed the keys to the kingdom , " what ever you bind on earth (declare to be unlawful) is bound in heaven, and what ever you loose (declare to be lawful) is loosed in heaven."

These are the seven (7) affirmations and seven (7) keys of RECOVERY:

AFFIRMATION: KEY #1. <u>REPENTANCE</u>
I admit that my addiction has been a sin before God, and I confess my sorrow about it. I ask the Lord Jesus Christ to forgive me my sin and to cleanse me from both the sin and the disease of addiction. I repent by turning my back on sin and turning my face toward the Father, Son and the Holy Spirit.

KEY #2. <u>RESURRECTION</u>
I believe that Jesus Christ was raised from the dead, not as a spirit but as a man who was physically dead and came back to physical life again, in a glorified body. I will walk in newness of life and live in the victorious

power of the resurrected Christ, transforming my tests, trials and tribulations into a purposeful ministry of love to others. I will be an effective witness for Jesus Christ, taking a firm, fixed and bold position to set others free. I will be salt and light to the world.

AFFIRMATION: KEY #3 REBIRTH
Not only have I perceived myself as a sinner and have experienced the godly sorrow of repentance, I also confess that I believe that Jesus Christ was raised from the dead. I surrender my life to His Lordship. I ask the Holy Ghost to come into my life and re-create my spirit. I confess with my mouth that I am "born again", saved, sanctified, adopted and justified before God the Father through the shed blood of His Son.

AFFIRMATION KEY #4. REVELATION
I submit myself to the Holy Ghost to lead me and guide me into the truth about myself, my character defects and the root causes of my addiction. I will learn the language of my spirit by recording my dreams, visions and intuitions. I will be careful to try the spirits to see if they be of God. I seek wisdom and revelation into the knowledge of Jesus Christ.

AFFIRMATION KEY #5. RESISTANCE
I admit that my addiction kept me in bondage and captivity to the devil. I will resist the devil by learning all that I can about his distractions, deceptions and devices. I renounce the powers of darkness and take back what the enemy of my soul has stolen from me. I am preparing myself to be released from every curse that addiction has brought to my life.

AFFIRMATION KEY #6. RENEWAL
I faithfully commit myself to accept the responsibility

not to be conformed to this world, but to be transformed by the renewing of my mind, so that I can get in touch with the Lord's divine thoughts, plans and purposes for my life. I will find my place in the body of Christ by submitting myself to the Holy Ghost.

AFFIRMATION KEY #7. **RESTORATION**
I dedicate myself to remain disentangled from the yoke of bondage. I will forgive my own failures and the failures of those who have hurt me. I can forgive my enemies because I recognize that the unseen world of principalities and powers have used my enemies to destroy me without their spiritual knowledge. My divine love for my enemies will restore my soul.

KEY #1: REPENTANCE
THE FIRST KEY TO RECOVERY AND VICTORY OVER SATAN IS

REPENTANCE!

AFFIRMATION: KEY #1. **REPENTANCE**

I admit that my addiction has been a sin before God, and I confess my sorrow about it. I ask the Lord Jesus Christ to forgive me my sin and to cleanse me from both the sin and the disease of addiction.

II Corinthians 7:10

For godly sorrow worketh repentance to salvation not to be repented of: but the sorrow of the world worketh death.

Background

The first message of the kingdom was preached by John the Baptist---a message of repentance. This message tells man that when Adam fell, sin entered the entire human race, spreading death and evil throughout the world in each successive generation. God gave Adam dominion over the whole earth. With his fall, Adam forfeited his dominion to Satan, thus placing mankind into Satan's kingdom. To come into the kingdom of God, you must recognize your own sinful nature and feel within your own soul a need to be brought into right fellowship with God through accepting the blood sacrifice of His Son, Jesus Christ. In other words, repentance is not only a change of mind about the Lordship of Jesus Christ but it is also an inner recognition and realization of your own personal sinful nature and your desire to be made pure in heart. It is characterized by an inner sorrow that will produce the fruits of the second key, which is rebirth or salvation. Unless you change your view on sin, on yourself, on the world and on the Lord, it is not possible for you to be reborn or "saved."

Repentance will also transform your thoughts by exposing you to your sinful nature. Addicts, criminals, and societal misfits can recognize quickly that they are sinners primarily because their lives have become unmanageable. However, when you blame an outside force such as the drug itself, society, peers, genetics or family upbringing, you make it difficult to repent. Why? Because repentance is activated by an acceptance of personal responsibility and an awareness that there is something evil within you that causes you to sin in spite of your good intentions. In other words, you must admit to yourself and confess to God that you are sick and that your sickness of soul goes even deeper than just being an addict whose life is merely "unmanageable."

In early recovery, you will find that you yielded and surrendered to what you have called the "Higher Power" mainly because you had no where else to turn. Drugs and alcohol had ruined your life. You lost family, friends, loved ones, cars, jobs---you had nothing else to hold on to. The consequences of your addiction was that you were broken and out of control. You didn't go to sleep at night. You passed out. You didn't wake up in the morning. You "came to." Satan manifested himself as the god of your addiction and you gave him worship. In spite of your adulation, your god stole your health, strength, sanity, potency and freedom and you crawled to God for protection and safety.

Once you repent, you must also confess. "Confess the Lord Jesus with your mouth and believe in your heart that God has raised Him from the dead and you shall be saved. (Romans 10:8) Confession is your outward expression of repentance. When you call on the name of the Lord, in that call is the realization that you need Jesus to make things right for you with His Father. Confession links repentance to salvation in that it is a verbal expression of your faith in Jesus Christ---like the crying aloud of "Mama" when a child recognizes his mother. You have recognized your Savior, your Redeemer and your Lord. Within this recognition is realizing that your fall goes far deeper than mere addiction. You discover that you are not a victim to disease, to hostile societal ills, but that your illness is a product of your own alienation from God and your natural inclination toward disobedience.

When you repent, you will be convicted of sin. As you are drawn to Jesus by the Holy Spirit, the Lord's light will expose your true nature before the Father. The Holy Spirit will use the situations and circumstances in your life to uncover your sinful nature and reveal it to you. Repentance will also act as a positive trigger toward the development of true humility where the hidden desires of your heart are revealed. God wants you to approach Him with humility. Without repentance, you will think more highly of yourself than you ought to think. There are many who believe that Jesus is the Christ but they are not saved because they have not been exposed to their sinful nature through repentance. **Consider the Apostle Peter.** He had been with Jesus. He was even given direct revelation from the Father that Jesus is the Messiah, yet he was not converted until after his true nature was exposed to him and he experienced sorrow that led to repentance. The pain of Peter's fall was necessary. In spite of being anointed by the Lord to heal the sick, he was also used by Satan.

When you repent, your conscience will be awakened. In your addiction, you were rebellious to Christ. Your world and your flesh taught you that getting high was acceptable. The Holy Spirit has used the thunders and lightnings of your life to shake your conscience so as to convince you that you have been a sinner and you have no way within your own ability to answer the Father's righteous demand. If you have merely heard the word of God with your mind and have been touched in your emotions, and you have decided with your will that God's way is better, you need more to be truly saved. **Your conscience must be convicted of sin.** Once your conscience is stirred up, you will be convicted of sin, particularly the sin of unbelief in Jesus Christ, and you will be sorrowful in a godly way. Godly sorrow is not the result of shame or guilt at being found out. It is a recognition that your violation of God's law has caused you to be lost and separated from the Father. This conviction will prepare you for salvation. "When the Holy Spirit comes, He will convince the world of sin and of righteousness and of judgement." (John 16:8)

When you repent, you will change your mind about Jesus of Nazareth. While a sinner, you could not understand why God Himself would come to earth and take upon Himself flesh. You could not understand that a man could be all human and all God at the same time. How could a man who lived for only 33 years also be the God of all creation? And why would He come to earth to die for man's sins? You could not comprehend such a God. You loved what the Lord hates and you hated what the Lord loves. Your thoughts have not been His thoughts and your ways have not been His ways. Therefore, you could not understand the Lord's sacrifice at the cross. It was foolishness to you. However, in the twinkling of an eye you will understand the crucifixion. You will instantaneously realize your inability to answer God's righteous demand. You will understand that heaven and hell are real.

When you repent, your heart is softened. With a hardened heart, you once justified yourself before people. In so doing, you established them as your Lord and you gave them authority in your life to mold you. You sought their support and you became rooted in the world's affirmations. However, with a softened heart, you have become more flexible. Whatever the word of God reveals about the Son of God, repentance prepares you to receive Him. Where your plans and purposes are concerned, your mind has been touched to flow with God. In other words, what ever you may have decided upon in the past is now subject to change. You are prepared to receive with meekness the engrafted word.

When you repent, your self esteem will be touched by the Holy Spirit. Peter the Apostle had high self esteem. He took care of himself. However, when he was faced with the sinfulness of his own soul after denying knowing the Lord three times, his self esteem was broken. His sinful nature was fully revealed to him. It is important to understand that the pain of his fall was very necessary. As a result, Peter lost all confidence in himself and gained the salvation of his soul. In the same manner, when you are placed in a situation where you too must face the reality of your own sinful nature, you will gain your soul.

When you repent, you will turn away from Satan's kingdom of unrighteousness and evil. Without repentance, we are all prey to demonic deception. When you maintain a heart of repentance, you will receive the light of spiritual discernment, where you will be able to recognize your own sinful nature. When you turn from darkness to light, you will begin to examine your own heart and lose your tendency toward self-righteousness. Repentance will help you to reject the tendency to justify your thoughts, opinions, perceptions and actions.

When you repent, the Holy Spirit will crucify your flesh by brokenness. Being broken is another way of "dying" or being crucified with Christ. In "To Curse the Root", brokenness is defined as weeding. Weeding is a spiritual process that involves self-examination and discovery, whereby you will uncover those attitudes, thoughts and habits that have been hurtful or have hindered your surrendering to the Lordship of Jesus Christ. The weeding process loosens the hard soil of your soulish nature by digging deep into your spirit. Weeding draws up experiences that may have been tightly packed and hidden beneath layers of denial, procrastination and rejection.

As the seat of human personality and consciousness, the soul acts as a mediator or "middle man" between the spirit and the body. Simply put, the soul is the seat of the self or the "I AM." Although each human personality has some hereditary characteristics or predispositions, the "I AM" has been trained by habit, experiences, and cultural or societal opinion. Moreover, even though the "I AM" may appear to have a mind, feelings and a will of its own, much of its makeup has been defined by people, including family, peers and other social systems. Your predominant world view has been progressively formed in you in direct relationship to the power of those messages or words that have been absorbed by you internally and subsequently computed into your personality makeup through the subconscious process of socialization.

Every system that does not have Jesus Christ as its Head is under the rulership of the god of this age, also known in scripture as "the prince of the power of the air." The word of God tells us that Satan is the god of this world and its systems. Even those systems that are considered good or positive fall under demonic power if Jesus Christ is not in control of them, including family, education, culture, and government. Jesus did not come to make peace with the systems of this world. In fact, He declared, "Do not think that I came to bring peace on earth. I did not come to bring peace but a sword. For I have come to set a man against his father and a daughter against her mother, and a daughter-in-law against her mother-in-law; and a man's enemies shall be those of his own household." When your heart is full of repentance, you will know in your heart that your righteousness before a holy God is as filthy rags. Even the good things of your world are filthy before a holy and righteous God.

When you repent, you will receive forgiveness and cleansing. I have heard of those who have received a full cleansing from addiction wherein the Lord wiped away all cravings and urges. However, this has tended the be the exception and not the rule. Cleansing has most often been progressive as opposed to instantaneous. In this regard, it is important that you seek the guidance of the Holy Spirit to understand your own experience of craving, and to realize that craving does not mean that you want to resume drug use. Rather, as you repent, you should seek the wisdom of God to help you identify triggers that are the most problematic and also developing a set of coping strategies from the word of God that will help you to overcome yielding to urges and cravings. It is important to realize that having a desire to use is not failure. Failure comes from yielding to the temptation.

Key Scriptures

About Peter's Repentance

Matthew 16:15 He saith unto them, But whom say ye that I am?

16 And Simon Peter answered and said, Thou art the Christ, the Son of the living God.

17 And Jesus answered and said unto him, Blessed art thou, Simon Barjona: for flesh and blood hath not revealed it unto thee, but my Father which is in heaven.

Matthew 16:21 From that time forth began Jesus to shew unto his disciples, how that he must go unto Jerusalem, and suffer many things of the elders and chief priests and scribes, and be killed, and be raised again the third day.: 22 Then Peter took him, and began to rebuke him, saying, Be it far from thee, Lord: this shall not be unto thee.

:23 But he turned, and said unto Peter, **Get thee behind me, Satan: thou art an offense unto me: for thou**

savourest not the things that be of God, but those that be of men.

Matthew 26:69 Now Peter sat without in the palace: and a damsel came unto him, saying, Thou also wast with Jesus of Galilee.: 70 But he denied before them all, saying, I know not what thou sayest.:71 And when he was gone out into the porch, another maid saw him, and said unto them that were there, This fellow was also with Jesus of Nazareth.:72 And again he denied with an oath, I do not know the man.:73 And after a while came unto him they that stood by, and said to Peter, Surely thou also art one of them; for thy speech betray thee: 74 Then began he to curse and to swear, saying, I know not the man. And immediately the cock crew.:75

And Peter remembered the word of Jesus, which said unto him, Before the cock crow, thou shalt deny me thrice. And he went out, and wept bitterly.

About Repentance

II Timothy 2:24: And the servant of the Lord must not strive; but be gentle unto all men, apt to teach, patient,:25 In meekness instructing those that oppose themselves; if God peradventure will give them **repentance** to the acknowledging of the truth;

:26 And that they may **recover** themselves out of the snare of the devil, who are taken captive by him at his will.

Acts 26:18 To open their eyes, and to turn them from darkness to light, and from the power of Satan unto God, that they may receive forgiveness of sins, and inheritance among them which are sanctified by faith that is in me.:19 Whereupon, O king Agrippa, I was not disobedient unto the heavenly vision::20 But shewed first unto them of Damascus, and at Jerusalem, and throughout all the coasts of

Judaea, and then to the Gentiles, that they should repent and turn to God, and do works meet for **repentance.**

Mark 2:16 And when the scribes and Pharisees saw him eat with publicans and sinners, they said unto his disciples, How is it that he eateth and drinketh with publicans and sinners?:17When Jesus heard it, he saith unto them, They that are whole have no need of the physician, but they that are sick: I came not to call the righteous, but sinners to **repentance.**

Man's Need for Repentance

Colossians 1:21 And you, that were sometime alienated and enemies in your mind by wicked works, yet now hath he reconciled In the body of his flesh through death, to present you holy and unblamable and unreproveable in his sight:

Philippians 3:18 (For many walk, of whom I have told you often, and now tell you even weeping, that they are the enemies of the cross:19 Whose end is destruction, whose God is their belly, and whose glory is in their shame, who mind earthly things.)

:20 For our conversation is in heaven; from whence also we look for the Savior, the Lord Jesus Christ:

II Peter 3:9 The Lord is not slack concerning his promise, as some men count slackness; but is longsuffering to us-ward, not willing that any should perish, but that all should come to repentance.

I Peter 5:6 Therefore humble yourselves under the mighty hand of God, that He may exalt you in due time, :7 casting all your care upon Him for He cares for you.

Philippians 3:8 Yea doubtless, and I count all things but loss for the excellency of the knowledge of Christ Jesus my Lord: for whom I have suffered the loss of all things, and do count them but dung, that I may win Christ,:9 And be found in

Repentance

him, not having mine own righteousness, which is of the law, but that which is through the faith of Christ, the righteousness which is of God by faith::10 That I may know him, and the power of his resurrection, and the fellowship of his sufferings, being made conformable unto his death;:11If by any means I might attain unto the resurrection of the dead.

Ezekiel 36:26 A new heart also will I give you, and a new spirit will I put within you: and I will take away the stony heart out of your flesh, and I will give you an heart of flesh.

Study And Reflection Outline

> **KEY STATEMENT:** Repentance is a humbling experience because you must admit to yourself and to God that you need a complete transformation of personality and character.

Point 1: You were once a chosen vessel of the enemy, Satan. Repentance will convert you from the kingdom of the anti-Christ into the true kingdom of the Christ.

    A. Satan has used your sinful nature to hinder God's purposes without your knowledge but with your implied consent through sin.

    B. In spite of this, the triune God has called and chosen you.

Point 2. Every unsaved person needs a recovery that embraces repentance.

    A. "All" have sinned and fallen short of the glory of God. (Romans 3:23)

B. "All" have been alienated and without God in the world. (Colossians 1:21)

C. Our friendship with the world has made us God's enemies. (James 4:4)

Point 3. Addiction is a sin that is similar to other sins of the flesh, including:

A. lasciviousness/lustfulness

B. licentiousness/disregard for legal, moral or sexual restraints.

C. idolatry

D. fornication or sexual uncleanness

E. theft and extortion (I Corinthians 6:10)

Point 4 The most outstanding sin of any unsaved person---addicted or not--- is a refusal to receive Jesus Christ as Lord.

A. Jesus is the Mediator between God and man.

B. Jesus is the only way to right relationship with the Father.

C. There is no recovery without reconciliation with Him. (Romans 5:6-19)

Point 5 Your first effort of repentance will be to change your mind about Jesus.

A. You will feel sorrow in your heart that you denied the Lord by your life of lust and lasciviousness.

B. You will realize that His sacrifice for you was essential to your complete recovery in Him.

C. You will cry out to Him for forgiveness.

Point 6   Repentance will be manifested by an inner sense of sorrow.

  A. You will have a spiritual recognition of sin in your spirit

  B. The feelings that are most pronounced are guilt and shame.

  C. Often you will find yourself weeping, groaning or wailing.

Point 7   The Holy Spirit is the force behind your repentance.

  A. His purpose is to awaken your conscience.

   1. An awakened conscience will give you the heart of a true worshipper

    a) to honor Jesus Christ with great respect

    b) to know the fear of the Lord

    c) to bask in the knowledge of how much Jesus loves you.

   2. His purpose is to teach you to judge yourself.

    a) seek the judgements of the Lord.

    b) be willing to receive correction.

    c) see the corruption that is within you.

  B. His purpose is to humble you.

   1. When you think that you are the least vulnerable, you are in the most danger.

   2. Humility will teach you that your victory is in walking close to the Lord

    a) He gives grace to the humble.

        b) Pride is an enemy that sneaks up behind you unawares.

Point 8 Repentance is the first step to breaking any curse over your life.

    A. Humbling yourself before the Lord Jesus Christ will bring you under His protection.

    B. Baptism is a sign of your renunciation of the world, the flesh and the devil.

        1. you will pass through the water of baptism out of Satan's kingdom into the kingdom of the Lord Jesus Christ.

        2. your baptism gives you the authority to take control over cravings.

Point 9 Repentance will quench your thirst and lead you to a satisfied life which is found only in the salvation of your soul.

    A. When you are dissatisfied, you will feel unfulfilled, incomplete and empty. Your emptiness is a major reason why you have abused drugs.

        1. you tend to always be wanting but never having

            a) indulgence in the flesh is always temporary and short-lived.

            b) your appetite is strong and insatiable.

        2. Your emptiness felt within will cause you to always want to be occupied or "doing something."

            a) you will be restless and anxious.

            b) you will tend to be bored easily.

    B. Satisfaction is a spiritual substance or force that cannot be obtained in the flesh.

1. Happiness is obtainable in the flesh. However, happiness can not fill your emptiness.

    a) happiness comes from outside stimulation (new car, job, etc.)

    b) outside stimulation is a product of circumstances

    c) lose the stimulation and the happiness is also lost.

2. Joy is a spiritual force that is not destroyed by outside stimulation.

    a) a joyous person is filled and strengthened from within.

    b) without repentance, you will never know the joy that comes from being forgiven by the Lord.

C. When you hunger and thirst after righteousness, you will be filled.

1. Righteousness is the opposite of unrighteousness or SIN.

2. You have been dissatisfied because you are or have been a sinner.

3. As previously stated, ADDICTION IS SIN!

4.

Workstudy Exercises

Exercise #1: Are you willing for God to do anything to re-create and mold your life? If so, write down a particular event,

To Curse The Root

personality change or situation that serves as evidence that you have repented. If you are not so willing, point out what is blocking you from repentance.

Exercise #2: Scripture states that rebellion is as the sin of witchcraft. What is the nature of your style of rebellion in regards to your former abuse of intoxicants?

Exercise #3: Read from "to Curse the Root", pages 42-46. Of the four (4) personality types, which one or more best describes you.

Exercise #4: Craving is uncomfortable, but in Christ you can deal with it without using. Each day this week, fill out the daily record chart of drug or alcohol craving you may have experienced and what you did to cope with it.

Repentance

Daily Record of Substance Abuse Craving

Date/Time	Situation: thoughts and feelings	Intensity of craving (1-100)	Length of craving	How I coped

To Curse The Root

Exercise #5 What is your experience of craving or of temptation? What triggers you? Check the statement that most represents you.

    a)__I get a feeling in my stomach
    b)__My heart races.
    c)__I start smelling it.
    d)__I can't get it out of my head.
    e)__It calls me.
    f)__I get nervous.
    g)__I get bored.
    h)__I get disappointed.

If you selected a,b,or c, then temptation comes to you through your body. If you selected d or e, then temptation comes to you primarily through your mind. If you selected f g or h, then temptation come to you primarily through your emotions.

Exercise #6 Repentance is about change. At this level of your recovery, how do you respond to the following statement?

a) I can go to parties, see friends who are users, have a beer or a glass of wine, and/or smoke marijuana without using myself.

_____

b) Read Psalm 1 In light of your response as written in part (a) of this exercise, how does your response compare to the word of God? If your response is in contradiction with the scripture, what do you intend to do about it?

_____

c) Now that you have read Psalm 1, also read II Corinthians 6: 11-18. Are you in a close relationship with someone that uses your drug of choice? What does the word of God reveal to you that you must do? What do you intend to do now that you know how the Lord feels about your relationship?

Exercise 7 Imagine every high risk situation where you might encounter someone who would offer you alcohol or drugs. Jot down in the following table what you plan to say in each situation.

People places and situations	What you will say or do

Exercise #8: If you are in agreement to any one of the following statements, the depth of your repentance will be revealed to you.

a) Life will never be the same. I love being high.

b) Life without drugs will be boring. I expect that I will slip once in a while.

c) Previous treatments haven't worked. The REC Program probably won't work either.

How do you stand in regards to these three (3) statements?

To Curse The Root

⁞ (blank lined writing space) ⁞

Exercise #9: Read pages 46-69 of "To Curse the Root." Where do you believe that you need to be broken the most.... your affections, your desires, or your feelings?_

KEY #2: RESURRECTION

THE SECOND KEY TO RECOVERY AND VICTORY OVER SATAN IS

RESURRECTION

AFFIRMATION KEY #7. **RESURRECTION**

I will walk in newness of life and I live in the victorious power of the <u>resurrected</u> Christ, transforming my tests, trials and tribulations into a fruitful ministry of soul winning. I will be an effective witness for Jesus Christ, taking a firm, fixed and bold position to set others free. I will be salt and light to the world.

Romans 6:4,5

Therefore we are buried with him by baptism into death: that like as Christ was raised up from the dead by the glory of the Father, even so we also should walk in newness of life. For if we have been planted together in the likeness of his death, we shall be also in the likeness of his resurrection.

Background

When the Christ walked on earth, He taught His disciples that to live for the self or the life of the soul is like a grain of wheat, once planted, refusing to die and thereby remaining alone. (John 12:24) Yet, if it dies, it will be extremely fruitful. In like manner, when you are bound too strongly to your mind, affection, emotions and desires, you will hinder spiritual power and productivity. In order to operate exclusively by the power of God, Jesus Christ calls for death. However, within a spiritual context, death does not imply utter destruction. Rather, the death of your soul life is manifested in His crucifixion, where your human personality becomes transformed and renewed in the fruitfulness of His resurrection.

God's breaking or pruning hand is His way of transforming your mind, emotions and will so that He can cause you to bare fruit, ...for if you become united with Him in The likeness of His death, you shall be also in the likeness of His resurrection." Rather than becoming intellectually or emotionally deprived, a spiritually empowered personality is one that has been recreated by the hand of God for spiritual productivity.

Paul the Apostle is one of the best biblical examples of a spiritually fruitful person. Once filled with pride over his scholarly achievements and his cultural and religious background, Paul's soul and his spirit figuratively died on the road to Damascus, while his physical body was blinded and struck down by the glory of the Lord Jesus the Christ. (Acts Ch 9). Though zealous and committed to God as he perceived Him, Paul did not realize that he was barren and unfruitful in spite of all of his efforts to serve God. Paul describes his symbolic death in his letters to the Galatians and to the Corinthians. To the Galatians Paul writes "I was crucified with Christ but nevertheless I live, not I but Christ who lives in me. To the Corinthians he writes: "baring about in the body the dying of the Lord Jesus Christ that His life might be made manifest in our mortal flesh."(IICorinthians 4:10)

This kind of death is neither a forced or contrived breaking of the soul through sacrifice or penance. Rather it is that you were made dead through the death of Jesus. The secret of victory is never to consider yourself apart from Christ. Since a dead person cannot relapse, God does not expect the corpse of a dead addict to struggle every waking moment in the abyss of sin and of the world in his mind and emotions, ever promising Him to "do better next time." He does not require a corpse to improve itself. He has no expectations of the dead, for the dead know nothing. Of course, you are to confess your faults and ask for forgiveness when you have failed. However, you must realize that the root of your failure is that you allowed the corpse to live. In other words, you yourself resurrected the old nature outside of Christ and consequently, you fell.

The water baptism of the Christian faith is a holy and symbolic ritual of the believer's death and resurrection in the Son of God. Its significance lies in its message of the burial of the soul and the flesh, followed by the rebirth of the spirit. Through His death and burial, Christ has redeemed you from the curse of the law and supplied you with God's grace in His resurrection. (Galatians 3:29, Ephesians 2:8) The curse of the law is the inborn weakness of your soul and your flesh to satisfy God's commandments, rules and demands. In short, you are an habitual sinner without Christ.

Nevertheless, when you symbolically rise out of the water of baptism, grace supplants the law and sin no longer has dominion over you. Grace is both unmerited provision, anointing and power of the Holy Spirit within us, Who overshadows your weakness and frailty with His supernatural and divine ability. (II Corinthians 12:7)

It is a great discovery to experience a victory that transcends the soul and the body. If you followed the 12 Steps model, you depended on your mind and your willpower to work the principles and traditions. Now you will find that true deliverance and freedom is trusting in the 13th step: the resurrection life of Christ, the True Vine Who is the source of ALL grace and ALL power.

The second key of resurrection is a place of joy that is beyond the reasoning of the mind and the determination of the will. In matters of sobriety, victory is obtainable when Christ is the life or the Vine of recovery. Jesus declared Himself to be the true Vine of fruitfulness and productivity. To His disciples in recovery, Jesus declares that He is the true Vine. Without Him, you can do nothing. In order to be fruitful and successful, you must satisfy your inner craving and thirst by drinking from the true Vine. The life of the Vine is the Holy Spirit within your reborn spirit. His life produces victory by supplying you with the strength to be sober and clean without your conscious awareness of the effort. (John 15)

Jesus would agree with AA in its evaluation of addicted flesh, for addicted flesh is hopeless and it cannot change. After suffering many relapses and defeats, some persons ultimately stop all treatment. Others hate their defeat and with renewed determination remain sober for a time, only to fall once more. The addict cries out in despair:

> For that which I do I know not: for not what I would, that do I practice; but what I hate, that I do. But if what I would not, that I do, I consent unto the law that it is good. So now it is no more that I do it, but sin which dwelleth in me. For I know that in me, that is, in my flesh, dwelleth no good thing: for to will is present with me, but to do that which is good is not. For the good which I would I do not: but the evil which I would not, that I practice. (Romans 7:15-19)

The source of victory is to abide in the Vine and believe that you were made dead to the law through the body of Christ, "that you should be joined to another, even to Him who was raised from the dead, that you might BRING FORTH FRUIT UNTO GOD." (Roman 7:4) When Jesus died, you died also. A dead person is neither fruitful nor barren, successful nor failing. Just as the Lord's resurrection followed His death, resurrection also follows your death. Just as Christ was raised by the glory of the Father Who is the Holy Spirit, you too are so raised, if you abide in the Son. In his book entitled "The Glory of His Life", Watchman Nee provides an excellent portrayal of this spiritual truth:

> "We who are resurrected in Christ will bring forth fruit to the glory of God. Since God has given the life of Christ to us, we hereafter are able to live out Christ's life.

> Whatever be the grain of wheat that is sown, there shall be the thirty, the sixty or the hundred grains which grow out of it. If a person plants barley he will not get wheat or squash. What is sown is that which grows. There can be no change. If what is sown is wheat, all which grows out will be wheat. How can we live like Christ and bear fruit to glorify God as Christ did? In only one way: by letting Christ live in us and letting Him live out of us. Consequently, Christ not only died for us on the cross but He also lives for us within us. Who can make us live like Christ? None except the One who gives the life of Christ to us. As we have the life of Christ, we may bear fruit to the glory of God." (Nee, 1976 pg. 95)

Resurrection life will be evident when you experience revelation, power, and discernment under the guidance and instruction of the Holy Spirit. Revelation is to receive God's own personal knowledge and wisdom about your life. Power is God's supernatural ability applied to your human frailty. The Holy Spirit within you will also reveal how to discern between good fruits and harmful weeds as well as provide the power to bear fruit.

> In order to strengthen your spirit, The Lord will use various "spiritual" fertilizers. A natural fertilizer is an earthly substance applied to the soil by a farmer or a gardener to enrich the soil's productivity so that it might bare fruit in an abundance. By comparison, within the field of human productivity, fertilization is the process of enhanced impregnation. Consider that as manure is a fertilizer to earthly ground,---faith---a spiritual substance--- is God's fertilizer for the human spirit. Faith enriches the spirit's ability to bare fruit in a barren land where past failures and defeats have depleted our source of hope, trust and courage.

Jesus is your resurrection and your life. In other words, He has raised you up out of the deadness of your addicted condition by the power of His life. By that same power, He can also keep you alive, clean and sober. Furthermore, if you review your past experiences, you will find that many times death was at your door without your knowledge but you are still here. You are here because you have not yet fulfilled your eternal destiny which was in the mind and heart of the Father, Son and the Holy Ghost when you were conceived before the foundation of the world. Before you entered into your mother's womb, the Lord knew you and purposed that you would be a light to the world and salt to the earth because you were already pre-ordained or chosen in Him in the spirit realm before your spirit entered your body. Therefore, you must resist death until your final work here on earth is finished.

Your victory over death is revealed in your revelation of your purpose as expressed in His vision to you. If you have a vision, you will not perish. Your vision is your proof to yourself and to the devil that you can walk in newness of the power of the Lord's resurrection by faith because God's word does not return to Him void or empty but it accomplishes the purpose to which it was sent. Therefore, you can hold on to your joy, remain steadfast and finish your course. The blueprint for your life is already built into you. Once your blueprint has been revealed to you, if you resist it, then not only will you be rebelling against the Lord, but you will also be rebelling against yourself.

Resurrection life will also be evident in the fruitfulness of your prayers for others. After Jesus was raised from the dead, those who believe on His name were given power to use His name to break every yoke. Jesus declared, "all power has been given unto me both in heaven and on earth. Now you go and use my name to cast out devils. Therefore, when you pray with resurrection power, you will be using words that you have spoken by your faith---words that are in accordance with the Lord's will and your authority to use His name. When God calls those things that be not ask though they were, the resurrection power manifested in you will be able to bring the life of Christ into those things that do not exist into reality through prayer, according to the will of the Lord Jesus Christ. The purpose of intercessory prayer is to confront the demonic world for the lost and to do battle with unseen forces with the fruit of your lips. A true prayer warrior will be able to loose the bands of wickedness, undo the heavy burdens, let the oppressed go free, and break every yoke. (Isaiah 58)

Key Scriptures

I Corinthians 15:13But if there be no resurrection of the dead, then is Christ not risen:

:14 And if Christ be not risen, then is our preaching vain, and your faith is also vain.

:15Yea, and we are found false witnesses of God; because we have testified of God that he raised up Christ: whom he raised not up, if so be that the dead rise not.

:16For if the dead rise not, then is not Christ raised::17And if Christ be not raised, your faith is vain; ye are yet in your sins:18Then they also which are fallen asleep in Christ are perished.:19If in this life only we have hope in Christ, we are of all men most miserable.:20But now is Christ risen from the dead, and become the firstfruits of them that slept.:21For since by man came death, by man came also the resurrection of the dead.:22For as in Adam all die, even so in Christ shall all be made alive.:23But every man in his own order: Christ the firstfruits; afterward they that are Christ's at his coming.:24Then cometh the end, when he shall have delivered up the kingdom to God, even the Father; when he shall have put down all rule and all authority and power.

:25For he must reign, till he hath put all enemies under his feet.:26The last enemy that shall be destroyed is death.:27For he hath put all things under his feet. But when he saith all things are put under him, it is manifest that he is excepted, which did put all things under him.:28And when all things shall be subdued unto him, then shall the Son also himself be subject unto him that put all things under him, that God may be all in all.

Romans 6:5For if we have been planted together in the likeness of his death, we shall be also in the likeness of his resurrection::6 Knowing this, that our old man is crucified with him, that the body of sin might be destroyed, that henceforth we should not serve sin.:7For he that is dead is freed from sin.:8Now if we be dead with Christ, we believe that we shall also live with him::9Knowing that Christ being raised from the dead dieth no more; death hath no more dominion over him.:10For in that he died, he died unto sin once: but in that he liveth, he liveth unto God.11Likewise reckon ye also yourselves to be dead indeed unto sin, but alive unto God through Jesus Christ our Lord.

Study and Reflection Outline

> **KEY STATEMENT:** Resurrection is symbolic of fruitfulness. If you abide in the Vine, you will be productive and you will walk in the power of the Holy Spirit.

KEY STATEMENT: Resurrection is symbolic of fruitfulness. If you abide in the Vine, you will be productive and you will walk in the power of the Holy Spirit.

Point 1: If you truly repented, your spirit has experienced resurrection. Therefore, it is impossible for you not to bare fruit. Not to bare fruit is like being dead.

Resurrection

A. Fruit can be defined in three ways: the character or holiness of Jesus Christ, drawing souls to salvation by your testimony, and positive results or outcomes.

   1. the character of Christ is represented by 9 fruits of the Holy Spirit

a) Love	d) Patience	g) faithfulness
b) Joy	e) Kindness	h) meekness
c) Peace	f) Goodness	i) self control

   2. Your testimony should be living evidence to the world that Jesus Christ is alive.

      a) Others will be drawn to the power of His resurrection that is within you and will pour out from you in your testimony

      b) Those that you reach for Christ will also draw fruit or souls to your account.

   3. Jesus came that we might have abundant life.

      a) Abundant life will be manifested as both natural and spiritual blessings.

      b) The anointing that is in your mouth will bless others in your intercessory prayer life.

         1) to loose others from demonic bondage

         2) to prosper and be in health

      c) Jesus said that you can know a person by his or her fruit.

B. The key to bearing fruit in all three categories is to submit to the Vine.

   1. The seeds are planted within your born again spirit but...

2. Only the Holy Spirit can give the increase when you abide in Christ.

C. The rebirth experience is about change. People tend to resist change.

1. They like to maintain their comfort zone.

2. They are attached to what they are doing in the world

3. They are self righteous and extremely proud

4. They are too attached to the former past life.

Point 2 To inherit the kingdom of heaven is to be fruitful in your spirit, soul and body. Jesus said that in order to inherit the kingdom you must be poor in spirit, in other words, meek. The fruitfulness of your recovery is dependent upon the level of your humility and meekness.

A. Meekness is enduring injury with patience and with gentleness

1. You will refuse to injure someone else for your own benefit

2. You will consider others more highly than yourself.

3. Meekness is not weakness.

B. Meekness is also being obedient to God's word and His will

1. The fear of the Lord is the beginning of wisdom.

2. Godly wisdom will cause you to be fruitful

3. You will set your own desires, thoughts and emotions aside.

4. Putting God's word above your pride will open you to blessings.

C. Meekness is the opposite of pride.

1. To die daily is to allow the cross to put your pride to death.

2. Pride will cause you to walk in the flesh.

a) jealousy and envy will lead you to strife and division

b) hypocrisy and conceit will lead you to deception and confusion.

D. Pride will cause you to do God's work in your own strength

1. You will be without His grace.

2. Your Christian walk will be a burden to you.

E. To be crucified with Christ involves the death of your pride

1. Being broken or pruned is a sacrifice that you must make to the Lord.

2. Pride blocks the flow of the Holy Ghost.

Point 3   The power of the resurrection is manifested when you walk in the spirit and not fulfill the lust of your flesh.

A. Walking in the spirit will bring what is unconscious in you into your conscious mind.

1. Everything that you need to know about your future has already beenplanted in you by the Holy Spirit.

2. The lust of your flesh will always desire to do what is contrary to the Lord's will. Your flesh has its own plans.

3. As you have delighted in the Lord, the Holy Spirit has already planted God's desires for you in your heart.

B. A vision of your assignment will help you to walk in the spirit.

1. a vision is inspired by God.

2. man's plan requires natural ability

3. God's vision requires supernatural ability.

C. Commitment is required to complete a vision.

1. commitment requires sacrifice

2. commitment requires patience

D. Besides commitment, a vision requires the following:

1. faith: the substance of hope, that requires corresponding action

2. hope: an expectation of the vision in spite of what you see

3. love: the substance that will not fail but will sustain you

4. desire: propels you and keeps you from giving up

5. joy: the source of your strength

Point 5 The Lord will sometimes give a foreshadowing of your direction to keep you focused on the right direction.

A. Sometimes your vision will be voiced by a prophet

1. a "word seed" is planted into the earth about you

2. that seed is the Word of God spoken into your spirit

3. faith added to God's word will produce God's plan

B. Prophecy is important because it is the foundation upon which God's plan for you is built upon.

1. His word creates a visual picture.

2. His word establishes hope in your soul.

C. God calls those things that be not as though they were, and then "THEY ARE!"

1. prayer calls into existence what does not exist.

2. prayer brings God's will into actuality on earth.

B. The first prophecy spoken by God into the earth was concerning the first coming of the Messiah, spoken to Satan in the Garden (Genesis 3:15)

1. from Abraham to John the Baptist, each saint was expecting His first coming.

2. they each had a personal vision linked to the coming Messiah.

C. The prophecy concerning the Lord's second coming should be at the center of each and every life since Jesus ascended into Heaven after His resurrection.

1. from His ascension until the present day, we wait on His second coming.

2. Your assignment is linked to His second coming.

Point 6 Your whole purpose for living is to complete your assignment.

A. The Lord will even use your mistakes and failures to develop you for your assignment.

B. Life will take you through a personal wilderness

1. to experience disappointment, rejection and misunderstanding

2. to learn how to endure hardship like a good soldier

C. You must prepare to lose what you thought was beneficial.

1. forget what was behind.

2. press forward

D. You must recognize when a similar assignment is not YOUR assignment.

1. cultivate patience and caution

2. fight the urge to be impulsive

E. The first place to look for your assignment is in your own heart.

1. delight in the Lord, ie. put nothing or no one before Him.

2. assess your flesh honestly, ie. are you extremely self interested?

F. The next place to look for your assignment is to evaluate your style of helping.

   1. maternal style or "mothering" is nurturing

   2. paternal style or "fathering" is training by example

Point 7 As you grow in Christ, you should be able to resurrect or reproduce your testimony in the life of another person or persons.

A. When you do your assignment legalistically, there will be no fruit for the Lord in His service.

   1. To be legalistic is to do things for the sake of pleasing your flesh, ie, being judgmental and intolerant of the failures of others, patting self on the back.

   2. Legalistic people are devoted to habits and rigid formulas

   3. Legalistic people make others feel incomplete and incompetent.

B. The fruit of help provided in the flesh will be a lack of peace, including:

   1. stress, frustration and fear

   2. anger, feeling abused, vindictive, violent

   3. lonely, isolated, feelings of failure and self loathing

C. You should become a spiritual father or a spiritual mother.

   1. to those who are babies in the Lord.

   2. to those struggling with bondages that you have overcome.

Point 8 You must make a covenant with the Lord to be committed to His business above your own.

A. You should be so committed to your destiny in Christ, that failure or defeat is never considered an option

B. Brave any consequence and refuse to be distracted by any problem.

   1. Satan will test you to see if you will wrongfully use your anointing.

      a) to fulfill your own fleshly needs

      b) out of religious pride

      c) to hurry God

      d) to rush in without sufficient preparation

C. Pain, persecution, disappointment and delays are crucial to your preparation.

   1. Don't waste your trials

      a) use them to obtain the kingdom.

Point 9 You should learn how not to be discouraged if it takes a long time for the fruit in you to be visible.

A. Look for the seed that will become the fruit.

   1. Keep His commandments by obeying His word.

   2. Abide in His love

      a) love the brethren

      b) bare one another's burdens

B. You must be willing to submit every thought to the foot of the cross.

a) meditate on the Lord's word

b) store His word in your heart

c) obey His word

C. Victory is obtained when you can identify the sin that has continued to trap you and keep you in bondage.

D. The way to fruitfulness is forgiveness.

1. The way that you receive persecution will influence your ability to be a soul winner.

2. Forgiveness sets the captives free.

Point 10 The abundant life is being fruitful or blessed in all that you put your hand to do.

A. You will be able to hear the still small voice within your spirit.

1. guidance and direction

2. divine help

B. Fruitfulness will be determined by how well you allow the Holy Spirit to renew your soul.

1. guard your spirit by controlling your mind and emotions

a) Christ must be at the center of your relationships

b) establish your relationships by your vision

2. realize that the only one who will completely understand you is the Lord.

C. "Whoever" you are trying to please will determine your level of success.

Point 11 The kingdom of God will come upon you in a fullness when you take the name of Jesus and go forth and cast out Satan's kingdom where you find it.

   A. You should become a witness with a testimony

      1. Don't rest on what you have done.

      2. Learn how to press forward.

   B. You should make your work and your life a ministry.

Workstudy Exercises

Exercise #1 To become fruitful in leadership, you must live out the phrase "NOT I, BUT YOU." On a scale from 1 to 5, how do you rate in the following areas:

   1. Objectivity--You can take your own likes and dislikes out of the situation__

   2. Understanding--You can move beyond yourself to listen to someone else__

   3. Tolerance---Not just you and yours is acceptable__

   4. Empathy---You can identify with someone else's pain even when you are suffering yourself__

Exercise #2 Conduct a role play with another Christian brother or sister. Let your partner play the part of a Jehovah witness or any other religion where Christ is not given complete deity. Describe the outcome of the role play._____
_____
_____
_____
_____

Resurrection

Exercise #3 What is the most important aspect of your testimony as a former addict? How can you target your testimony to the souls that will be most challenged by it?____

Exercise #4 What areas of giftedness are you manifesting? Are there hindrances to your fruitfulness that need to be removed? Describe.

To Curse The Root

Exercise #5 What quality of the life of the Lord would you like to see evident in your life by the power of His resurrection? Which fruit of the Spirit do you seek first?

Exercise #5 Describe here how you would plan an evangelistic home group for unbelievers in recovery that you know? How would you create a conducive atmosphere where souls can be saved in your home?

Exercise #6 Read 2 Peter 3:18 and I John 4:16-17 What are some areas in which you can experience spiritual growth?

Resurrection

Are you aware of your purpose and your place in the body of Christ. What are the clues from your life as an addict that might give you understanding about your purpose? Explain.

Exercise #8 As a prayer assignment, go before the Lord in your quiet time and make a commitment to Him that you will serve Him in His way and not your own. Make a commitment to do what is necessary to complete your assignment. As you read Romans 12: 1 and 2, what must you do to fulfill your assignment?

Exercise #9 To be steadfast is to be consistent, unwavering and reliable. When you become steadfast, you will be fixed in your pursuit of your divine purpose---secure, solid and strong, solid as a rock. What can make you unsteady?

Exercise 10 The more truth you know about who you are, the more skillful you will be at discerning the truth in other people, even though they have gone to great lengths to hide the truth from you. Describe ways that you once used to hide things from others that have helped you to recognize the "games others play."

KEY #3: REBIRTH

THE THIRD KEY TO RECOVERY AND VICTORY OVER SATAN IS

REBIRTH!

AFFIRMATION: KEY #2 **REBIRTH**

I have already confessed that I believe that Jesus Christ was raised from the dead. I surrender my life to His Lordship. I ask the Holy Ghost to come into my life and re-create my spirit. I confess with my mouth that **I am "born again"**, saved, sanctified, adopted and justified before God the Father through the shed blood of His son.

II Corinthians 5:17

> Therefore if any man be in Christ, he is a new creature: old things are passed away; behold, all things are become new.

Background

To understand salvation, you need to view mankind as a connected species that renews itself through passing on its essence into the bloodline of the fruit from its own body through what is biologically called "genetics." From the days of the fall of the first created human beings, the human bloodline has been contaminated and subject not only to corruption and decay but to sin and evil. When Adam fell, sin entered the entire human race, spreading death and destruction. Through the sin of this one man Adam, everything began to grow old and die. God had given Adam dominion over the whole earth.

With the fall, Adam forfeited his dominion to Satan and took into his own bloodstream the nature of "the god of this world." The kingdom of God consists of those who have come to the Lord Jesus Christ and have been brought out of bondage to the forces of the kingdom of darkness and have been delivered from Satanic enslavement.

The two kingdom's---God's and Satan's---stand side by side in direct opposition to each other. Both kingdoms are spiritual. One major feature of salvation is the process of changing families or dominions through adoption. God's plan from the very beginning of creation was to gather His children through the redemptive work of His Son at the cross. Jesus became sin for you so that you could be reunited with His Father. In this role, Jesus is referred to as "the second Adam." Adam's failure is the Lord's victory. You are reunited to the Father through the mediation of His Son. As a result, if you have received His Son as your Lord and Savior, you leave Satan's dominion and enter into God's family. All those who come to Him shall become like His Son, so that His Son would become the first born out of the human race, with may brothers and sisters.

This family relationship is based upon a blood covenant that God will never break. Only you can break it. Blood covenant was a common practice in Abraham's day, still practiced today among Indian and African cultures and tribes. Each tribe or nation varied in their practices of blood covenant but there were some common elements: <u>the mixing of human blood, the pronouncing of a curse if the covenant is ever broken, the scaring of fidelity and loyalty, the changing of names, the pronouncing of the terms of the covenant, partaking of a special ceremony and the serving of a ceremonial meal usually of bread and wine.</u> Families and tribes entered covenant with other families and tribes in order to help each other in times of need. The strengths of one family would be applied to the weakness of the other. One family might excel at war while another might be skillful in raising food. So both families who entered blood covenant would share everything, both strengths and weaknesses. In short, they would die for each other and live to bless each other.

The blood covenant is similar to a contract. The contract or agreement is sealed in the blood like a present day contract would be made official and binding by a signature and the seal of a notary. Another word for covenant is "testament." In the days of Abraham, individuals and groups would form binding contracts by the shedding of blood. When God entered into blood covenant with man, He was doing something with which the people were very familiar, as blood covenants were their culture's primary means of survival. One of the reasons that the so-called civilized world does not have a full revelation of God's love toward man is because the civilized world do not understand the blood covenant and what it entails. Blood has turned to ink on paper. Blood has been "watered down" until contracts lose their binding effect. For example, marriage was intended to be similar to blood covenant in the principle of "til death do us part."

The covenant was first established between God the Father and Abraham through the blood of circumcision. It consisted of both natural and spiritual promises and blessings that would come upon Abraham and his seed or descendants. "The seed" who is Jesus Christ was first spoken of by God in the garden to the devil and to Adam and Eve. Paul wrote the Galatians that if all who believe on Christ become Abraham's seed and therefore are heirs to the promises.

The blood covenant was the most powerful agreement that could be made---an agreement breakable only by death. So the event of the circumcision in Genesis the 17th chapter was an extremely serious symbolic ceremony, entered into by God with Abram (named changed after the blood ceremony to Abraham). With it, the Father marked Abraham's mind with a vision that would anchor his faith to believe God's promises. He also marked the minds of Abraham's descendants with each circumcision. In this way, the Father communicated his love in a way that Abraham could understand.

The deep seriousness of entering the blood covenant came from those in covenant vowing to forever give themselves to each other. The Father took upon Himself a practice that would forever bind Him to Abraham and Abraham's seed. Since the Father has no weakness, all that He had to contribute to the blood covenant relationship was strength, might, power, glory and grace. Abraham's enemies became God's enemies. God would supply for Abraham according to his every need, by His own riches in glory. When Abraham was weak, then God would be strong in him and for him.

In Hebrews the 11th chapter, God asked Abraham to do a very strange thing. He asked him to present his only son Isaac on the altar of sacrifice. Even more strange is the fact the Abraham set out to comply with killing his son without hesitation. Furthermore, as recorded in the 22th chapter of Genesis, Abraham told his two servants that he and Isaac would be going up into the mountains. He said "I and the lad will go yonder and worship and come again to you." Although God had told Abraham to sacrifice his son, Abraham remained assured that both he AND his son would be coming back down that mountain.

It is clear that Abraham believed that if his boy was sacrificed, that the Father would raise his son from the dead. This demonstrates how strongly Abraham believed in his blood covenant with God. He did not know if God could raise anyone from the dead, but he knew that his son Isaac would have to produce some offspring or "a seed." Since no seed had yet been born, Abraham believed that the Father would have to raise his son from the dead because God had made a promise to him, cut in BLOOD! How could the Father do any less. He too would offer up His Son as a sacrifice of blood in the new covenant or testament. He would also raise Him from the dead by the power of the Holy Spirit.

Abraham's covenant was filled with many material blessings to his natural seed, the Israelites. However, the most profound spiritual promise and benefit of Abraham's faith is salvation and the born again experience--- a blessing that would only be fulfilled through the sacrifice of the Father's seed, the Lord Jesus Christ. The righteous would never be forsaken or his seed begging bread because Jesus would come down from heaven and feed His people. Jesus is the living bread of the covenant meal of the new covenant cut in His own precious blood. Jesus instructed His disciples to use the ceremonial meal of the Holy Communion to remember the terms of His covenant with those who believe upon Him. Jesus declared that the bread is His body and the wine of the meal is His blood. When Jesus tells you to "take and eat", you should very seriously re-affirm your blood covenant relationship with Him. Jesus is saying to YOU personally, "I died and I gave my life for you. I was raised so that you might never die but have everlasting life. Remember and enjoy the blessings of your salvation."

Another joy of the blood covenant of salvation is the freedom you have obtained from the curse of the law. Mankind continued to sin from the time of Adam until the days of Moses yet God did not judge them guilty of death for breaking His laws until He had given them through the prophet Moses. Moses wrote that if a person could be perfectly good and hold out against temptation all of his life and never sin once, only then could he be pardoned or saved. Thus, the giving of the law began a system of trying to please God through obedience to His laws. The old system of Jewish laws required blood sacrifices year after year yet this system was incapable of saving those who lived under its rules. If it could have, then one animal offering would have sufficed once and for all and the feeling of guilt would be gone. However, this very sacrificial process only served as a constant reminder to the people of their disobedience and guilt instead of relieving their minds.

When Jesus laid down His life, He cancelled this first system in favor of a far better one. Under the new covenant or "contract", we have been forgiven and made clean by Christ's dying once and for all,--- for ALL sin, both past, present and future. Under the old covenant, the priest stood before altar continually offering sacrifices that could only cover sin for a season, but never take sins away completely. Christ's offering of Himself to God for our sins is one sacrifice for all time. Christ has redeemed us from the curse of the law because His blood answered the law's demand which requires punishment for all sin. Christ's shed blood saves you. Without the blood, you cannot be saved. Because of God's righteousness, God cannot help but save you because His Son's blood has paid the price for your sin and the Father's righteous demand for your punishment has been satisfied. You therefore are saved by the righteousness which Jesus has accomplished in His death at the cross.

However, without resurrection, there is no salvation. You must not only believe that Jesus died for your sins but that He was raised from the dead. Resurrection broke the power of death, giving you victory over death. Death has lost its sting. Jesus Christ is resurrected to live within you. Such a demonstration of Almighty power not only defeats death, but ensures that you, as a believer, receive a new life in a body that one day will be resurrected and made immortal as was the Father's original intention in Adam. Your physical body is now dying yet upon the Lord's return to earth for the children of the kingdom, your dead body will either rise from the grave or if still alive, will be changed instantly from mortality to immortality. If you had remained a part of Satan's kingdom, at your death, your spirit and soul would have been ushered into hell by the devil's demonic cohorts. Now that you are saved, to be absent from the body is to be present with the Lord in heaven and the angels will come for you.

You are saved through faith and not of works because salvation is a free gift from God. There is no other requirement then to first repent, and then to believe in your heart that God raised the Lord Jesus from the dead. You should have good works once you are saved. But none of the works thought to be good before you were saved will earn you salvation. Because of your ancestor Adam, nothing outside of receiving His Son as Savior and Lord will earn you salvation. You cannot please God the Father in your flesh. Therefore, you cannot rely on your own righteousness for salvation. Once you ARE saved, then faith in Jesus Christ will produce righteousness and you can earn a crown in heaven by your good works.

Although salvation is eternal, you must live out your salvation on a daily basis as the image of Christ is formed in you. The gospel is "good news" and your salvation is filled with hope and joy because of the birth, death, resurrection and ascension of Jesus Christ. You have been delivered from the judgement of your sins, the curse of the law, the threat of death, the punishment of hell and the power of Satan.

THE GOOD NEWS OF THE GOSPEL OF JESUS CHRIST IS THAT THE SHAME AND GUILT FROM OUR PAST HAS BEEN WASHED AWAY BY THE BLOOD OF JESUS CHRIST!There is no condemnation to those who are in Christ Jesus because the sins of our past have not only been covered but they have been washed away by the Lord's blood. When we base our self-worth on past failures, bad habits or dissatisfaction with personal appearance **we often develop a false belief.** That false belief says: I am what I am. I cannot change. I am hopeless.

You have been given the keys to the kingdom: both kingdoms. You can bind Satan and his demons on earth and heaven will back you up. You can loose the angels by your prayers to bring forth God's will on the earth. On top of all of these blessings, a special joy of salvation is that you have God residing in your spirit forever, through the personhood of the Holy Ghost. This is salvation!

To be born again also means that you have been adopted, justified, and sanctified. Christ is your Lord. If you confessed your belief in Him with sincerity in your heart and truly believe

Rebirth

that Jesus Christ was raised from the dead, change has already begun to take place. In the natural, to be adopted is to relinquish one's birth parents and enter into a new family. In the spirit, you were formerly alienated and without God in world because you were conceived in sin. God is your Creator but He was not your Father until you received His Son as Lord and Savior. Jesus is the Mediator or "Go Between" who has brought you into His Father's Family. You were formerly trained and reared by your father, the devil, for he is the god of this world. Now that you have repented and sought the Lord, you have been "adopted" by Him.

Adoption has brought you into the family of God. You have taken on a new name, which is the name of Jesus Christ, now called "a Christian." **You have been given the power to use His name over all the power of the enemy.** Why, because you are now in the family and have all the rights and privileges of a son of God. (If you are a woman, you are still a SON of God, for in the spirit, there is neither male nor female.)

You have also been justified. Justification says that you are treated by God as though you had not sinned.---EVER!--- This is why the gospel is such "good news!" Since addiction is "sin", once you have been born again, you are treated by God as though we never sinned. You must believe that God has accepted you by faith. If you remain in shame after you are born again, then you have doubted God's ability to change you. Therefore, you will not please God because without faith, it is impossible to please Him.

You have been sanctified. Sanctification means to be "set apart" for God's use. God puts the gift of the Holy Spirit in human vessels. He knows that in the flesh you are nothing. But God's strength is made perfect in your weakness. He cannot use you if you feel condemned or ashamed because you were once an addict, a criminal, mentally ill, etc.

Finally, you have been made the righteousness of Christ. The first key of repentance opened the door for you to receive His righteousness. You are given God's own righteousness through your faith in Jesus Christ. Your faith in Christ has given you the free gift of God's own righteousness. Once you have humbled yourself to the fact that there is no good work that you can do in your flesh that the Father God would consider righteous and you have become a born again Christian, you are no longer dependent upon your ability "to do good." Jesus said that those who hunger and thirst after His righteousness will be filled or "satisfied." In other words, the source of satisfaction, wholeness and stability is seeking God's way of doing things. When temptations come your way, ask yourself "how would Jesus do this?" "What does He think of this?"

Another word for unrighteousness is sin. Sin will bring dissatisfaction into your life. Your lack of fulfillment may cause you to be overly zealous toward immediate gratification leading you to impulsive and compulsive behavior. When you are filled with the stress of always having to fulfill your needs, you will be filled with complaints, denials and accusations. Now that you are saved, when you find yourself unfulfilled, do an inventory to find where there might be sin in you life.

Key Scriptures

On Adoption

Ephesians 1:5 Having predestinated us unto the **adoption** of children by Jesus Christ to Himself, according to the good pleasure of his will,1:6To the praise of the glory of his grace, wherein he hath made us accepted in the beloved. 1:7In whom we have redemption through his blood, the forgiveness of sins, according to the riches of his grace;1:8 Wherein he hath abounded toward us in all wisdom and prudence;

Romans 8:15 For ye have not received the spirit of bondage again to fear; but ye have received **the Spirit of adoption,** whereby we cry, Abba, Father.

8:16The Spirit itself beareth witness with our spirit, that we are the children of God:

8:17And if children, then heirs; heirs of God, and joint heirs with Christ; if so be that we suffer with him, that we may be also glorified together.

Galatians 4:6 And because ye are sons, God hath sent forth the Spirit of his Son into your hearts, crying, Abba, Father. 4:7Wherefore thou art no more a servant, but a son; and if a son, then an heir of God through Christ.

On Justification

Romans 5:18 Therefore as by the offense of one judgment came upon all men to condemnation; even so by the righteousness of one the free gift came upon all men unto **justification** of life. 5:19For as by one man's disobedience many were made sinners, so by the obedience of one shall many be made righteous.

Romans 4:24 But for us also, to whom it shall be imputed, if we believe on him that raised up Jesus our Lord from the dead;

4:25Who was delivered for our offenses, and was raised again for our **justification.**

On Sanctification

I Thessalonians 5:23And the very God of peace **sanctify** you wholly; and I pray God your whole spirit and soul and body be preserved blameless unto the coming of our Lord Jesus Christ.

John 17:19And for their sakes I **sanctify** myself, that they also might be **sanctified** through the truth.17:20 Neither pray I for these alone, but for them also which shall believe on me through their word;:21 That they all may be one; as thou, Father, art in me, and I in thee, that they also may be one in us: that the world may believe that thou hast sent me.

John 3:18 He that believeth on him is not condemned: but he that believeth not is condemned already, because he hath not believed in the name of the only begotten Son of God.:19And this is the condemnation, that light is come into the world, and men loved darkness rather than light, because their deeds were evil.:20For every one that doeth evil hateth the light, neither cometh to the light, lest his deeds should be reproved.

On Righteousness

Romans 10:3For they being ignorant of God's righteousness, and going about to establish their own righteousness, have not submitted themselves unto the righteousness of God.:4 For Christ is the end of the law for righteousness to every one that believeth.

Matthew 5:6Blessed are they which do hunger and thirst after righteousness: for they shall be filled.

Philippians 3:8Yea doubtless, and I count all things but loss for the excellency of the knowledge of Christ Jesus my Lord: for whom I have suffered the loss of all things, and do count them but dung, that I may win Christ ,:9 And be found in him, not having mine own righteousness, which is of the law, but that which is through the faith of Christ, the righteousness which is of God by faith:

I John 2:28And now, little children, abide in him; that, when he shall appear, we may have confidence, and not be ashamed before him at his coming. :29If ye know that He is righteous, ye know that every one that doeth righteousness is born of Him.

Matthew 6:31 Therefore take no thought, saying, What shall we eat? or, What shall we drink? or, Wherewithal shall we be clothed?:32 (For after all these things do the Gentiles seek:) for your heavenly Father knoweth that ye have need of all these things.

:33But seek ye first the kingdom of God, and his righteousness; and all these things shall be added unto you.

On The Kingdom

Luke 17:20 And when he was demanded of the Pharisees, when the kingdom of God should come, he answered them and said, **The kingdom of God** cometh not with observation: :21Neither shall they say, Lo here! or, lo there! for, behold, the kingdom of God is within you.

Matthew 18:4Whosoever therefore shall humble himself as this little child, the same is greatest in the **kingdom of heaven.**

Matthew 16:19 And I will give unto thee the keys of **the kingdom of heaven**: and whatsoever thou shalt bind on earth shall be bound in heaven: and whatsoever thou shalt loose on earth shall be loosed in heaven.

On Your Rights and Privileges

Romans 8:16The Spirit itself beareth witness with our spirit, that we are the children of God:17And if children, then heirs; heirs of God, and joint heirs with Christ; if so be that we suffer with him, that we may be also glorified together.

James 2:5 Hearken, my beloved brethren, Hath not God chosen the poor of this world rich in faith, and heirs of the kingdom which he hath promised to them that love him?

James 5:13Is any among you **afflicted?** let him pray. Is any merry? let him sing psalms. 5:14Is any sick among you? let him call for the elders of the church; and let them pray over him, anointing him with oil in the name of the Lord.::15And the prayer of faith shall save the sick, and the Lord shall raise him up; and if he have committed sins, they shall be forgiven him.:16Confess your faults one to another, and pray one for another, that ye may be healed. The effectual fervent prayer of a righteous man availeth much.

Galatians 4:7 Wherefore thou art no more a servant, but a son; and if a son, then an heir of God through Christ.:8Howbeit then, when ye knew not God, ye did service unto them which by nature are no gods.:9But now, after that ye have known God, or rather are known of God, how turn ye again to the weak and beggarly elements, whereunto ye desire again to be in bondage?

Isaiah 53:5 But he was wounded for our transgressions, he was bruised for our iniquities: the chastisement of our peace was upon him; and with his stripes we are healed.

I Corinthians 6:9 Know ye not that the unrighteous shall not inherit the kingdom of God? Be not deceived: neither fornicators, nor idolaters, nor adulterers, nor effeminate, nor abusers of themselves with mankind,:10Nor thieves, nor covetous, nor drunkards, nor revilers, nor extortioners, shall inherit the kingdom of God.

Rebirth

6:11And such were some of you: but ye are washed, but ye are sanctified, but ye are justified in the name of the Lord Jesus, and by the Spirit of our God.

Romans 8:4 That the righteousness of the law might be fulfilled in us, who walk not after the flesh, but after the Spirit.:5For they that are after the flesh do mind the things of the flesh; but they that are after the Spirit the things of the Spirit. 8:6For to be carnally minded is death; but to be spiritually minded is life and peace.:8 So then they that are in the flesh cannot please God.:9But ye are not in the flesh, but in the Spirit, if so be that the Spirit of God dwell in you. Now if any man have not the Spirit of Christ, he is none of his.:10 And if Christ be in you, the body is dead because of sin; but the Spirit is life because of righteousness.11 But if the Spirit of him that raised up Jesus from the dead dwell in you, he that raised up Christ from the dead shall also quicken your mortal bodies by his Spirit that dwelleth in you.:12Therefore, brethren, we are debtors, not to the flesh, to live after the flesh.:13 For if ye live after the flesh, ye shall die: but if ye through the Spirit do mortify the deeds of the body, ye shall live. 8:14For as many as are led by the Spirit of God, they are the sons of God.For ye have not received the spirit of bondage again to fear; but ye have received the Spirit of adoption, whereby we cry, Abba, Father:The Spirit itself beareth witness with our spirit, that we are the children of God::17 And if children, then heirs; heirs of God, and joint heirs with Christ; if so be that we suffer with him, that we may be also glorified together.

:18 For I reckon that the sufferings of this present time are not worthy to be compared with the glory which shall be revealed in us.

Galatians 5:21Envyings, murders, drunkenness, revellings, and such like: of the which I tell you before, as I have also told you in time past, that they which do such things shall not inherit the kingdom of God.:22But the fruit of the Spirit is love, joy, peace, longsuffering, gentleness, goodness, faith,23Meekness, temperance: against such there is no law.:24And they that are Christ's have crucified the flesh with the affections and lusts.

Galatians 5:25 If we live in the Spirit, let us also walk in the Spirit.

Study and Reflection Outline

> **KEY STATEMENT:** The only part of you that has experienced rebirth is your spirit. Your soul (mind, emotions, will and personality) must be RENEWED daily through your surrender to the cross.

Point #1 When you are in Christ and Christ is in YOU,

    A. God sees you at your best when you are at your worst.

        1. give Him what you have been.

        2. He will mold you into His original plan for you.

    B. You have the mind of Christ or Christ's mind.

        1. you are holy and without sin.

        2. you are blameless and without accusation.

        3. you are above reproach and without judgement.

Point #2 You have been sanctified from the moment of your salvation. This means that you have been set apart from the world, for the Lord Jesus Christ.

A. Sanctification is not based upon what you do. It is based upon what Christ has already done.

   1. you are sanctified by the work of the Holy Spirit and
   2. by the blood of Jesus.

B. As a sanctified person, you are set aside for special benefits.

   1. provision (blessed)

      a) the Lord will supply your needs
      b) the Lord will see that you find favor

   2. protection (safety)

      a) the Lord will place you in a safe place
      b) the Lord will lead you to new friendships

   3. purification (clean or pure at heart)

      a) the Lord will cleanse you from cravings for drugs
      b) the Lord will restore your desire for righteous living.

Point #4 A major factor to freedom from addiction is to realize that you belong to a "new kingdom". Jesus brought you into this new kingdom by His sacrifice at the cross.

   A. Addiction is a part of the kingdom of Satan

      1. Satan's nature is to kill, steal and to destroy
      2. Satan is at the root of all bondages.

   B. Recovery and healing are a part of the kingdom of God.

1. Jesus came that we might have abundant life
2. Jesus heals all that are oppressed of the devil
3. Jesus has given you the keys to the kingdom of healing and recovery from addiction.
   a) you can bind the devil in your own life
   b) faith in the name of Jesus will bring victory

Point #5 The way to healing and recovery is to become born again.

A. If you are not born again, you can neither understand the kingdom nor can you enter into or appropriate the benefits of the kingdom for yourself.
   1. As a Christian in recovery, you have rights and privileges.
      a) you have the promise of healing and recovery.
      b) you can use the authority of the name of Jesus.
   2. As an heir in the kingdom, you have an inheritance.
      a) salvation includes deliverance from temporal evils, ie. the bondage of addiction.
      b) you have the right to expect that your prayers offered in the will of God will be answered.
   3. A part of your inheritance is to be set free from your addiction.
      a) you have been given a measure of faith to believe that in Christ you can remain drug free.

b) Satan no longer has a legal claim to you.

Point #6: Your HELMET OF SALVATION is your weapon against the power of the past to control your present and to dictate your future.

A. You may look back to the past only when the Holy Spirit guides you to look back.

1. to enhance your spiritual growth and discernment or to

2. to stir up your faith on our past victories

3. to heal unconscious wombs

4. to cast out a demon or demons from your mind and emotions

5. to close the door of the past to the devil.

B. You must forget what is behind because you are pressing toward your destiny.

1. God has thoughts and plans for the rest of your life in Christ.

2. Vision and hope will keep you focused on the future instead of the conditions of the past and the present.

3. The Lord doesn't need a lot of time to fulfill His purpose. Ex.: Jesus lives for 33 years but His purpose was not fulfilled until the last 3 years of His earthly life.

C. Don't look at your past as a waste of time.

1. The past is an opportunity for you to move more steadily and wisely toward the Lord's purpose for your life.

2. God will take every sinful experience of your past and use it for His glory in the present and in the future.

3. When you are low in spirit, go back and revisit the joy of your salvation, ie, return to your testimony of how you got born again.

D. Sometimes your past and your present will unite in one climatic moment where your life's purpose is revealed.

1. God can take the failures and weaknesses of your past and restore you completely in a year, a month, a week, a day, a minute or a second.

2. You don't even have to look for your blessing when the Lord is looking to use your weakness to manifest His glory.

E. Once God heals or delivers you, don't hide the glory.

1. Don't let the shame of your past cause you **not** to reveal what the Lord has delivered you from. ie., a life of prostitution, homosexuality, incarceration, HIV etc.

    a) If you do, chances are you will lose your healing.

    b) If you do, the Lord will deny you before His father.

2. There is no condemnation to those who are saved or born again.

    a) You do not need to live in shame

    b) You are no longer guilty because of His blood sacrifice.

3. Someone who is not yet delivered needs to hear your testimony to increase their own faith to obtain their particular blessing.

    a) We overcome by the word of our testimony

    b) When you confess your faults or weaknesses to another believer, you will be healed.

F. When God delivers you from your past, He will cause your family, neighbors and associates to witness it. He will do this to manifest His own glory to the people.

    1. Do not use your testimony to try to defend yourself **by proving** you have changed.

        a) Those who "knew you when" **still** will not believe you!

        b) Only Jesus has the power to judge you.

    2. Let your love and surrender to Jesus be your response to "the critics."

        a) Christians are known by our love for each other

        b) Set your example by the word of God.

Point #7 Complete recovery of your spirit, soul and body can only be found in the anointing of Jesus Christ. The Lord's mission is recovery.

A. Every human needs recovery because we have all been lost.

    1. Even though you were lost, the Lord always knew where you were.

    2. To be lost, is not to be able to find your way.

To Curse The Root

   a) Your "way" is your destiny as ordained by God.

   b) You will not find your destiny until you find Jesus.

B. Jesus is the Way, the Truth and the Life. He is also the Light.

   1. The Light has been shining around you but you could not see Him.

   2. Satan blinded your mind so that you could not understand that Jesus is the only way to your destiny.

      a) He tried to distract you with the "broad" way of the world.

      b) When you relapsed, you walked into Satan's door

      c) Satan locked the door and hid the key

Point #8 Victory over relapse was obtained in the blood sacrifice of Jesus Christ at the cross.

A. Jesus asked the Father for you as His inheritance for His sacrifice.

   1. Satan no longer has any rights to you because of the blood.

   2. Don't let Satan steal your joy

B. Those that Jesus owns become His friends.

   1. When you relapse, you have sinned against the blood

      a) Satan will use your relapse to mock Jesus

Rebirth

      b) Relapse is a sign of disloyalty to the One who died for you

  2. All of those "in Christ" are Satan's enemies

      a) the world will rejoice at your fall from grace

      b) you have no place to go but back to the saints

  1. they will anoint you with oil

  2. they will pray for your forgiveness.

      c) you must repent AND confess to be restored in fellowship.

Workstudy Exercises

Exercise #1: Read Acts. Chapter 9. How did Paul overcome His past as a persecutor of the early church and as a murderer of Christians? Select the correct response.

1. Paul heard the word and he _____ it. (received/rebelled against)

2. Paul_____on the next step. (searched for/waited for)

3. The next step was that he_____(went on his missionary journey/was baptized and healed.

4. How did Paul learn of his purpose and assignment? Do you know what your purpose and assignment is? If you do, write it down. If not, pray to the Lord this entire week to know your assignment. Then come

To Curse The Root

back to this part of your assignment and complete it.

Exercise #2 The following words define recovery from a Christ-centered perspective known as " The Five "R's"

1) restoration--when the Lord repairs that which was broken.

2) renewal--when the Lord revives and refreshes one's mind.

3) redemption--when the Lord sets free that which was bound.

4) reconciliation---when the Lord reunites us with His Father.

5) rebirth---when the Lord brings us out of darkness and fills us with the spirit of God.

According to this definition, what have you recovered since you have been saved? Be specific.

Exercise #3 Read Psalm 37 in its entirety. Note or underline in your bible the word "righteous" each time you locate it. How many times is it mentioned? In your own words, describe how the blessings of righteousness far outweigh the temporary pleasures of your flesh.

Exercise # 4 Read pages 101-110 in "To Curse the Root." Can you identify with Gertrude? What has been **your** cycle of addiction?

Exercise 5: Dissatisfaction or a feeling of emptiness within is a clear sign that you are not receiving the blessings of your rebirth--- a sense of peace and satisfaction. Listed below are

Rebirth

several areas of life. Identify any area where dissatisfaction is a problem and convey in your own words discussing how this condition manifests itself.

Relationships_____

Career or Occupation_____

Recovery_____

Desires and aspirations_____

Body image_____

Christian witness and service_____

Exercise 6: Read chapter 5 in "To Curse the Root." What is the nature of your ground? Are you a leader, thinker, feeler or worker?

_____

Pray and ask the Lord to show you what you need to offer up from your personality to the Holy Spirit to be changed? When you believe that you have heard from God, write it down here.

_____

Exercise 7: As noted in this lesson, you have left an old kingdom and are now adopted into a new one. Much of "who you are" has been shaped by the verbal and non-verbal messages you received in your natural family. What are some the messages and experiences of the past that are block you from believing that you are completely cleansed and forgiven by God in the blood of Jesus Christ?

_____

Exercise #8 Write down and memorize a scripture that tells you how much the Father God values and loves you. Are you a people pleaser? How do you feel now that you know that the Lord is pleased with you?

_____

To Curse The Root

Exercise #9 Although they didn't realized it, those people who were the most significant in your life were used by the devil to hurt you. True recovery from the emotional damage you suffered must first be acknowledged, confronted and resolved. You must bring it out before Jesus and put it on the cross. Complete the following phrases:

The most outstanding damage that I have endured is

_____

Who are you most angry at and why?

_____

How has this study on the key of salvation helped you to address your anger?

_____

KEY #4: REVELATION

THE FOURTH KEY TO RECOVERY AND VICTORY OVER SATAN IS

REVELATION

AFFIRMATION KEY #4. **REVELATION**

I submit myself to the Holy Ghost to lead me and guide me into the **truth** about myself, my character defects and the root causes of my addiction/bondage. I will learn the language of my **spirit** by recording my dreams, visions and intuitions.

John 16:13

"However, when He, the Spirit of truth, has come, He will guide you into all truth; for He will not speak on His own authority, but whatever He hears He will speak; and He will tell you things to come."

Background

God's first human beings, Adam and Eve, literally "walked in the spirit." Their physical bodies did not dominate them, as evidenced by the fact that clothing was incidental and went unnoticed prior to their fall. It was sin that caused Adam and Eve to depend upon their physical senses. Actually it was the sense of sight and taste that drew them into sin in the first place. So sin is what caused man to depend upon his human skills and reasoning. As Paul wrote, "the law of sin is in our members." That same sin will cause you to depend upon everything else but the Lord Jesus Christ for your recovery.

As they "walked in the spirit", Adam and Eve talked to God face to face. It was an everyday occurrence. They probably were even able to see God with their "spiritual" vision. For although the triune God is a Spirit, He also has a form. He has substance. He is invisible to you now, but He was visible to them. With sin, they lost for you and everyone else the capacity to look upon a holy God. If you could look upon His face in your fallen condition, you would immediately die. This is why Jesus came to earth in a human body. When we look upon Jesus, we see and know the Father. When Jesus ascended, He left behind the Holy Spirit to show us the Father and the Son.

Your spirit is that part of you that enables you to communicate and worship the Father, the Son and the Holy Spirit. It is by your spirit alone that you will be able to understand the triune God. When you were a sinner, you did not have spiritual comprehension because your spirit was dead in sins and in trespasses. You could not even understand the things of God, and therefore you were out of touch with the truth. Only through your born again spirit can you become truly aware of the meaning of spirituality. By your spirit, you touch the spiritual world. By your body, you touch the physical world. Your spirit cannot act directly on your body and therefore needs an interpreter. Your soul stands between these two worlds, yet belongs to both, acting as the mediator or "go-between".

Your spirit can influence your body through your soul. Likewise your body can influence your spirit through your soul. Sometimes the bible uses the word "flesh" to describe the mixture of soul with spirit and soul with body. When Jesus said "the spirit is willing but the flesh is weak", the "flesh" in this context was the body. Jesus was referring to the fact that His apostles were sleeping at a time that they should have been praying. A synonym for the word "flesh" is the word "carnal." Carnality refers not to the body but to the soul.

All final decisions concerning matters of the spirit and the body are made by the mental, emotional and volitional powers of the soul. For example, you are asleep. Your body wants to urinate but your spirit wants to continue sleeping. Therefore, with the creative imagination of your spirit, you envision a bathroom or some other place where you can relieve your bladder. You see yourself urinating but you feel no actual release. Your soul then makes the decision to wake up your spirit so that your body can find a toilet. When your soul is weak in its decisionmaking powers, you may wet the bed!

Many people do not make a distinction between the soul and the spirit. However, this distinction is very important, particularly to a person who is born again but who is still in recovery from an addiction or a similar bondage. Even though you are now born again and therefore no longer an addict in your spirit, your body does not know this. Your body will still crave only for substances. Your soul will support your body because it too will crave and lust after the lifestyle i.e. the people, places and things of addiction. For this reason, your soul needs to be renewed. The renewal of the soul is the subject of the fifth key of renewal. However, through the third key of revelation, it is important for you to know that your soul cannot discern the things of God. Your spirit is your direct communication and connection to the spirit world: to God, His thoughts, plans and purposes.

All Godly revelations must come through and by the Holy Spirit within your newly created, born again spirit. If you are truly a spiritual person, your life will be directed by the Lord's will and not your own. You must receive God's revelations in your spirit first, as you become practiced at communing with God while meditating upon His word, in worship and in prayer. You will learn how to order your steps by the quite guidance of the Holy Spirit, listening to the still, small voice within you in His work as the Spirit of truth.

Real truth is connected to the spirit world. Truth is sincerity in character, action and speech. Truth gives you a clear, conscious view of your own opinions and judgements. Truth is faithful and constant. The truth can also be defined as the absence of lies. Since God the Father is not a man that He should lie, God Himself is the complete and total truth without any lies in Him at all. An inference is something considered to be true but in reality it is only a maybe. Logic is man's truth. It is conformity to fact or to actuality. Fact is something put forth as objectively real or true because it has been demonstrated. Facts are connected to the natural world.

Since God's people were limited in their access to God under the old covenant, they were also limited in their ability to comprehend Him or to understand His heart. The old covenant believers had to depend upon the truth about the Father revealed to the them through the prophets. In this sense, the pre-born again believers could not worship the Father in spirit and in truth because truth is knowing God. Truth is "spirit knowledge." On the contrary, the born again believer under the new covenant has been given a new heart and a new spirit. We also have an unction from the Holy Ghost---the Spirit of Truth. The Holy Spirit will lead us and guide us into all truth. In other words, it is the job of the Holy Spirit to teach us about the heart of our Father by presenting to us a true picture of Jesus Christ.

Jesus Himself said "I am the way the TRUTH and the life. No man comes to the Father but by Me." Another way of expressing this thought is that no one comes to know the truth except by Jesus because Jesus Himself is the truth. If I want to know the truth in a particular situation, I need to know the heart of the Father in regards to those issues involved in this particular set of circumstances. I need to know His will. I will only know His will by seeking the Father in the Name of Jesus. The Holy Ghost will reveal to you what He has heard from the Father and the Son about your future and the Father's will for your life.

Therefore, your spiritual ear must be properly trained so that you can hear what the Holy Spirit wants to reveal to you.

The Lord's way is truth and it is life. A major inaccuracy of the 12 Steps model is to suggest that you can choose how you want to understand God. This is not only presumption but it is an insult to the majesty and glory of the Lord. Jesus declared that He is the only way to the Father and that there is no other way.

If you want to improve your conscious contact with the Father God, then you must know Him and perceive Him as He is, and not as you believe Him to be according to your own whim. With the first and second keys, you were drawn to Jesus Christ by the Holy Spirit. Once drawn, He then convicted your heart and caused you to repent. He also gave you the faith to believe that Jesus Christ was raised from the dead. When you confessed this truth with your mouth and believed it in your heart, you got saved or born again. As the Spirit of adoption, the Holy Spirit performed the official task of bringing you into the family of God. He indwelt you, He sealed you in the Lord's name so that you became the property of Jesus Christ of Nazareth.

The brother of our lord, James, learned a lot about truth by growing up with Jesus and walking with his Master during His three year ministry on earth. James wrote: If you have bitter envying and strife in your hearts, glory not and lie not against the truth. This wisdom descendeth not from above. This wisdom is sensual or devilish. For where envying and strife is, there is confusion and every evil work. But the wisdom that is from above is pure peaceable, gentle, easy to be entreated, full of mercy and god fruits, without partiality and without hypocrisy.

It is clear from these words that the devil wants to block you from the truth. Jesus said "And you shall know the truth and the truth shall set you free." God, who is a spirit, often reveals the truth through symbols. Jesus Himself is a living, flesh and blood symbol sent from heaven. He was made natural or physical so that we who are natural and physical could comprehend the Father who resides in another galaxy which the bible calls the "third heaven." Called the Lamb of God, the Living Bread, the Rock, the Rose of Sharon, the Lily of the Valley, and many other symbolic names, the flesh and bone Jesus, is a living picture or representation of the Father God. Since no man can look upon the holy Father's face and live, the Father sends us a living photograph of Himself in His Son Jesus. We can look in the face of Jesus and live, for He is our life. As such, God speaks to us in symbols so that we can know the truth about Himself through symbols we earthlings can understand.

Throughout the gospels, we read where Jesus would say to the people, "he that has an ear to hear, let him hear what the spirit says." An ear to hear or an eye to see is not a physical organ. Jesus is alluding to the ability to move beyond the physical 5 senses of the flesh and receive a spiritual truth. If we can overcome the flesh, we will be able to receive the true knowledge of God. If we cannot overcome the flesh, we are both deaf and blind. The deaf cannot hear the truth and the blind cannot see the truth. It is our flesh that keeps us from the truth. Therefore, we must crucify the flesh by yielding our soul to the Holy Spirit's scrutiny. The more your flesh is crucified, the clearer will be your understanding of spiritual truths because, Christ--who is the Truth--- will live out His life IN YOU! (Galatians 2:20)

As your body has eyes and ears for the purpose of sight and sound, as you wear clothing to protect yourself from inclement weather conditions and for the sake of modesty, your spirit has eyes and ears also. If you are spiritually blind, you cannot see or perceive the nature of your own character defects nor can you comprehend the character of God. If you are spiritually deaf, you cannot hear the Lord's voice, even though He speaks to you constantly. If you do not know His character, if your are out of touch with your own character defects, and if you cannot hear His voice, you will not know His will nor what He created you to fulfill on earth within your divine purpose.

Revelation

Your spiritual life is like a journey. You are travelling "up the King's Highway", you climb "Jacob's Ladder" or you journey through valleys to find your mountaintops. You will find that life is a trip to find your purpose. The Holy Spirit has a rather detailed travel plan and map prepared by the Lord Jesus Christ. However, if your flesh is not crucified or "broken of its self centeredness", you will live and eventually die and never discover the hidden meaning of your life. You have become accustomed to travelling alone, and without a map. You have been walking for a long time and your addiction has brought you to a crossroad. Now you must make a decision.

Your usual pattern has been to select the road or path of least resistance which includes unconscious patterns of escape into deceptions, vicious circles of behavior and defenses that your soul perceives to be easier to live with then facing the truth. Therefore, your moral inventory of yourself without the help of the Holy Spirit is limited by half truths and Satanic lies. You are wearing spiritual clothing that only the triune God can see. You cannot know the exact nature of your wrongs if you do not discern the style of your clothing. Consequently, if you want to know the root cause of your addiction, you need the Holy Spirit to reveal to you the truth about your most prominent character defect.

Motive is the driving force that reveals our spiritual nature. Just as a district attorney searches for a motive to convict a defendant, the motive is the key to spiritual perception and discernment. As a serial killer may have a recurrent motive, so does the spirit of man. A spiritual motive is a recurrent, repetitive spiritual theme that is at the root of every action that the soul persuades the body to take. Anyone who remains ignorant to his or her primary spiritual motive is spiritually blind, deaf and naked.

Contingent upon the extent of activity of the flesh and the soul is the spirit's ability to receive God's enlightenment and translate His knowledge and wisdom to the soul and the body.

This is why most religious systems emphasize various forms of meditation. Meditation slows down the activity of the soul and the flesh, causing the spirit to become more receptive and active. Hypnosis is a more intense form of meditation where the activity of the spirit passively responds to the direction of the hypnotist. It is my belief that hypnosis is dangerous because it is the most blatant example of the "blind leading the blind." Since the hypnotist is blind to the invisible world of the spirit, he cannot see where he is directing his subject. It is like a blindfolded man leading a crippled person who has lost his wheelchair across a dangerous highway. The cripple sees the oncoming truck, but he cannot get out of the way without his wheelchair. The blindfolded man could get out of the way, but he is handicapped without his vision to see oncoming traffic.

To avoid such danger, it is important that the spirit not be handicapped by spiritual ignorance. To be empowered, your spirit must have clear vision. It must be able to distinguish between good and evil. It must be able to engage, encourage and enlighten the mind. Your spirit must be able to help our will to choose God's will above our own. Therefore, meditation should be active. You are not obligated to obey the Lord mechanically. Instead, you must choose and do His will in full and conscious awareness. Even if you are unaware of His will, your spirit must be free to decide to choose His will. In and of itself, such a decision will be enough to empower your spirit to know the will of the God intuitively, allowing your spirit to govern your flesh.

Motive also foreshadows the success or failure of recovery. For example, a recovering substance abuser must avoid a tendency towards self love. Too strong a motive to be alcohol or drug free has led some patients to become so self absorbed that they end up in "self-love" or indulgence. Within their anxiety to remain "clean", their thoughts endlessly dwell on their own recovery. Countless hours may be exhausted thinking about their own sobriety that they find no time to meditate on God or on what He desires to accomplish in their lives.

Likewise, within the cycle of addiction, an excessive concern for oneself may cause a person to become addicted to his sickness. You must ask yourself, " If all you desire is that the Holy Spirit deliver you from pain, are you really being led by Him?" Therefore, your prayer, meditation and fasting should actively concentrate on entreating the Lord to:

1. open your spiritual eyes and ears so that you can perceive your true condition before Him;

2. reveal to you the language of your own spirit that you may know His will; and

3. provide you with His strength in your spirit to choose His will, once you know it.

In this regard, dreams can provide countless benefits. I have found that these benefits can be categorized in the following ways:

1. dreams that REVEAL

2. dreams that REBUKE

3. dreams that RESTORE

Dreams that reveal are those that inform, enlighten and explain. They can provide insight into personal motivations as well as the motivations of others. They can illuminate the meaning of our past, give us directions about the present and provide a glimpse into the future. A significant purpose of a revelatory dream is to present a symbolic meaning for your life. When your spirit learns to translate the meaning of a symbol, your dreams will be less metaphorical. In fact, dreams can be a helpful storehouse of specific, concrete information. For example, I have receive five (5) consecutive dreams, over a span of ten (10) years, that have provided specific information about my overall purpose in life. Each dream is like an additional chapter in a book where the plot is unfolding, line by line.

Although dreams that rebuke can also reveal, their overall purpose is to present a reprimand in a way that urges, cautions, and/or warns in a dramatic style. The goal is to bring about correction. When the Holy Spirit chastens you, it is because He loves you. The more you run from the chastening, the more dramatic, even frightening the dreams may become. Every apparently frightening dream is not a nightmare. Sometimes the Lord creatively confronts you so that you will become motivated to be fruitful. This kind of confrontation is a part of the purging process. A common dream among those in recovery is to see yourself searching for the drug and not being able to find it. These kinds of dreams can be very upsetting. It could be a demon trying to stir up craving within you to cause you to relapse. It could also be the Lord showing you not to be too overconfident by showing you exactly where you stand in your recovery. The dream will be like a movie where you are the leading man or lady. Were you resisting the drug or were you longing after it? The dream could also be prophetic in that the Lord may be warning you about a temptation that Satan is about to bring your way in the near future. If your motives are pure and you are seeking after the truth, the Holy Spirit will reveal to you the meaning of the dream or send someone anointed in dream interpretation to you to provide you with understanding. In all cases, you need to pray!!!!.

Notwithstanding, when you are rebuked, you also need to be restored. As calm follows a storm, as growth follows pruning, you will need to see the mountains when you are in the valley of the shadow of death. Dreams that restore provide you with strength, healing, assistance, help, support and relief while we are in the midst of hardships and distress. Such dreams will help you not to fear evil, because the Lord is with you.

The unconscious or the invisible belongs to the realm of the spirit. Consequently, the spirit has developed its own set of strategies by which to blind itself from the truth and to protect the mind and the emotions from the pain of self discovery. Repression and projection are but two of the defense mechanisms that attempt to enable the self to avoid the truth. Repression is the spiritual force that deceives the emotions by believing that "all is well when all is NOT well." To protect the mind against the anxiety of responsibility, projection is a spiritual state of denial that operates by blaming other people and circumstances for virtually everything. In each individual case, it is the task of the Holy Spirit to break the power of the spirit's unconscious defense mechanisms that protect you from the truth of God's ways and purposes. Very often, it is difficult for you to yield because you do not understand the Lord's methods of breaking or pruning you.

Categories of Personality

Basically there are four "different" personality types or categories: the leaders, the thinkers, the feelers, and the workers. Although most people have elements of all four types within their personality, usually one or two sides is predominate. For example, the leader who is also a feeler will tend to be dramatic, emotional and charismatic, while "a leader" who is "a worker" will be down in the trenches, working with the people. When we repent and we receive a reborn spirit, we allow the Holy Spirit to change our personalities on a daily basis.

Key Scriptures

On the Human Spirit

On the truth

John 8:44 Ye are of your father the devil, and the lusts of your father ye will do. He was a murderer from the beginning, and abode not in the **truth,** because there is no truth in him. When he speaketh a lie, he speaketh of his own: for he is a liar, and the father of it.

John 18:37 Pilate therefore said unto him, Art thou a king then? Jesus answered, Thou sayest that I am a king. To this end was I born, and for this cause came I into the world, that I should bear witness unto the truth. Every one that is of the truth heareth my voice.

Hebrews 10:26 For if we sin wilfully after that we have received the knowledge of the truth, there remaineth no more sacrifice for sins,

I Timothy 6:5 Perverse disputings of men of corrupt minds, and destitute of the truth, supposing that gain is godliness: from such withdraw thyself.

John 4:24 God is a Spirit: and they that worship him must worship him in spirit and in truth.

Galatians 3:1 O foolish Galatians, who hath bewitched you, that ye should not obey the truth, before whose eyes Jesus Christ hath been evidently set forth, crucified among you?

II Corinthians 4:2 But have renounced the hidden things of dishonesty, not walking in craftiness, nor handling the word of God deceitfully; but by manifestation of the truth commending ourselves to every man's conscience in the sight of God.

I John 1:6 If we say that we have fellowship with him, and walk in darkness, we lie, and do not the truth:

On the light

John 12:35 Then Jesus said unto them, Yet a little while is the light with you. Walk while ye have the light, lest darkness come upon you: for he that walketh in darkness knoweth not whither he goeth.:36 While ye have light, believe in the light, that ye may be the children of light. These things spake Jesus, and departed, and did hide himself from them.

Luke 11:33No man, when he hath lighted a candle, putteth it in a secret place, neither under a bushel, but on a candlestick, that they which come in may see the light. :34The light of the body is the eye: therefore when thine eye is single, thy whole body also is full of light; but when thine eye is evil, thy body also is full of darkness. :35 Take heed therefore that the light which is in thee be not darkness. :36If thy whole body therefore be full of light, having no part dark, the whole shall be full of light, as when the bright shining of a candle doth give thee light.

Ephesians 5:8For ye were sometimes darkness, but now are ye light in the Lord: walk as children of light:

John 3:19 And this is the condemnation, that light is come into the world, and men loved darkness rather than light, because their deeds were evil.:20 For every one that doeth evil hateth the light, neither cometh to the light, lest his deeds should be reproved.:21But he that doeth truth cometh to the light, that his deeds may be made manifest, that they are wrought in God.

Colossians 1:12 Giving thanks unto the Father, which hath made us meet to be partakers of the inheritance of the saints in light:13Who hath delivered us from the power of darkness, and hath translated us into the kingdom of his dear Son:

I Thessalonians 5:5Ye are all the children of light, and the children of the day: we are not of the night, nor of darkness. 5:6Therefore let us not sleep, as do others; but let us watch and be sober. 5:7For they that sleep in the night; and they that be drunken are drunken in the night.:8But let us, who are of the day, be sober, putting on the breastplate of faith and love; and for an helmet, the hope of salvation.

To Curse The Root

5:9For God hath not appointed us to wrath, but to obtain

> KEY STATEMENT: The Holy Spirit is the only genuine source of complete truth about you and He will reveal it to you if you will follow Jesus Christ--He is the Light, the Way, the Truth and the Life.

salvation by our Lord Jesus Christ,:10Who died for us, that, whether we wake or sleep, we should live together with him.

Study And Reflection Outline

Point 1   You have no way of knowing the truth unless God reveals it to you by the Spirit of Truth.

    A. The truth is in heaven, in the throne room.

        1. The Holy Spirit is the Spirit of Truth.

            a. He repeats what He hears said in the throne room

            b. He will reveal the truth about your life to you.

        2. In the spirit world, time as we know it does not exist.

            a. Satan lives in the spirit world but he doesn't know the truth.

            b. Satan is the father of lies.

            c. You were held captive by Satan to the facts, the lies and the sins in your life.

B. Jesus is the TRUTH.

   1. You cannot change in the spirit if your foundation is based upon lies.

   2. Jesus cleansed you from the power of facts, lies and sin at the cross.

   3. The truth shall set you free by giving you a conscious view of your own opinions, perceptions and attitudes. (John 8:31,32)

   4. Jesus prayed that His people would be sanctified by truth (set apart and protected)

C. Real truth can only be found in the spirit through the Holy Spirit

   1. Truth goes deeper than mere knowledge, facts or information.

   2. Much of what is true is hidden in your subconscious.

      a. your soul will distort the truth by protecting secrets

      b. feelings, opinions and prejudices will deny the truth

D. Until your soul rises to a level with your spirit, you shall not know the truth.

   1. Your spirit was re-created (made new) but your soul remains the same.

   2. You must sacrifice your soul to the Holy Spirit for renewal.

      a) soul is renewed by the word of God.

      b) soul is renewed by breaking

Point 2: Jesus is the Word, Jesus is the Truth, Jesus is the Light. Logic states that A=B, B=C, Therefore, A=C. It follows that Jesus =Truth, Truth =Word, Therefore, Jesus is the Word.

   A. Truth is a synonym to the word "light."

      1. To be spiritual is to have light enter your spirit.

      2. You came out of the kingdom of darkness into the kingdom of light.

   B. Light is synonymous with OIL.

      1. You have an unction from the Holy Ghost--

      2. An unction is anything that soothes or comforts.

         a) quality or manner of utterance

         b) its purpose is to arouse a deep spiritual inward feeling.

      3. Light is supernatural information received from God.

         a) There is no doubt that it is the Lord.

         b) You must obey first, and reason later.

         c) Watch and pray.

   C. Oil is a symbol of the Holy Spirit.

      1. The purpose of oil in a lamp is to supply light.

      2. The spirit of man is the candle of the Lord. (Proverbs 20:27).

   D. One of the main purpose of the newborn spirit is to serve as a receptor of the light of the Lord Jesus Christ.

1. God is light and in Him there is no darkness at all.

   a) The Holy Ghost will provide clear revelation, without any darkness.

   b) In the Holy Spirit is the blueprint of your vision, purpose and a plan.

2. Very seldom does God give all the information at one time.

3. He also does not fulfill His word according to your timetable.

4. If you have envy or self interest in your heart, you lie against the truth.

E. An intuition is inner knowing without natural evidence or logic. (FAITH).

   1. the immediate knowing of something

   2. knowing without the conscious use of reasoning.

   3. to quicken or to come alive.

Point 3 When you walk in the light, you are walking in the glory of God.

A. In order to walk in the light, you must be dedicated to the truth.

   1. Within your own spirit is access to the truth about you:

      a) --to control yourself

      b) --to fulfill your destiny

      c) --to know the will of God for you

d)--to find self worth

e)--to reshape your personality

f)--to take the beam out of your own eye

g)--to be a spiritual leader to others

2. You must surrender every day by allowing the soul life to die.

   a) You will come into constant conflict between the world, the flesh and the devil.

   b). You need to discern between good and evil (Hebrews 5:;14)

3. You can become spiritually deaf, dumb and blind.

   a) set our minds on things of the spirit.

   b) be always ready to repent and to forgive others

B. The tongue will ultimately prove the nature of its anointing. (Luke 6:45)

1. You can grow in truth by the level of progress that you make in controlling your tongue.

   a) Demons flash you thoughts on a regular basis.

   b) Demons know that their thought penetrated your mind is by listening to your words.

2. Your anointed tongue is equipped to confuse and confound the devil, and to cast down imaginations and thoughts sent to you.

Point 3 You cannot have complete recovery without anointing.

A. Anointing is the power of the Holy Spirit upon your life.

   1. Anointing is God's supernatural ability applied to man's inability.

   2. To be anointed is to have:

      a) a divine **Appointment**-the Lord has called and chosen you.

      b) a divine **Assignment**-the Lord has a job for you.

      c) a divine **Ability**--the Lord will place His power upon you.

B. To be anointed you must be filled. To be filled you must be emptied or "swept clean, To be fully recovered

   1. you must be emptied of self

   2. you must be set free of demons.

   3. you must be filled with the Holy Spirit

Point 4: The spirit speaks to us in symbols.

A. A symbol is a natural, every day example that gives meaning to a spiritual truth.

   1. Symbols make spiritual things easier to understand and receive.

   2. Symbols make comparisons between the natural and the spiritual.

      a) a simile is a comparison connected by the word "like" or "as" ie, the blessed man is like a tree planted by the river of water

       b) a metaphor is a stronger comparison which treats that natural as if it were the spiritual. ie. Jesus is the Rock, Jesus is the lily of the valley.

  B. Symbols ignore the self or the conscious mind within your soul.

    1. You know that you didn't "make it" up

       a) you don't know what the symbol means

       b) the meaning of the symbol is beyond your own level of creativity

    2. Since you didn't make it up, the symbol is coming from one of two sources:

       a) a message from God as sent by one of His angels

       b) a message from Satan as sent by one of his demons

Workstudy Exercises

Exercise #1: The Lord can speak to you in visions, dreams, prophecies, as you meditate on scripture, while in prayer and from your circumstances or situation. The Lord's voice can be audible and strong or it can be a still small voice from within your spirit. How does the Lord most often speak to you?

Exercise #2 Read 1Timothy Chapter 4: 1-5 and Matthew Chapter 24:3-13. It is evident from these scriptures that there is a danger to be open to visions, dreams and prophecies in these last days. After completing your study of the third key of revelation, describe your reaction to the following statement: There is a much greater danger if you are not open to them.

Exercise #3 Conduct a study of each of the following words that have similar symbolic meanings in the bible. : the tree in Psalm 1, the ground in Matthew 13:1-9, the house in Matthew 12:43-45. What do they symbolize or represent?

Exercise #4 Suppose you have had a certain thought or feeling that you know is not yours? How are you going to tell whether that particular thought in your mind is from the Lord the devil? In answering this question, use a specific thought or feeling.

Exercise #5 Have you ever had a dream that actually came to pass? Summarize it. Where did it come from---The Holy Spirit or the devil? How do you know?

Exercise #6 Truth is most profitable when you can receive your own personal revelations. Summarize your most recent revelation concerning your recovery.

Exercise #7 Read Hebrews 5:12-14 and I Corinthians 3: 1-11. As a newborn Christian, you need a teacher to operate as a coach to "feed you" and guide you through your spiritual development. What are some of the characteristics of your teacher that causes him or her to be the right teacher for you?

Exercise 8 When you remember a dream and it is clear and not confused, it is probably inspired by the Holy Spirit. If you have such a dream, answer the following questions about it:

What is the central point of the dream?

If you are in the dream, why are you acting in the way that you are portrayed in it?

If others are in the dream, who are they, and what is their significance in the dream ie. what message does their behavior convey to you about you and about them?

How does this dream relate to the issues that are most outstanding in your life right now, particularly if you are in recovery from an addiction?

List a series of questions that have occurred to you about this particular dream.

Exercise #9 Dreams frequently will show you some issue or theme related to your personality that is calling you to greater completeness and maturity in Christ. In what ways has a particular dream brought up some attitude, value, behavior, habit, opinion, bias etc. that suggests a change or a correction on your part?

Exercise #10 It is essential that you write down your dreams or whatever you can recall as soon as you are awake. If you are not a writer, jot down a few notes, sketch a picture or a diagram, or speak into a tape recorder. Make sure that you date the dreams. You can begin your dream dialogue by using the blank sides of pages in this workbook or you can select another notebook as a dream diary or journal. Include images, symbols, actions, reactions, thoughts, attitudes, feelings, conversations, characters. Here are some other pointers:

> write fast, not concerned for grammar---improve it later.

Revelation

share your dream with someone close---you will remember it better.

if the dream is prophetic, write down the date of when the dream came to past.

note any differences between the dream and what actually happened.

KEY #5: RESISTANCE
THE FIFTH KEY TO RECOVERY AND VICTORY OVER SATAN IS

RESISTANCE

AFFIRMATION KEY #5. **RESISTANCE**

I admit that my addiction kept me in bondage and captivity to the devil. I will resist the devil by learning all that I can about his distractions, deceptions and devices. I renounce the powers of darkness and take back what the enemy of my soul has stolen from me. I am preparing myself to be released from every curse that addiction has brought to my life.

JAMES 4:7

Therefore, submit to God. <u>Resist</u> the devil and he will flee from you.

Background

The spirit world consist of God and His angels, Satan and his demons, and the human spirits of the deceased who are either with God of the devil. The Book of Genesis suggests that It was God's will that Adam and Eve only be in touch with that aspect of the spirit world that was good. In the beginning, they were so filled with the glory of God, that they were protected from evil. I believe that the reason that Satan had to speak to them through the flesh of a serpent is because their spiritual eyes were not opened to perceive evil. Although evil was in the spirit world, Adam and Eve were only in touch with God and His angels. In other words, they could not see the countless demons that were surrounding them.

Therefore, Satan had to resort to deception by appealing to their five senses. Satan told Eve a "half truth" which is a lie. Satan was correct when he told Eve that only God has all knowledge. The Lord knows evil because He created Lucifer. Lucifer is the father of evil. The lie that Eve believed was that if she ate of the tree of good and evil that her eyes would be opened and she would be as God, knowing both good and evil. In short, Satan suggested that not only would she and Adam be able to see God and His angels, but that they would be able to see Satan and his demons. The first humans believed that if they obtained the spiritual capacity to see all of the spirit world, both angels and demons, they would be like God.

However, once their eyes were opened and they became capable of seeing evil spirits, God in His great mercy shut down their ability to see into the spirit world <u>at all!</u> In so doing, they could no longer perceive the good. They lost their capacity to have face to face communication with God and His angels. Once the ability to function in their spirit nature was dormant or inoperative, they then had to become dependent upon their minds, emotions and their five physical senses. It was truly a blessing from God for it to be so. For if you as a human being were able to see your filthy, disgusting, demonic surroundings in the spirit world, you would not be able to function in your right mind, for you would become insane.

As I revealed in the first chapter of this book, I have caught a glimpse of the evil side of the spirit world when I was a student and a practitioner of the occult. I learned from these experiences that Satan most definitely can transform himself into an angel of light. However, he is truly grotesque, as are the demons under his command. I believe that mental illness is a term that needs to be redefined in light of God's word and the gospel accounts of the Lord and His ministry of casting out of demons. To be mentally ill is "to have one's eyes opened to perceive evil." It is to be in such touch with the evil in the spirit world, that the person identifies himself almost totally with that world. The evil in the spirit world becomes the person's reality because it IS reality! Evil spirits, the very same ones that were in the garden of Eden, the very same ones that caused God to destroy the earth with the flood, are the very same ones that exist today. Spirit never dies. Whether it be angelic, demonic or human,--- spirit has eternal existence.

Likewise alcohol and narcotic drugs as well as psychedelic drugs like peyote and LSD, will open your eyes to the evil side of the spirit world. Drug induced contact can jeopardize you to demons that specialize in torture and defilement. The essential feature of those that torture particularly through drug withdrawal or detoxification is an hallucination with vivid or loud voices. These voices will address you directly, but they will also discuss you in the third person. When these voices are threatening, Satan is trying to force you to either commit suicide or to attack those that he accuses. You may react not so much because of the command, but to avoid the believed consequences of the torture such as disgrace, injury or even death. The torture of demons of defilement will be threatening in a derogatory and shameful way.

How should you guard against deception? You need to discern what is God's operation and what is the evil spirits' operation; what is the work of the Holy Ghost, and what is the work of Satan. All of the works of the Lord Jesus Christ are done by the Holy Spirit through the spirit of man. The works of Satan are done through man's soul. You should know the Holy Spirit as well as the enemy so that you will never mistake his words for the Lord's words. To know the third person of the Holy Trinity and His work is most important to resisting Satan. It is by the power of the Holy Spirit in the name and the blood of Jesus Christ of Nazareth that demons are cast out.

As a Person, the Holy Spirit speaks, teaches, witnesses, guides, comforts, convicts, commands, helps, converts and performs miracles. He can be obeyed, lied to, resisted, grieved, quenched, insulted and blasphemed. The work of the Holy Spirit on earth centers on lifting up the Son, just as the Son ever lived on earth to glorify the Father. The Father too glorifies the Son and calls Him Lord, just as the Holy Spirit is called the Spirit of Christ and the Spirit of the Father. All three Persons are One. As our Teacher of spiritual truths, the Holy Spirit will enlighten your mind with insights into the mind of Christ, and as in the third key of revelation, He will unlock the spiritual doorways to the secret things of God.

The only way that you can come to know Christ more intimately is through the revelation of the Holy Spirit. Therefore, you must give the Holy Spirit His place of honor in your life by surrendering totally to Christ. You do this by spending unhurried time in fellowship and prayer. As you keep your attention focused on His indwelt Spirit, He will continue to fill you. Filling is a result of surrender, obedience, trust and faith. Once filled, the scriptures will become alive to you. Your prayers will become powerful.

However, just as the Holy Spirit drove Jesus into the wilderness to do battle with the devil, He will also do the same to you. The Lord not only wants you to know Him. He wants you to know your enemy and He will arrange your wilderness for you! The Holy Spirit knows that it is crucial that you not be ignorant to Satanic deception, for the demons have access to you through your soul. Therefore, it is imperative that you learn how to tell the difference between what is spiritual and what is soulish or carnal. An obedient surrender of your will to Jesus Christ is a major step toward overcoming evil---as outlined in AA's first three (3) steps. The self-examination process as defined in step four (4) is also important. Self-knowledge equips you to be able to discern thoughts and feelings that are alien to your own character and personality. However, more is required. You must also know the will and the ways of the enemy.

A crucial facet of spiritual empowerment and recovery is to know the wiles, schemes and plots of the "evil one" and to receive power from God to be victorious in each maneuver that the demons will inevitably attempt against you. Clearly, there are destructive people, systems and circumstances in the world --- obviously evil in motives, methods and results. Moreover, Satan is a destroyer who leaves a conspicuous trail of destructive evidence behind him. Even so, you may still blame the Lord for acts of senseless loss, mayhem and violence as "an act of God." False accusations of this kind point to clear evidence that you do not possess an intimate knowledge of the Holy Spirit. If you do not know God's thoughts and ways, you remain ill equipped to recognize Satan's influence.

Satan's greatest advantage is to be allowed to work in your life without being recognized. In his masquerade as God, he skillfully uses the same words of his apparent opposition to fully attack and disavow himself. This kind of "counter espionage" is a trick, where the spy brings back information about the enemy, solely for the purpose of deceiving the agency or persons who have employed him. Satan's goal is to win your confidence by virtually attacking himself through those who appear to be his enemies, but who, in fact are either his avowed, or uninitiated friends and servants. Many professed believers in Jesus Christ fall under this category. They verbally attack demon forces yet a closer scrutiny will uncover extremes and excesses---either a repressive, judgmental morality or an opposing tolerance of man's sinful nature that borders on moral weakness, disguised as mercy, grace and love. Within BOTH ethical extremes, though anonymous and disguised, Satan and his demons maintain a vital continuum of power and control.

Satan is not only the father of lies, but he is also the author of "half-truths".It is important to know that a "half truth" is a lie, and can be even more deadly than a complete lie. Demons love to snare prey with half truths rather than with complete lies because a half truth can set a more believable trap. You say to your self, if this is true, then that must be true and then you are trapped. This is the scheme that is the foundation of all false religions. There is at least one truth about God in all of them, perhaps more. But 99 percent of truth is no truth. It is a lie. God is 100 percent truth as there are no lies in Him. God is light and in Him there is NO darkness AT ALL! Ninety-nine percent of the truth is from the devil.

Your human struggle with the evil side of the spirit world is a daily event. With a well known biblical prayer, we ask the Lord not only to give us our DAILY bread, but we ask Him to deliver us each day from evil or "the evil one." Therefore, we must take heed to the scriptural advice of the Apostle Simon Peter when he tells us to be sober and vigilant because of the tricks of the devil.

To be sober is to take demonic influences seriously and realistically, without exaggerating or under-estimating their power. In this sense, sobriety is marked by a sound and stable mind that is neither seduced by excesses of emotion, habit or opinion nor pushed or hurried by cognitive or emotional extremes. We who are sober will not allow our thoughts, emotions or feelings to motivate us to form an unhealthy opinion that will ultimately lead to "giving Satan place" to operate in our lives. For recovering people, the term "sober" or "sobriety" used in this biblical context should signify that the state of being drunk or otherwise intoxicated is an open door to Satanic intervention.

Within this framework, vigilance is more than just being watchful or cautious, for the hallmark of vigilance is self examination and self knowledge. We must know ourselves down to our patterns, habits and motives. As the treatment of a disease begins with an assessment and a diagnosis, vigilance is operationalized by opening ourselves to the Higher Power for scrutiny and by our willingness to come to terms with his assessment and His correction, without defending or minimizing our weaknesses. Watchman Nee, a Chinese Christian philosopher puts it this way in his book entitled "The Spiritual Man:

"Should the child of God desire freedom, his folly must be removed. In other words, he must know the truth. He needs to appreciate the real nature of affairs. Satanic lies bind, but God's truth unshackles. Naturally the knowledge of truth is going to be costly, for it will shatter the vainglory one has assumed due to his past experiences. He looks upon himself as far more advanced than others, as being spiritual and infallible. How hard hit he will be if he confesses the possibility of his being invaded or if he is shown to have been so invaded! Unless God's child sincerely adheres to all the truth of God, it becomes very rough for him to accept this kind of painful and humiliating truth. One encounters no difficulty in accepting that truth which is agreeable; but it is not easy at all to take in a truth which blasts one's ego. To acknowledge himself as liable to deception is relatively easy; whereas to confess that he is entrenched by the enemy already is most difficult. May God be gracious, for even after a person has known the truth he may yet resist it. The acceptance of truth is thus the first step to salvation. The child of God must be willing to know all the truth concerning himself. This requires humility and sincerity. Therefore let him who vehemently opposes such truth beware lest unknowingly he actually be enslaved. (Nee, p 122, 1968)

The spoils of the "invasion" to which Watchman Nee refers is the ground or territory of our souls that has been surrendered to Satan---territory that my first book, To Curse the Root--- is devoted to ensuring that you reclaim.

To be truly sober is to take demonic influences seriously, realistically, without exaggerating or under-estimating their power. In this sense, sobriety is marked by a sound and stable mind that is neither seduced by excesses of emotion, habit or opinion or pushed or hurried by cognitive or emotional extremes. If you are truly "clean" and "sober" you will not allow your thoughts, emotions or feelings to motivate you to form an unhealthy opinion that will ultimately lead to "giving Satan place" to operate in your life. For recovering people, the "sober" or "sobriety" used in this biblical context should signify that the state of being drunk or otherwise intoxicated is an open door to Satanic intervention.

Within this framework, vigilance is more than just being watchful or cautious, for the hallmark of vigilance is self examination and self knowledge. We must know ourselves down to our patterns, habits and motives. As the treatment of a disease begins with an assessment and a diagnosis, vigilance is operationalized by opening yourself to the Holy Spirit for scrutiny and by your willingness to come to terms with His assessment and His correction, without defending or minimizing your weaknesses.

Demonic influence has many styles of deception. Where addictive behavior is concerned, demons revel in depression, oppression and vexation of spirit because these three (3) emotional conditions are open doors to relapse during the recovery process. Depression is spiritually nurtured by a poor sense of esteem, dissatisfaction, and alienation---each rooted in a lack of patience. Evil spirits thrive on the three "d's" of doubt, disappointment and despair to lower our physical energy and vitality. Their method is to entangle weeds of negative thoughts, emotions and attitudes into a stronghold or spiritual underground root system that develops into a solid fortress or base of operation from which demons can function unhindered. Condemnation and accusations are central to the guilt experienced by the depressed.

Oppression brings a sense of being smothered or weighed down with the burdens of a troubled, problematic life. In such cases, the demon assigned to oppress you is by metaphor a "monkey on the back", hovering around and pressing you down with a persistent attack, until your spiritual back breaks and you relapse. At times sudden and shocking, the demon will apply a steady and relentless attack with persecution and disarming calamities of all sorts.

Vexation of spirit takes several forms. Restlessness can lead to a feeling of annoyance or irritability. In this regard, evil spirits will employ sequentially ordered petty harassments to cause worry and a disquieted state, akin to mild or even acute stages of paranoia. In the mental realm, vexation also brings confusion and disorientation. The demonic weapons of choice are fear and intimidation. Demons will use others close to us to create situations that incite your emotions. The agitation you feel may become so intense that you might literally "lose it" and attack somebody. The evil spirit's goal is to take advantage of and condemnation for past failures, coupled with the worry and fear over the consequences you may face for your actions. The demons will maneuver these circumstances to motivate relapse. When you are ignorant to Satanic devices, evil spirits can repetitively and consistently employ the same strategies to defeat us simply because we are ignorant to the fact that "that devil did make you do it!"

Attempting to control your addiction with human will power alone is an exhausting struggle that Satan will ultimately win. Human will power cannot outlast Satan's power. However, when you are able to rest in Christ by ceasing from your own works, the Holy Spirit will empower your spirit with strength that exceeds the capacity of your will. You will be able to walk in the spirit and not fulfill the lust of your flesh without much effort because you have sought the kingdom and found righteousness.

Key Scriptures

On Spiritual Warfare

Matthew 4:1**Then was Jesus led up of the Spirit into the wilderness to be tempted of the devil.**:2 And when he had fasted forty days and forty nights, he was afterward an hungered.:3And when the tempter came to him, he said, If thou be the Son of God, command that these stones be made bread.:4But he answered and said, It is written, Man shall not live by bread alone, but by every word that proceedeth out of the mouth of God.:5 Then the devil taketh him up into the holy city, and setteth him on a pinnacle of the temple,:6And saith unto him, If thou be the Son of God, cast thyself down: for it is written, He shall give his angels charge concerning thee: and in their hands they shall bear thee up, lest at any time thou dash thy foot against a stone. :7Jesus said unto him, It is written again, Thou shalt not tempt the Lord thy God.:8Again, the devil taketh him up into an exceeding high mountain, and sheweth him all the kingdoms of the world, and the glory of them;:9And saith unto him, All these things will I give thee, if thou wilt fall down and worship me.:10Then saith Jesus unto him, Get thee hence, Satan: for it is written, Thou shalt worship the Lord thy God, and him only shalt thou serve.:11**Then the devil leaveth him, and, behold, angels came and ministered unto him.**

Ephesians 6:11**Put on the whole armour of God, that ye may be able to stand against the wiles of the devil.**:12For we wrestle not against flesh and blood, but against principalities, against powers, against the rulers of the darkness of this world, against spiritual wickedness in high places.13Wherefore take unto you the whole armour of God, that ye may be able to withstand in the evil day, and having done all, to stand.

:14 Stand therefore, having your loins girt about with truth, and having on the breastplate of righteousness;:15And your feet shod with the preparation of the gospel of peace;:16Above all, taking the shield of faith, wherewith ye shall be able to quench all the fiery darts of the wicked.:17And take the helmet of salvation, and the sword of the Spirit, which is the word of God::18Praying always with all prayer and supplication in the Spirit, and watching thereunto with all perseverance and supplication for all saints;

II Corinthians 10:3For though we walk in the flesh, we do not war after the flesh:

:4(**For the weapons of our warfare** are not carnal, but mighty through God to the pulling down of strong holds;):5 Casting down imaginations, and every high thing that exalteth itself against the knowledge of God, and bringing into captivity every thought to the obedience of Christ;:6And having in a readiness to revenge all disobedience, when your obedience is fulfilled.:7 Do ye look on things after the outward appearance? If any man trust to himself that he is Christ's, let him of himself think this again, that, as he is Christ's, even so are we Christ's.

II Corinthians 11:13For such are false apostles, deceitful workers, transforming themselves into the apostles of Christ :14And no marvel; for Satan himself is transformed into an angel of light:15 Therefore it is no great thing if his ministers also be transformed as the ministers of righteousness; whose end shall be according to their works.

I John 4:1Beloved, believe not every spirit, but try the spirits whether they are of God: because many false prophets are gone out into the world: 2Hereby know ye the Spirit of God: Every spirit that confesseth that Jesus Christ is come in the flesh is of God::3

And every spirit that confesseth not that Jesus Christ is come in the flesh is not of God: and this is that spirit of Antichrist, whereof ye have heard that it should come; and even now already is it in the world.:4Ye are of God, little children, and have overcome them: because greater is he that is in you, than he that is in the world.I John 4:They are of the world: therefore speak they of the world, and the world heareth them.

I John 4:We are of God: he that knoweth God heareth us; he that is not of God heareth not us. Hereby know we the spirit of truth, and the spirit of error.:7Beloved, let us love one another: for love is of God; and every one that loveth is born of God, and knoweth God.I John 4:8He that loveth not knoweth not God; for God is love.

(I Peter 5:8,9) Be sober, be vigilant; because your adversary the devil walks about like a roaring lion, seeking whom he may devour. Resist him, steadfast in the faith, knowing that the same sufferings are experienced by our brotherhood in the world.

Matthew 12:24But when the Pharisees heard it, they said, This fellow doth not cast out devils, but by Beelzebub the prince of the devils.:25 And Jesus knew their thoughts, and said unto them, Every kingdom divided against itself is brought to desolation; and every city or house divided against itself shall not stand::26 And if Satan cast out Satan, he is divided against himself; how shall then his kingdom stand?:27And if I by Beelzebub cast out devils, by whom do your children cast them out? therefore they shall be your judges.:28But if I cast out devils by the Spirit of God, then the kingdom of God is come unto you.12:29Or else how can one enter into a strong man's house, and spoil his goods, except he first bind the strong man? and then he will spoil his house.

Matthew 12:43When the unclean spirit is gone out of a man, he walketh through dry places, seeking rest, and findeth none.:44Then he saith, I will return into my house from whence I came out; and when he is come, he findeth it empty, swept, and garnished.

:45Then goeth he, and taketh with himself seven other spirits more wicked than himself, and they enter in and dwell there: and the last state of that man is worse than the first. Even so shall it be also unto this wicked generation.

On Love, Giving, Obedience and Meekness

Luke 6:35But love ye your enemies, and do good, and lend, hoping for nothing again; and your reward shall be great, and ye shall be the children of the Highest: for he is kind unto the unthankful and to the evil.:36Be ye therefore merciful, as your Father also is merciful. :37Judge not, and ye shall not be judged: condemn not, and ye shall not be condemned: forgive, and ye shall be forgiven:

38Give, and it shall be given unto you; good measure, pressed down, and shaken together, and running over, shall men give into your bosom. For with the same measure that ye mete withal it shall be measured to you again.

Luke 6:39And he spake a parable unto them, Can the blind lead the blind? shall they not both fall into the ditch?40The disciple is not above his master: but every one that is perfect shall be as his master.41And why beholdest thou the mote that is in thy brother's eye, but perceivest not the beam that is in thine own eye?

42Either how canst thou say to thy brother, Brother, let me pull out the mote that is in thine eye, when thou thyself beholdest not the beam that is in thine own eye? Thou hypocrite, cast out first the beam out of thine own eye, and then shalt thou see clearly to pull out the mote that is in thy brother's eye.:43For

> KEY STATEMENT:The personality of an addict is so broken down that demons of all kind have had free reign. You must submit yourself to Jesus Christ to take back control of your soul.

a good tree bringeth not forth corrupt fruit; neither doth a corrupt tree bring forth good fruit.

:44For every tree is known by his own fruit. For of thorns men do not gather figs, nor of a bramble bush gather they grapes.:45A good man out of the good treasure of his heart bringeth forth that which is good; and an evil man out of the evil treasure of his heart bringeth forth that which is evil: for of the abundance of the heart his mouth speaketh.

Resistance

Luke 6:46And why call ye me, Lord, Lord, and do not the things which I say?:47

Whosoever cometh to me, and heareth my sayings, and doeth them, I will shew you to whom he is like::48He is like a man which built an house, and digged deep, and laid the foundation on a rock: and when the flood arose, the stream beat vehemently upon that house, and could not shake it: for it was founded upon a rock.49But he that heareth, and doeth not, is like a man that without a foundation built an house upon the earth; against which the stream did beat vehemently, and immediately it fell; and the ruin of that house was great.

Galatians 6:1Brethren, if a man be overtaken in a fault, ye which are spiritual, restore such an one **in the spirit of meekness;** considering thyself, lest thou also be tempted.

:2Bear ye one another's burdens, and so fulfil the law of Christ.

:3 For if a man think himself to be something, when he is nothing, he deceiveth himself.

:4But let every man prove his own work, and then shall he have rejoicing in himself alone, and not in another.

Study and Reflexion Outline

Point 1: The ascension of the Lord gives me the authority to bind demons and loose angels in the spirit realm. This is spiritual warfare(Matthew 18:18)

A. There are demons operating in the spiritual command center located in the heavens. (first and second heaven) (II Corinthians 12:2)

B. What goes on in the heavens is controlled by the words of our mouth

   1. Death and life are in the power of the tongue

   2. Angels stand by us to hear the word of God from our lips so that they can heed or obey the word of the Lord (Psalm 103)

Point 2: The crucifixion of the Lord gives us the power to "plead the blood."

A. We plead the blood for

   1. **power**/ authority over demons

   2. **pardon**/forgiveness

   3. **purification**/cleansing

   4. **protection**/deliverance

   5. **piety**/holiness

B. The cross provides us with death---

   1. to the world(its customs, habits, opinions have lost their pull or influence.

   2. to the devil (he is no longer our father)

   3. to the curse of the law (we are free from guilt and shame)

   4. to ourselves (our souls are consecrated to the breaking of the Holy Spirit

   5. to sin (sin has lost its dominion or power to control us)

   6. to the past (our old, former spiritual condition) (2 Cor 7:12, 5: 16-18)

Point 3: You must learn how to try the spirits to see if they be of God.

Satan searches for your weaknesses of character in order to block God's power and plan for your life. Therefore, character development is a part of your spiritual armor as we allow the sword of the Spirit--the word of God---to break and develop you.

   A. As you develop character, you will develop wisdom. With wisdom comes spiritual discernment. (Hebrews 4:12)

      1. The nine fruits of the Holy Spirit represent the character of Christ.

      2. Love is the most important weapon because love does not fail.

   B. THE WORD divides the soul from the spirit. It is:

    piercing---it cuts

    powerful---it confronts

    probing--- it corrects

   C. Try the spirits to see if they be of God.

      1. The first step to trying the spirits is to examine your own heart or "judge yourself" so as not to give demons any place in you.

      2. The next step is to examine the fruit.

         a) become a skilled listener

         b) be slow to speak

         c) be wise as a serpent but harmless as a dove.

Point 4: Dealing with your own prideful nature is an important step to spiritual warfare and resisting the devil.

A. Definition of pride

1. excessive self esteem or "to think more highly of yourself then you ought to think.

2. pride can "put you to sleep" about yourself. The truth about how you think and feel will be hidden from you.

   a) it will create a false image

   b) it will call truth a lie and a lie the truth

   c) it will cause you to be spiritually ignorant of who you are

3. the behavior of pride can be disdainful, haughty, arrogant, narrowminded, critical, self-pitying, defensive, offensive, critical and judgmental.

   a) you will not be able to endure insult

   b) you will be susceptible to failure. (Proverbs

4. pride will lose out on God's grace. Grace is the Lord's favor and power. An unearned gift from God, grace is the power of the Holy Spirit to cause you to be able to perform in ways that are not natural to you.

   a) without grace and power, you will do the Lord's work in your own power.

   b) you will place too much emphasis on material things.

   c) God is not concerned with "fairness" according to our human understanding.

> 1) He applies His grace to the humble (James 4)
>
> 2) He recognizes differences in people yet He is not a respecter of persons.

5. pride will go to great lengths to protect your soul.

   a) pride will block your blessing

   b) pride will block your spiritual understanding

6. pride will insult God

   a) pride stands in the way of your fear of the Lord

   b) pride will cause you to trust yourself rather than Him

7. pride will lead to strife

   a) stay in harmony and agreement will other believers

   b) a hot temper will hinder prayer

B. Resist pride by putting on humility. To be humble is to:

1. endure injury with patience

2. overcome resentment

3. obey the word even when it contradicts your thoughts, feelings and emotions.

4. recognize when you are wrong and make corrections speedily

5. refuse to injure someone else for your own vindication.

Point 5 Since character defects thrive on unforgiveness, unforgiveness opens a doorway of opportunity to demons to be victorious in your situation.

    A. Forgiveness looses or sets free, while unforgiveness binds and enslaves.

        1. hatred is a powerful Satanic force.

        2. demons will use negative emotions to attack the unforgiven

    B. Satan uses unforgiveness in progressive increments to destroy your fruits by destroying your peace.

    C. When you resist the devil, you remove yourself as the source of evil by:

        1. fighting the impulse to answer back

        2. being slow to speak

        3. being swift to hear

        4. being slow to anger

        5. learning how to receive correction and criticism

        6. seeking to make adjustments to your personality

        7. yielding to the needs of others.

        8. being quick to forgive and to seek forgiveness

            a) you will forgive but you will not compromise for the sake of peace

b) you will learn to separate what people do from who they are

c) you will forgive but be wise enough not to trust until trust is rebuilt.

D. Meekness or humility will cause you to be fruitful.

1. You will steal souls out of Satan's kingdom, setting the oppressed free.

2. You will draw souls to Christ by rendering good for evil.

a) If you are abused, you will not strike back

b) If you are wrongfully accused, you will not blame

c) If you are exploited, you will share your assets

d) If you are slandered, you will uplift what is right

e) If your are rejected, you will embrace a the outcast

3. Compassion is an important weapon in spiritual warfare.

a) Love never fails.

b) Fervent prayer of the righteous is powerful

Point 6 The Lord needs to break you in order to remove your impurities.

A. Trials, tribulations and persecutions are used by God to build character

1. You must pass the tests of life to grow and bare fruit

> 2. Your failures are clues as to what the Lord is breaking in you
>
>   a) each relapse is an indication that you have failed the test
>
>   b) within each relapse is a clue to the root of your addiction
>
> B. Trials and tribulations and persecutions are used by God to build trust
>
>   1. Rest is freedom from demonic oppression and confidence that the battle is already won in Christ.
>
>   a) Satan cannot use any spiritual knowledge that is beyond our human understanding or ability to resist
>
>   b) Jesus defeated Satan at the cross.
>
>   2. When you trust the Lord, you will be unconcerned about public opinion
>
>   3. The Lord will use trust to help you overcome your anxieties and fears

Point #7 If you are going to resist the devil, you must learn to be vigilant. To be vigilant is to be watchful, cautious and wise.

> A. You must be vigilant about your social relationships with the world.
>
>   1. Do not be conformed to the world
>
>   a) avoid being a people pleaser
>
>   b) learn what pleases God and obey it.
>
>   c) draw people to Christ and not to you.

2. Do not allow the world to define your self concept.

   a) submit yourself to God's word to mold and correct you

   b) realize that without Christ you can do nothing.

Point 8 Faith mixed with the word of God will profit you in battle.

A. Without faith disobedience will ultimately follow.

   1. Faith involves trust

   2. You cannot trust God without faith.

B. If you cannot trust God, then you cannot wait on Him

   1. Waiting helps you to know the Lords ways.

   2. Faith mixed with patience can help you to endure

      a) when things look bleak

      b) when plans are delayed

Point 9 The Lord will use circumstances to change you, before He changes your circumstances.

A. Faith without works is dead.

   1. You must be tried.

      a) faith cannot stand on untried information

      b) you need to know the level of your own endurance

B. The Lord Himself does not change.

1. He does new and different things in your life to cause you to change
2. Flexibility is to have skill at adjusting and accepting new situations
   a) a lack of flexibility can distort your thinking
   b) rigidity can lead to mental illness.
3. Grace involves flexibility. It is the opposite of the law which demands rigidity.

C. We need grace to uphold us while we wait on the Lord for deliverance.
   1. Grace is divine assistance where your ability is not sufficient
   2. Grace is also unmerited favor in undeserving times.

D. Grace dictates that you don't have to fight the devil in your own strength.
   1. the fight is conducted by angels
   2. disobedience and rebellion will provoke angels
   3. to provoke an angel is to incite, anger or agitate them.
      a) they will be hindered in fighting off Satan's demons
      b) you will empower the demons that are assigned to you.
      c) you will weaken the angels that are assigned to you.

Point 9 Seduction is a major tactic of Satan, including flattery, feigned affection and forwardness.

A. To be seduced is to be deceived into doing wrong or committing sin.

   1. To be seductive is to be strongly attractive and enticing.

   2. Until you recognize within yourself what traits YOU have that make you vulnerable to the traits in others, you are at risk to ANYTHING.

B. In order to overcome the Seducer, you must learn to be discrete and to use discretion.

   1. To be discrete, one must be able to: Rightly Divide, Distinguish and Discern.

      a) Discretion involves freedom to make godly choices,

      b) power to judge or to act and

      c) being careful about what you say and do.

   2. You will be discrete when wisdom comes into our hearts.

      a) Discretion will preserve you. (Look up scripture)

      b) Your soul will be renewed.

C. Be careful who you share your troubles with and your dreams with.

   1. Spiritual warfare between demons and angels will take place.

      a) You don't want to give demons any advantage.

      b) You don't want forfeit your supply of anointing

2. The doubt and unbelief of others will hinder your hope, peace, trust and faith

    a) Keep hope alive by controlling your tongue.

    b) Constant replay of troubles will weaken the power of your hope

    c) Too much talk will increase the power of hopelessness.

3. Be careful of who you allow to pray for you.

    a) Avoid people with grasshopper mentality

    b) Avoid people who don't have a body concept of Oneness in Christ. (talebearers and strife setters)

    c) Avoid people with a narrow vision or no vision at all.

4. The purposes and plans of ungodly people will steal your wellbeing.

Workstudy Exercises

Exercise #1: A SPIRITUAL PERSON IS ONE WHO HAS ADEQUATELY EXAMINED HIS OWN PERSONALITY AND WHO HAS TAKEN ACTION TO CORRECT HIS OR HER CHARACTER DEFECTS. What are your character defects?

___

Exercise #2 Pick your most outstanding character defect. How does it manifest itself in your thought, your emotions, your personality and your actions?

___

Exercise #3 What is your style of pride? Do you tend to:

The pleaser

    a. desire to please other people with your abilities?

The judge

    b. attempt to be right and to prove others to be wrong?

The superior

    c. perceive yourself as a "cut above others?"

The manipulator

    d. attempt to control others with your personality?

The pretender

    e. hide your feelings so that no one sees you sweat?

The gifted

    f. admire your own intelligence?

The arrogant

    g. enjoy "lording" it over others?

The headstrong

    h. refuse to receive counsel or help from others?

For each letter that you circled, give a specific example of situation where your style of pride was recently evident. Exercise #4 Where do you stand? Some test questions are as follows:

1. Are you able to stand in the midst of a storm in your life without using?

2. Are you able to be content with what the Lord is doing in your life right now without comparing yourself to someone else?

To Curse The Root

Exercise #5 As you grow up in the Lord, your test and trials will become increasingly difficult. Describe a level of growth that you have obtained through trial and error.

___

Exercise #6 How did you come to recognize Satan's devices in this particular situation and how did you take a stand against him?

___

Exercise #7 Satan will use the mouth of a scorner to penetrate your spirit. Look up Proverbs 18:4. This scripture suggests that you must guard your spirit if you are to keep joy in your life. Wounded spirits seem to attract one another. You can recognize a scorner by his words, for Jesus said that out of the abundance of the heart or the spirit the mouth speaks. Describe some of the "scorners" in your life and plan some strategies to guard your spirit against their words.

___

Exercise #8 Although they didn't realized it, those people who were the most significant in your life were used by the devil to hurt you. True recovery from the emotional damage you suffered must first be acknowledged, confronted and resolved. You must bring it out before Jesus and put it on the cross. Complete the following phrases:

Part A The most outstanding damage that I have endured is_

___

Part B Who are you most angry at and why?

___

Part C Have you ever become resentful, bitter or vengeful because of unresolved anger? If so, describe._

___

Part D Does knowing that those who hurt or damaged you may have been used by demons to torture or destroy you without their knowledge help you to forgive them?___

Part E How has the RIC Program helped you to address your anger

---

KEY #6: RENEWAL

THE SIXTH KEY TO RECOVERY AND VICTORY OVER SATAN IS

RENEWAL

AFIRMATION KEY #6. **<u>RENEWAL</u>**

I faithfully commit myself to accept the responsibility not to be conformed to this world, but to be transformed by the <u>renewing of my mind</u>, so that I can get in touch with the Lord's divine thoughts, plans and purposes for my life. I will find my place in the body of Christ by submitting myself to the Holy Ghost.

ROMANS 12:2

Be not conformed to this world, but be ye transformed by the renewing of your mind that you may prove what is that good and acceptable and perfect will of god.

Background

In spiritual terms, the world is any person, place thing or system where Jesus Christ is not the Head. Therefore, to understand the world is relatively easy. The world then includes our family, relatives, peers, education and teachers, politics and politicians, the police department, social clubs and community, (if it is not Christ centered), television, movies, magazines,---the list is endless. Jesus declared that all power has been given unto Him both in heaven and in earth. He has the keys to the kingdom. However, the systems of this world refuse to submit to the Lord's authority. Satan, the exile from heaven, is referred to by Paul the Apostle as being "the god of this world" and "the prince of the power of the air." There are only two kingdoms on earth: the kingdom of God and the kingdom of the devil. When you were born into this world you entered into Satan's kingdom because of your sin nature. When you chose Jesus Christ as your Lord and Savior, you left Satan's kingdom and you now belong to the Lord Jesus Christ.

Jesus declared in the gospels that if you belong to Him, you will be hated by the world. He purchased you with the price of His blood and the cross is a symbol of that purchase. <u>You are no longer your own.</u> You have been bought with a blood price. The ritualistic symbol of your separation from the world is baptism. When you go down into the water, you are saying goodbye to the world. Since you have been redeemed by the blood, you have become both a stranger and a pilgrim to the world. The blood of Jesus separates the people of God from the people of this earth. To be separated from the world is to come out of it as a system, but of course, not to come out of it as a place. The reality is that you have left the world as a system. Undoubtedly, you will go to school, vote, interact with people in the world, ride the bus, watch television and shop in most of the same stores as the people in the world. The difference will be in your attachments and affections. You must love what Jesus loves and hate what Jesus hates. Your involvement with the world should be as a spectator. Morally and spiritually speaking, you do not belong. You need to adopt a spectator's attitude toward all the affections, opinions and relationships that you developed in the world. That which may be highly esteemed among your family, peers, friends and your social setting may be an abomination to God. You insult Him when your continual attachment to the world causes you to seek the support and approval of others and to adopt their ways, when their ways are contradictory to His.

Every born-again believer will find separation from the world a difficult process. The world has planted seeds into you from the time you were born and in this way has shaped and formed your soul. As the seat of human personality and consciousness, the soul acts as a mediator or "middle man" between the spirit and the body. Simply put, the soul is the seat of the self or the "I AM." Although each human personality has some innate or genetic characteristics or predispositions, the "I AM" has been trained by habit, experiences, and cultural or worldly opinion. Moreover, even though the "I AM" may appear to have a mind, feelings and a will of its own, much of its makeup has been defined by those from whom the most messages have been computed or internalized within socialization as controlled by the predominant world view. Within your soul, the words from those messages have been planted into you. These words have grown within your soul and have developed into weaknesses and strongholds.

The primary message in "to Curse the Root" is that behind every outward manifestation of weakness or dysfunction, there is a root cause. It should also be understood that at times the root cause for your behavior may be grounded in mental and/or emotional conflicts that you are not conscious of. Your mind is a major component of you soul. Your soul is a mixture of your emotions, your mind and your will. Where your mind is concerned, a thought is a means to activate your intellect. The intellect is the seat of reasoning. As your body has a built-in system to eliminate wastes, the intellectual activity of your mind controls your thoughts. Thought life is extremely important because your personality and character is reflected in the way you think.

The more steadfastly you fix your mind on a particular thought, the thought then becomes "an imagination." The stronger the "imagination," the closer you come to taking the action that the particular thought suggested. You can determined how close you are to making a mistake by monitoring your thoughts. In most cases, the innermost voice of the spirit will break through to your mind and tell you not to take the particular action you were about to take. However, if you are out of touch with your spirit, you will generally yield to the thoughts of your mind. If your reasoning is defective, your thoughts can manipulate you in a negative manner. For example, consider the person who thinks: "I can shoot heroin just once and I won't get hooked or I can take just one drink and I will be okay." Such a thought will bring about an action that will ultimately produce a major repercussion.

Rationalizations and justifications are the products of an unrenewed mind. In such cases, you make excuses for yourself by blaming others. In order to correct the thoughts of your mind, you must take the following actions:

1. open your intellect to examination by being honest with yourself;

2. stop a thought in mid-stream and analyze it;

3. change the words of your mouth;

4. say "no" to that thought, out loud if necessary.

People who negotiate life through their minds are very often confused or "doubleminded." A doubleminded person is unstable in all of his or her ways. (James 1:8) Such a person will use the world's standards of money, status, clothes and the like to prove to himself that he is valuable. A doubleminded person compares himself to others. He has a "grass is greener on the other side of the street" mentality, and therefore, is never satisfied. This lack of satisfaction causes such a one to place impossible demands on the people who love him or her. He also seeks to fill his inner unrest or dissatisfaction with immediate gratification by fulfilling the lust of his flesh. Furthermore, the doubleminded will minimize or exaggerate the facts when discussing his life of pleasure seeking.

People who are doubleminded also tend to be procrastinators. They "reason" that something that ought to be done now, can be done later. For example, such a person will stay in an unsatisfying relationship because he is so consumed by his thoughts that he is out of touch with how he really FEELS. His thoughts tell him that he should not forsake the present relationship until he has found a romantic replacement. "A bird in the hand is better than one that is in the bush."

Out of touch with his emotions, the "doubleminded" will reason in his mind that he is "in love." His feelings become so disguised, that he loses the ability to be genuinely affectionate. He reasons that to be emotional is to be too "soft". In an effort to emotionally survive, he may hide his real self from others. Such behavior creates an emotional blindness, where the doubleminded person is out of touch with his own true feelings. For example, the "macho" image is rooted in masculine hardness as a way to avoid painful feelings. You may need to rediscover your emotions by quieting your thoughts long enough to feel what you need to feel.

A person who acts from the emotions cares neither for principle nor for reason, but only for his feeling. Under the power of the emotions, the mind becomes undependable. With a powerless mind, you cannot distinguish between right and wrong. Consider the person who tries to collect his emotional debts from the opposite sex because someone of that sex hurt him in a previous relationship. In this regard, some men hate all women because their mothers hurt them. Similarly, some women hate or distrust all men because some man in their past hurt or betrayed them, ie, a father, brother, friend, etc

Rooted in emotional dysfunctions, repetitive scenarios become habitual re-plays, where similar patterns evolve in every relationship. Unable to break this emotional cycle, the emotionally disabled person cannot trust other people and therefore does not make lasting commitments in a relationship. It is difficult for such a person to accept love from others. Whether real or imagined, feelings of victimization or rejection will lead to a need to victimize or reject others. To obtain victory over such feelings, it is important that you develop other parts of your soul, particularly the mind. To instill rational thinking, you as the caretaker of your own spiritual empowerment and recovery should realize that very often those that you are hating are not even thinking about you. They are simply moving on to a new conquest, and literally having themselves a "grand ole time."

Anyone who makes decisions either by the influence of the mind or the emotions is usually weak in his or her will. Your will is the organ that examines, distinguishes, judges and makes decisions based upon the information received from your mind and your emotions. Choices can be enduring and long-lived. Unfortunately, you can make the decision but you cannot choose the repercussion.

The way to victory is to establish a value system or a set of principles that will be followed regardless of the emotional situation. Since feelings generated by our emotions are so changeable, we should never take any action during highly emotional times. Moreover, you should not allow any external force to create any feeling in you that is against your will. If you follow the leading of strong, negative feelings, your whole being will learn to thrive on these sensations, your willpower will be paralyzed, and your mind will become undependable.

In order to renew your mind, there are some key points that should be underscored:

1. You are what you THINK you are. Your thoughts have power to draw both positive and negative energy. If you have practiced negative "self talk", in the same manner, you should consciously practice positive "self talk." Positive thought will bring forth positive talk. Positive talk will bring forth the fruits of victory and success.

2. A part of renewing the soul is to learn how to deal with what is uncomfortable. Struggles and failures supply the necessary preparation. You must learn to picture in your mind a positive outcome in "all things."

3. Once you discover what you need to learn about your own inner struggles, there are other people who will need your testimony and your influence so that they too can be victorious. A major purpose of struggling is that you can become consolers of those who are struggling in those areas where you have become triumphant. By planting new seeds of power into your minds, old patterns and habits will be destroyed. In a metaphorical context, the seeds are the "words of power."

The Lord speaks to you entirely in your spirit. Your soul cannot perceive or understand God. Once your mind has been renewed by the word of God and the Holy Spirit, your mind will be able to explain to your soul what your spirit has revealed to it and to form the message into words that you and others can understand. A renewed mind will cooperate with your spirit and the Holy Spirit. Only the Holy Spirit knows the Lord's will for you and He is the only one who can convey this knowledge to your spirit. Without a renewed mind that is no longer conformed to this world, you will confuse the voice of the Lord with the thoughts, emotions and desires of your own soul.

You will obtain your renewed mind by presenting yourself... spirit, soul and body... as an act of consecration. When you consider the blood covenant of Jesus of Nazareth, it becomes clear why Paul says that presenting your body as a living sacrifice as our part of the contract is a reasonable service. (Romans 12:1) With the shedding of His blood at the cross, you are brought into an inheritance that requires you to give your all to Him as He has given His all to you. You will receive within the terms of the contract or covenant all that is His to give---salvation, righteousness, faith, healing, justification, forgiveness, deliverance, abundant blessings. In exchange, the life you live on earth belongs to Him. Your contribution to the contract is more than reasonable since your life had been worthless when you consider that a sentence of death was placed upon you at birth, for all have sinned and come short of the glory of God. (Romans 3:23)

Nevertheless, to God, you are valuable. He has a work to do in you. He has His own expectations of you. Since the Christ gave all, He expects all. No one would even die for a righteous man much less for a sinner. (Romans 5:7) Yet, the blood of the Lord's crucifixion bought you from Satan. You were chained to the devil's slave block, sold to the highest bidder. Jesus is the highest bidder. He bought you and put His seal on you in the same way that a rancher brands his cattle. You are His sheep, and as a good shepherd, Jesus brands you as His own and became your Master. Once purchased and branded, He then transformed you into His equal. What a Master! He is your Master yet He refers to Himself as your Servant. You have been transformed from servant or slave to friend. You are washed and clothed in the fine spiritual linen of righteousness and caused to:

1. sit in heavenly places with Christ Jesus;

2. walk in the spirit; and

3. stand your ground against the fiery darts of Satan.

There are many born again believers, both in and out of recovery, still positioned in the wilderness. They have not entered into God's rest. They have seen the kingdom but they have not enter it. Moreover, they have an inheritance that they have not claimed as their own by faith. Such people sit in worldly places, walk according to the vanity of their minds and cannot stand their ground against the trials and tribulations of the wicked one. Once the reality of who they are in Christ becomes sealed in their spirits and renewed in their minds, they will become spiritually empowered. The Holy Spirit will begin the developmental process where the ground of the soul is prepared to transform its conceptual position into an actual spiritual reality.

The developmental process begins with a desire to be different. You have been like a leopard who desired to change its spots but could not. You cannot change yourself. Nor can you change anyone else. This is the job of the Holy Spirit. Michael Jackson had a hit record in 1988 which told the world to look in the mirror and change our ways. This is an impossibility. The change man makes upon himself is an illusion. It is like putting clean clothes on a dirty body. Clean clothes may fool others for a time, the odor is still there. Those who follow the 12 Steps or a secular treatment model of "self" development are fooling themselves that what they do is "spiritual." Such a path is merely putting new wine into old wineskins.

The desire to be different should be followed by a recognition of pride in yourself. To be renewed, you must see your pride as an evil, ugly thing. For example, when you feel offended, you should know that it is your pride, ego and your vanity that has raised its ugly head. When you believe you have been disrespected, then you should realize that you have sought some kind of recognition or dignity for yourself. When you are embarrassed, then know that you have been overly concerned with how others view you. If you keep a pure heart, maintain the right motive and obey that much of the Lord's will that you are aware of through His word and through your own conscience, then you will not grieve or quench the Holy Spirit. When the Holy Spirit is not hindered, He will give you a clear picture of the truth.

Renewal

Key Scriptures

On Pride

Psalms 10:4 The wicked, through the pride of his countenance, will not seek after God: God is not in all his thoughts.

Proverbs 13:10 Only by pride cometh contention: but with the well advised is wisdom.

Proverbs 8:13The fear of the LORD is to hate evil: pride, and arrogance, and the evil way, and the froward mouth, do I hate.

Proverbs 29:23A man's pride shall bring him low: but honor shall uphold the humble in spirit.

I John 2:16For all that is in the world, the lust of the flesh, and the lust of the eyes, and the pride of life, is not of the Father, but is of the world.

Mark 7:21For from within, out of the heart of men, proceed evil thoughts, adulteries, fornications, murders,:22 Thefts, covetousness, wickedness, deceit, lasciviousness, an evil eye, blasphemy, pride, foolishness::23All these evil things come from within, and defile the man.

I Timothy 3:5(For if a man know not how to rule his own house, how shall he take care of the church of God?):6Not a novice, lest being lifted up with pride he fall into the condemnation of the devil.

Proverbs 21:23Whoso keepeth his mouth and his tongue keepeth his soul from troubles.

:24Proud and haughty scorner is his name, who dealeth in proud wrath.

Psalms 119:21Thou hast rebuked the proud that are cursed, which do err from thy commandments

Proverbs 28:25He that is of a proud heart stirreth up strife: but he that putteth his trust in the LORD shall be made fat.

I Peter 5:5Likewise, ye younger, submit yourselves unto the elder. Yea, all of you be subject one to another, and be clothed with humility: for God resisteth the proud, and giveth grace to the humble.

I Samuel 2:3 Talk no more so exceeding proudly; let not arrogance come out of your mouth: for the LORD is a God of knowledge, and by him actions are weighed.

Psalms 123:4 Our soul is exceedingly filled with the scorning of those that are at ease, and with the contempt of the proud.

Psalms 138:6 Though the LORD be high, yet hath he respect unto the lowly: but the proud he knoweth afar off.:7Though I walk in the midst of trouble, thou wilt revive me: thou shalt stretch forth thine hand against the wrath of mine enemies, and thy right hand shall save me.:8 The LORD will perfect that which concerneth me: thy mercy, O LORD, endureth for ever: forsake not the works of thine own hands.

Psalms 40:4Blessed is that man that maketh the LORD his trust, and respecteth not the proud, nor such as turn aside to lies.

Psalms 101:5Whoso privily slandereth his neighbor, him will I cut off: him that hath an high look and a proud heart will not I suffer.

Proverbs 16:19Better it is to be of an humble spirit with the lowly, than to divide the spoil with the proud.

Proverbs 16:5Every one that is proud in heart is an abomination to the LORD: though hand join in hand, he shall not be unpunished.

-Proverbs 6:16 These six things doth the LORD hate: yea, seven are an abomination unto him::17A proud look, a lying tongue, and hands that shed innocent blood,

:18An heart that deviseth wicked imaginations, feet that be swift in running to mischief:19A false witness that speaketh lies, and he that soweth discord among brethren.

Proverbs 21:4An high look, and a proud heart, and the plowing of the wicked, is sin.

Peter 5:5 Likewise, ye younger, submit yourselves unto the elder. Yea, all of you be subject one to another, and be clothed with humility: for God resisteth the proud, and giveth grace to the humble.:6Humble yourselves therefore under the mighty hand of God, that he may exalt you in due time:

II Timothy 3:2For men shall be lovers of their own selves, covetous, boasters, **proud,** blasphemers, disobedient to parents, unthankful, unholy,:3 Without natural affection, trucebreakers, false accusers, incontinent, fierce, despisers of those that are good,

:4Traitors, heady, highminded, lovers of pleasures more than lovers of God:5Having a form of godliness, but denying the power thereof: from such turn away.

James 4:6 But he giveth more grace. Wherefore he saith, God resisteth the proud, but giveth grace unto the humble.:7Submit yourselves therefore to God. Resist the devil, and he will flee from you.:8 Draw nigh to God, and he will draw nigh to you. Cleanse your hands, ye sinners; and purify your hearts, ye double minded.

I Timothy 6:3If any man teach otherwise, and consent not to wholesome words, even the words of our Lord Jesus Christ, and to the doctrine which is according to godliness;

:4He is **proud,** knowing nothing, but doting about questions and strifes of words, whereof cometh envy, strife, railings, evil surmisings,:5Perverse disputings of men of corrupt minds,

> **KEY STATEMENT:** Your soul (mind, emotions, will and personality) must be RENEWED daily, to be conformed into the image of Jesus Christ.

and destitute of the truth, supposing that gain is godliness: from such withdraw thyself.:6But godliness with contentment is great gain.:7 For we brought nothing into this world, and it is certain we can carry nothing out.

Malachi 4:1For, behold, the day cometh, that shall burn as an oven; and all the **proud,** yea, and all that do wickedly, shall be stubble: and the day that cometh shall burn them up, saith the LORD of hosts, that it shall leave them neither root nor branch.

Exercise # Compare the benefits of being conformed to the world to being conformed to the Lord as demonstrated in the lives of Daniel, Shadrack, Meshack and Abendiggo.

On meekness

Psalms 25:9The meek will he guide in judgment: and the meek will he teach his way.

Psalms 37:11But the meek shall inherit the earth; and shall delight themselves in the abundance of peace.

Psalms 22:26 The meek shall eat and be satisfied: they shall praise the LORD that seek him: your heart shall live for ever.

Psalms 147:6 The LORD lifteth up the meek: he casteth the wicked down to the ground.

Renewal

Psalms 149:4 For the LORD taketh pleasure in his people: he will beautify the meek with salvation

Isaiah 29:19 The meek also shall increase their joy in the LORD, and the poor among men shall rejoice in the Holy One of Israel.

Study and Reflection Outline

Point #1: The soul can deceive itself.

- A. Deception comes when you think more highly of yourself and the world then you ought to think.
  1. Self esteem as defined by the world is when the world has high regard for you.
     a) you are accepted
     b) you are found worthy
     c) you are considered competent
  2. Worldly self esteem is rooted in what others think of you.
     a) you will seek the world's approval through compromise
     b) you will try to fit in.
     c) you will disobey the Lord's will to please others.
  3. You must purpose or establish in your heart that your self esteem is found in Christ.
     a) the Lord is the only one you need to please.

b) the Lord makes you worthy by dying for you.

   c) the Lord is your competence.

 B. Deception will also come from those that Satan has planted in the church as spies and troublemakers.

   1. you should be able to recognize the world within the church

      a) they have the spirit of the anti-christ

      b) they were never true believers

      c) they can transform themselves into angels of light

      d) you will know them by their lack of fruit

Point 2 Truth will be hidden when the motives of your soul are not pure.

 A. To be pure is to be

   1. clear---articulate, unclouded and visible

   2. clean--- unblemished and spotless

   3. not confused---understandable and easy to grasp

   4. not covered up or clandestine

   5. chaste---modest, righteous and honorable

 B. To defile is to contaminate or to pollute. Defilement comes from within.

   1. Pride is a defilement.

   2. Pride begins with what you say in your heart and believe in your mind

a) pride is an evil thought

b) the evil thought will manifest itself in your actions

3. Jesus links pride to adulteries, fornications, murders, thefts, covetousness, wickedness, deceit, lewdness, an evil eye, blasphemy, and foolishness. (Mark 7:20-22)

4. A proud mind is not pure because it thinks, feels and behaves in ways that suggest that one thinks more highly of oneself than one ought to think.

C. Pride, self esteem and vanity will deny and conceal the truth.

1. These three traits will pull you away from the Lord's will by quenching and grieving the Holy Spirit

   a) your spirit will become blocked from God's revelation about your future.

   b) you will be denied His power which cause you to be successful.

   c) as pride goeth before destruction, failure will be imminent. (Proverbs 16:18)

2. Pride is deceptive because it misrepresents your thoughts and feelings in order to put forth a facade or an act.

3. Pride is also easily hurt or injured because it is always insecure. Other facets of pride are that it:

   a) will block you from experiencing genuine feelingsof love and commitment

   b) will cause you to deny your feelings

- c) lead you to "front" before our enemies in your efforts to appear to be in control;
- d) will cause you to over compensate and be over-confident, hindering us from success;
4. will prevent you from admitting that you need help and therefore block you from crucial resources;
5. will bring you into danger because you can't abide an insult or a slight. (Don't dis ME!!!)

D. Those who are concerned about public opinion are those who are the most proud.
1. Proud people must always appear knowledgeable
   - a) they will hide the fact that they do not know something.
   - b) they are concerned that others will think they are stupid.
   - c) they will lie to cover their ignorance or their weakness.
2. Proud people will hide the truth to protect their public image.

E. Esteem has some additional negative qualities:
1. it is outraged when others think that they are superior;
2. it will cause you to defend and justify yourself;
3. it will cause you to tear down others in order to build up yourself;
4. it will cause you to hunger for prestige by seeking the praise and approval of others.

F. As vanity is excessive pride, a vain person's conceit will bring about selfdeception.

1. Self deception is a doorway to failure.

    a) Others will recognize your weakness and flatter you.

    b) Vanity is foolish because it anchors itself in features of the flesh that are fragile, impermanent and transient.

    c) It causes you to live in the past

2. Vanity will blind your spirit from a relationship with the Lord.

3. the Lord may use people and circumstances as a refiner's tool to chisel vanity from your spirit.

Point 3 In order to be renewed in your mind, you must be consecrated.

A. The world did not create you. The world did not redeem you. The Lord did!

1. To justify yourself before men is to

    a) establish them as your Lord with authority to control your behavior.

    b) seek their support and approval

    c) adopt their way of doing things

2. Consecration is committing your life to the Lord

    a) Commitment involves trusting Him in all things.

    b) Presenting yourself to Him is delighting in Him

        c) He will put His desires into your heart to give you His plans for your life

        d) Your plans must be surrendered to Him before You can receive His plans

        e) Your life consists of the affections, emotions, thoughts and desires of your soul.

        f) Your life also consists of all of your habits, including use of substances.

Point 4 In order to be renewed in your mind, you must develop a spirit of meekness.

    A. Meekness is bringing your "I will" or your power to make decisions into submission and into obedience to Jesus Christ.

        1. a meek person is reasonable and yielding.

        2. a meek person is not rebellious, defiant or resistant.

    B. Meekness is learning not to defend yourself, even if you are right.

    C. Meekness is not thinking more highly of yourself than you ought to think.

        1. Do not compare yourself to anyone other than to Jesus Christ.

        2. Stop looking to your crowd for self esteem.

        3. Stop making everything "personal."

        4. Learn how to receive correction.

Point 5 Soulish people know others after the flesh or the outward condition.

    A. They can't discern God's greatness and glory in someone else.

      1. They underestimate others.

      2. They overestimate themselves.

  B. They can't discern God's greatness and glory in themselves.

      1. They overestimate others.

      2. They underestimate themselves.

Point 6 Your self esteem must be examined and renewed in Christ.

  A. To find your true self esteem, you need to find out the Lord's will for your life.

      1. His life in you should be the foundation of your self esteem.

      2. You obtain your self worth by pleasing Jesus.

  B. Your competence ought to be based on the Lord's standards.

      1. Did He ordain it?

      2. Did He appoint it?

      3. Did He assign it?

      4. Did He anoint it?

Point 7 It is not for you to improve yourself. Once you surrender to Jesus, the Holy Spirit will improve you.

  A. You can please God by studying and obtaining competence in applying His Word.

  B. You can please God by separating yourself from distractions.

      1. shun unsavory relationships (people)

2. shun activities that hinder your testimony (places)

3. shun the works of darkness (things)

Point 8 Consecrating yourself involves presenting your uncleanness to the Holy Spirit.

A. Satan does not cast out Satan

1. love not the world

2. do not hear only, but obey the word of God.

3. Examine self for sins unknown to you.

B. Those who are humble will want an inner cleansing

1. the humble are not embarrassed.

2. the humble are true when no one is looking.

Workstudy Exercises

Exercise #1 An important way to become consecrated is to know what is "still in you" from the world. List some of your triggers to relapse. Explain how they are manifested._

Exercise #2 Also, what are some of your inner needs and longings? For example, do you long to be accepted or are you constantly trying to please people to avoid rejection?_

Exercise #3 Have you recently found yourself in a situation where you had to demonstrate in your behavior your separation from the world? If so, describe. How would you set your own standards by the word of God if this situation were to arise again?

KEY #7: RESTORATION

THE SEVENTH KEY TO RECOVERY AND VICTORY OVER SATAN IS

RESTORATION

AFFIRMATION KEY #7. **RESTORATION**

I dedicate myself to remain disentangled from the yoke of bondage. I will forgive my self and those who have hurt me. I will also forgive my enemies for they did not know that Satan was using them against me. My divine love for my enemies will <u>restore my soul.</u>

JOEL 2:25,26

And I will <u>restore</u> to you the years that the locust hath eaten, the cankerworm, and the caterpillar, and the palmerworm, my great army which I sent among you. And ye shall eat in plenty, and be satisfied, and praise the name of the LORD your God, that hath dealt wondrously with you: and my people shall never be ashamed.

Background

The seventh key of restoration involves cultivation of all that you have learned about yourself, Satan and the Lord through study, care and labor. Thus far you have uncovered some of the attitudes, thoughts and habits that have been hurtful or have hindered your growth. The focus of this key is to unlock the door to freedom from being ensnared by the same traps that caused your original defeat. Facing the truth through self-examination leads to self determination. You will continue to examine the sins and weights that so easily beset you. You will also continue to strive to know yourself better than the demonic world knows you. The first six keys have now produced in you a steadfast determination never to yield to any person, place, thing or circumstance that originally caused your defeat. In a manner of speaking, this key is a form of weed control geared toward avoiding relapse for the addict and remaining free from demonic infestation, which I refer to as spiritual recidivism or backsliding. While self-examination kills and breaks, restoration builds and strengthens. These processes occur simultaneously and continually throughout life. God ever tears down in order to rebuild and restore.

In the natural realm, a recidivist is one who gives up by relapsing into a previous condition or mode of behavior---a term most often used to describe the failure of rehabilitation and a return to a life of crime. In this context, rehabilitation is restoration to a former capacity that is socially acceptable. Similarly, the old testament used the term "backslider" to describe one who falls away from a life of faith and returns to a life of unrighteousness or sin.

However, in the new testament, the concept of regeneration transcends rehabilitation and the term "backslider" is not mentioned. On the contrary, in Christ, rehabilitation is impossible because the work of the cross is to symbolically "kill" the life of the soul so that from the spirit will spring forth newness of life wherein the soul will be renewed daily. As Paul declared to the believers in Galatia, "I am crucified with Christ, nevertheless, I live; yet not I, but Christ liveth in me. And the life I now live in the flesh I live by faith of the Son of God, who loved me, and gave Himself for me." (Galatians 2:20). Therefore, regeneration or "rebirth" involves the death of the soul life and the infilling of new life. This new life is God Himself dwelling within our spirits.

Restoration is an ongoing process that involves a permanent surrender to this significant spiritual truth---YOU MUST DIE DAILY! As you have been using the keys to your recovery, you have been "working out" the salvation of your soul with fear and trembling, "for it is God which worketh in you both to will and to do His good pleasure." (Philippians 2:12,13) You labor in vain when you attempt to rehabilitate or revive what Jesus Christ compels to die! It is God's good pleasure to crucify the soul life, because the carnal human mind is His enemy, having been molded by the world. (Romans 8:7 and James 4:4). Death and rebirth are well described by Dr. M. Scott Peck in "The Road Less Traveled:"

> The pain of giving up is the pain of death, but death of the old is birth of the new. The pain of death is the pain of birth, and the pain of birth is the pain of death. For us to develop a new and better idea, concept, theory or understanding means that an old idea, concept, theory or understanding must die. (Peck, p. 74)

The downfall of the spiritual recidivist is a belief in man's capacity to change himself. Consistent and intense cultivation will ultimately bring you to the revelation that without the divine essence of God working within you, you cannot affect a lasting self change. Even strong will power and discipline are no match for the desires and appetites of the human flesh.

Furthermore, you will discover that the Lord creates the best out of the worst. Within every relapse is the seed of a breakthrough if you learn how to understand the symbolic language of the spirit. Through study, care and labor that is guided by the Holy Spirit, you can become empowered to find the strength to resist temptation, to overcome persecution and to triumph over challenging circumstances.

Recorded in the old testament book of Number and summarized in the third chapter of the book of Hebrews beginning with the thirteenth verse---is an account of the Israelite's reaction to the giants in Canaan. At God's command, Moses sent 12 men to spy out the land which God promised to give to the Israelites. At the end of forty days, the twelve spies returned to the people, ten with a negative report, and two with a positive report

The negative report was quite clear. Ten spies declared: "Look here, Moses! We came to the land to which you sent us; it flows with milk and honey, and this is its fruit. Yet the people who dwell in the land are strong. The bottom line is that there are giants in the land, and we are like grasshoppers in our own sight." By contrast, Joshua and Caleb spoke power packed words: "Let's go up at once and occupy Canaan, FOR WE ARE WELL ABLE TO OVERCOME IT. Do not rebel against the Lord and do not fear the giants because they are bread for us; The Lord is with us. DO NOT FEAR THE GIANTS!" (Numbers Ch 13)

The writer of the book of Hebrews further explains why the Israelites did not enter into the Lord's rest for four reasons: they hardened their hearts, they did not know God's ways, they were rebellious, and they did not believe. As a result, they wandered about in the wilderness for forty years until each person died, except for Joshua and Caleb. Less than a day's trip took forty years because God removed His guidance and direction, and the people remained ineffectual and confused.

The Lord revealed to me that the cycle of addiction is akin to the Israelites wandering around in circles, never reaching the land of promise because they are fixated on faulty beliefs about Him. Challenging an addict's myths that have multigenerational roots is a formidable task, even for God. For example, the quest for unwavering self control is a time consuming giant that can only result in harmful preoccupation and bondage. The fact that substance abuse can be controlled for years and then suddenly and elusively re-appear is a perplexing paradox within the addictive cycle that fosters overconfidence on the one hand, and shame, doubt and depression as the aftermath of a relapse. This "gigantic" dilemma keeps the addict's life unmanageable, as the abyss between victory and defeat deepens and becomes hell on earth.

Restoration

Addicts arrive at the doorstep of a 12 Step program as though it were the land of Canaan, seeking solutions, only to hear familiar testimonies of vulnerability that confirm the tenacity of the addictive cycle, namely, that there are "giants in the land." As a part of the recovery process, they develop a network of associates, --- the ten spies--- each of whom are bound to the same cycle of victory and defeat---each anxiously counting days of sobriety---sporting their number of days clean as a tangible badge of their momentary self worth. Sadly after each relapse, they must recount their clean days from day one following their fall. In other words, they lose all of their clean days prior to the relapse.

I believe that the Lord Jesus Christ's prophetic word to the addict is a word of warning and rebuke:" You do not know Me. You are in disobedience and rebellion for by My stripes you are healed. Not only are you healed physically, but I have even bore your anxiety, shame and frustration on Calvary's cross. Yet, in your rebellion, you refuse me as your Higher Power. I have asked you to come unto Me, all of you who are heavy laden with this addictive cycle, yet you refuse. My yoke is easy. My burden is light. In Me, you will find freedom. In Me, you will enter into rest. Yet, you have hardened your heart with doubt and unbelief. You refuse to give Me my proper place as God. AA is your God and not Me! Therefore, YOU SHALL NOT ENTER INTO MY REST! You will wander about in your self created wilderness, and Satan will continue to make it a living hell for you."

Since as a son of God you are no longer an addict, the Lord does not have a word of rebuke for you. The essence of your restoration can be found in the covenant or contract that Jesus made with you in His blood. The revealed truth of God's word is that the blood of Jesus cleansed your conscience from the dead works of you past. This truth is not for you mind to understand. It is for your spirit to receive the Lord's grace and for your soul to believe His word. You overcome by the blood of the Lamb and the word of your testimony. (Revelation 12:11)

Your testimony is that it is impossible for you to make amends for even a tenth of your wrongdoing, for even a tenth would be insurmountable. The Lord is looking for those in recovery who can testify that when they received the shed blood of Jesus at the cross for the atonement of their own souls, their conscience was cleansed from the dead works of their past wrongdoing.

Who could possibly make amends, without the blood of Jesus? To compensate for the contamination of your soul, God Himself provided His own solution in the blood of Jesus Christ:

> For the life of the flesh is in the blood: and I have given it to you upon the altar to make an atonement for your souls: for it is the blood that maketh an atonement for the soul. (Leviticus 17:11)

> And almost all things are by the law purged with blood; and without shedding of blood is no remission. (Hebrews 9:22)

> How much more shall the blood of Christ, who through the eternal Spirit offered himself without spot to God, purge your conscience from dead works to serve the living God? (Hebrews 9:14)

> Giving thanks unto the Father, which hath made us meet to be partakers of the inheritance of the saints in light;

> Who hath delivered us from the power of darkness, and hath translated us into the kingdom of his dear Son: In whom we have redemption through his blood, even the forgiveness of sins: (Colossians 1:12-14)

To summarize these four passages of scripture, God has declared in His word that the purging or cleansing of the soul---the mind, emotions, willpower and personality of man---can only be obtained through shed blood. In reading the old and new testament, various scriptures suggest that blood, both animal and human, has the capacity to speak when it falls to the ground. In some supernatural way, the Father God can hear a voice cry out to Him from the ground and He is compelled to respond. (Genesis 4:10) To Cain in the first book of old testament, God declared that the voice of his brother Abel's blood cried out to Him for justice. Consistent with this explanation is a scripture in the last book of the new testament which indicates that the blood of the martyrs continually cries out to God for vindication. (Revelation 6:10). Therefore, I suggest that human blood spilt to the ground has a compelling voice.

This would explain why the Israelites would continually offer blood sacrifices of lambs, bulls and turtledoves at the altar of God. The blood of innocent, non-violent animals such as lambs, bullocks, goats and turtledoves voiced a temporary atonement. Similar to the eighth step in recovery, the Israelites were required by law to make amends for their wrongdoing on an ongoing basis. However, the blood offering of God Himself through His Son is a remarkable provision. The blood of Jesus speaks better things than the blood of Abel. (Hebrews 12:24) For within the dispensation of God's grace, you have obtained an extraordinary atonement by the blood of Jesus your Redeemer.

Consequently, to strive to make amends by the efforts of your own flesh is to refuse the Father's grace provided in His Son's sacrifice. Grace is not only God's unmerited favor but it is also the power of the Holy Spirit to do a work in you for His own glory. God offers you grace because He knows that it is impossible for any of us, particularly those who have lived lecherously, to make amends for each and every mistake. It is true that the former addict does not deserve such mercy, but this is the meaning of God's grace. It is beyond your human reasoning and understanding. You have been saved by faith through grace and not of yourself, for it is a gift from God.(Ephesians 2:8) That same grace that is capable of washing your spirit and renewing your mind, can also cleanse and restore your soul from a lust for an unclean life of addiction.

Moreover, you could not understand such mercy since you have found it difficult to even forgive yourself. Perhaps you have believed that God could not remove your affliction without you doing some form of penance. Therefore, you have felt more comfortable attempting to make amends in your own strength. Your rational mind does not conceive that such an easy way out is fair when you consider the extent of your wrongdoing.

Redemption is an eternal atonement that sets you free from the bondage of your tainted soul. Oh, to be set free from the bondage of addiction! Yet it seems too simple a process for you to believe by faith in the blood atonement of the Christ. You can understand punishment, suffering and penance, but you cannot fathom the grace of God. Human nature compels us to cling to our personal testimonies of the shame, guilt and disgrace of drunkenness. You prefer to relive the sordid debauchery of our addiction, hoping that the remembrance of the past will somehow prevent you from repeating it.

Yet, continued public sharing of past excess and indulgence only energizes the ravenous hunger of the flesh for more alcohol or drugs. The best examples to support this premise are the many confessions I have heard from recovering addicts who have revealed to me that their cravings for substances invariably has increased after an AA meeting, where the memories of the past were revived as a result of hearing the testimonies of other addicts. The revealed truth of God's word is that the blood of Jesus cleansed your conscience from the dead works of the past and this is complete restoration.

As depicted in Paul's letter to the Corinthians, the drunkard is included with a group of former sinners who have been washed and cleansed of unrighteousness- - - the thief, the homosexual, the adulterer, the troublemaker, the worshipper of false gods AND the drunkard have been declared righteous by

God Himself. This righteousness is manifested in a spiritual renewal that has transformed them from sinners into the righteousness of God.

As the nature of the former thief is to steal no more, he is no longer a thief. As the nature of the former adulterer is to cheat no more and to be faithful to his wife, he is no longer an adulterer. In keeping with this comparison, as the nature of the drunkard is to drink no more, he is no longer a drunkard or an alcoholic. Consequently, when a drunkard declares before his peers that he is an alcoholic and as such, is afflicted with an incurable disease, not only are his thoughts, emotions and spirit negatively affected by the faith that he has in his own words, but he is also denying the power of God to cure and to heal. Crucial to recovery is to have your conscience washed and cleansed from evil thoughts and the memory of the addiction removed from the cells of your flesh by the Holy Spirit.

Jesus provides you with a comprehensive deliverance of spirit, soul and body. Once an addict has been restored, Jesus no long views him or her as an alcoholic or a drug addict. A believer should not use such negative labels to define himself, once he or she has been set free. To even call yourself a "recovering" addict is to remain captive to the lust and hunger of the flesh for intoxicants. Complete deliverance is available in Christ Jesus wherein the captive is completely set free from the lust or hunger for drug or drink. This freedom includes even the very pain of your conscience as a former addict. Jesus blotted out the handwriting of ordinances that were against you, which were contrary to you. He took the pain of your conscience, the sting of your own self hatred. To actualize this truth is to be set free to forgive yourself and to allow the Holy Spirit to impress and convict those you have wronged to eventually forgive you.

An understanding of the invisible and unseen nature of demonic warfare and spiritual attack is an important answer to your ability to forgive your enemies. Your parents, relatives, peers, spouses, significant others, co-workers, teachers, policeman, etc. are all under the authority and power of Satan if they are not born again. It is important to realize that those you love can hinder your spiritual growth, especially if you are yoked together with an unbeliever. Even a carnal Christian opens the door to a demon using him or her against you if he or she is not walking in love. Jesus was able to forgive His enemies from the cross based upon their ignorance of spiritual warfare. As the crowd yelled for Barabas to be spared, the Lord's spiritual eyes were opened to discern that the power behind that crowd were the bulls of Bashan and the dogs that surrounded Him. (Psalm 22:12-16)

The bulls and the dogs are metaphors for ferocious demons that were invisible to everyone except the Lord. The Lord died for His enemies because God so love the world that He sacrificed His Son so that no human being would have to be eternally lost. As you consider this revelation, you can ask yourself whether or not your hatred of your enemies is so strong that you would desire that they would perish eternally. In other words, does your enemies' attack on you or yours justify that they should spend all of eternity in hell when Jesus died for them that they might go to heaven. Are you bold and stubborn enough to defy the Lord for one of those that He has died for and has commanded you to convert with your preaching and your testimony?

Jonah is a classic example in the Bible of a judgmental, unforgiving person. He preferred that 120,000 enemies of God enter into eternal damnation. Even though Jonah knew that the Father loved the people of Nineveh so much that He ordered Jonah to go and convert them, Jonah hardened His heart against the Lord's will and ended up in the belly of a whale for His disobedience. Jesus commands you to pray for your enemies. Your prayer should come out of His desire in your heart that no soul should have to go to hell and that all will come to Him for salvation. When you pray for your enemies in this manner, the love of God that was shed in your heart by the

Holy Spirit at the moment of your rebirth will rise big within you and will restore your soul. Otherwise, the Lord will prepare a special whale just for you!

Key Scriptures

Hebrews 10:22 Let us draw near with a true heart in full assurance of faith, having our hearts sprinkled from an evil conscience, and our bodies washed with pure water.

Titus 3:4-6But after that the kindness and love of God our Savior toward man appeared, not by works of righteousness which we have done, but according to his mercy he saved us, by the washing of regeneration, and renewing of the Holy Ghost; which he shed on us abundantly through Jesus Christ our Savior;)

Isaiah 58:10And if thou draw out thy soul to the hungry, and satisfy the afflicted soul; then shall thy light rise in obscurity, and thy darkness be as the noon day::11 And the LORD shall guide thee continually, and satisfy thy soul in drought, and make fat thy bones: and thou shalt be like a watered garden, and like a spring of water, whose waters fail not.:12And they that shall be of thee shall build the old waste places: thou shalt raise up the foundations of many generations; and thou shalt be called, The repairer of the breach, The restorer of paths to dwell in.:13If thou turn away thy foot from the sabbath, from doing thy pleasure on my holy day; and call the sabbath a delight, the holy of the LORD, honorable; and shalt honor him, not doing thine own ways, nor finding thine own pleasure, nor speaking thine own words:::14Then shalt thou delight thyself in the LORD; and I will cause thee to ride upon the high places of the earth, and feed thee with the heritage of Jacob thy father: for the mouth of the LORD hath spoken it.

Psalms 103:1{ A Psalm of David.} Bless the LORD, O my

> **KEY STATEMENT:** Your soul (mind, emotions, will and personality) is restored when you resolve with your will to experience on a daily basis complete freedom from the powers of darkness.

soul: and all that is within me, bless his holy name.:2Bless the LORD, O my soul, and forget not all his benefits:

:3 Who forgiveth all thine iniquities; who healeth all thy diseases;:4Who redeemeth thy life from destruction; who crowneth thee with lovingkindness and tender mercies;

:5Who satisfieth thy mouth with good things; so that thy youth is renewed like the eagle's.

John 10:9I am the door: by me if any man enter in, he shall be saved, and shall go in and out, and find pasture.:10 The thief cometh not, but for to steal, and to kill, and to destroy: I am come that they might have life, and that they might have it more abundantly.:11I am the good shepherd: the good shepherd giveth his life for the sheep.

Mark 11:25 And when ye stand praying, forgive, if ye have ought against any: that your Father also which is in heaven may forgive you your trespasses.:26 But if ye do not forgive, neither will your Father which is in heaven forgive your trespasses.

Luke 6:37Judge not, and ye shall not be judged: condemn not, and ye shall not be condemned: forgive, and ye shall be forgiven:

Luke 6:38Give, and it shall be given unto you; good measure, pressed down, and shaken together, and running over, shall men give into your bosom. For with the same measure that ye mete withal it shall be measured to you again.

Matthew 6:31 Therefore take no thought, saying, What shall we eat? or, What shall we drink? or, Wherewithal shall we be clothed?:32 (For after all these things do the Gentiles seek:) for your heavenly Father knoweth that ye have need of all these things.

:33But seek ye first the kingdom of God, and his righteousness; and all these things shall be added unto you.:34Take therefore no thought for the morrow: for the morrow shall take thought for the things of itself. Sufficient unto the day is the evil thereof.

Study and Reflection Outline

Point 1: In order to be fully restored, you must make sure that you have dealt with generational and personal curses.

- A. A curse is an evil outcome that has been spoken or professed by either God, man or the devil.
    1. Negative words pronounce an evil destiny
    2. A curse is often connected to an abomination.
        a) an abomination is something considered extremely disgusting
        b) an abomination is also loathsome, vile or shameful.
        c) some examples of an abomination include incest, idolatry, sodomy, bestiality
- B. Generational sins that lead to curses as outlined in Deuteronomy 27 include idolatry.

1. idolatry is the worship that is offered to Satan either knowingly or unknowing.

    a) Satanism today is open acknowledgement of Satan as God using various forms of witchcraft

    b) The New Age Movement also known as the occult is also idolatry

2. idolatry is also manifested in the church through religious demons that have infiltrated Christian worship

3. Other generational sins are:

    a) sodomy

    b) incest

    c) injustice

    d) oppression of the weak

    e) dishonoring of parents

    f) theft

C. For the most part, the curses emanate from the breaking of the 10 Commandments.

   1. The Israelites sacrificed their children to the god call Molech and brought curses upon themselves and future generations.

   2. The present day descendants of Molech are people that literallysacrifice their children to such things as drugs, shoplifting, in otherwords, people who support and condone their children to partake of demonic activities.

       a) the celebration of demonic holidays like Halloween

b) homage to mythological beings such as Santa and the tooth fairy

c) demonic cartoons and video games

d) cursing with the Lord Jesus Christ's name

Point 2 Your goal is to recognize hidden battles or potential curses in your own life so that you can experience complete cleansing and restoration so that you can find and maintain victory in the blood of Jesus.

A. You are responsible not to touch the unclean thing.

1. Unclean things include anything connected to your addiction.

   a) pipes, flasks, hypodermic needles etc. must be destroyed

   b) books, movies, games that glorify the addictions

   c) orgies, shoplifting, drug dealers, ie. the street life.

2. Unclean things also includes "the stuff" of your past that must be left behind.

   a) You can't bring a good thing out of a cursed place.

   b) You need to be delivered from "your crowd.

3. The Lord Jesus Christ will receive you if you will come out from among them in thought, word or deed.

4. You will be consumed in all of the sins of the unrighteous if you continue to touch the unclean thing. (Numbers 16:26, 2Cor. 6:17, II Peter 2:8,9

To Curse The Root

B. The blood of Jesus Christ has cleansed your conscience from the dead works of the past.

1. The Holy Communion is an important ritual in the exchange of a curse for a blessing

2. You will not be blocked in the fulfillment of God's plan for you life.

Workstudy Exercises

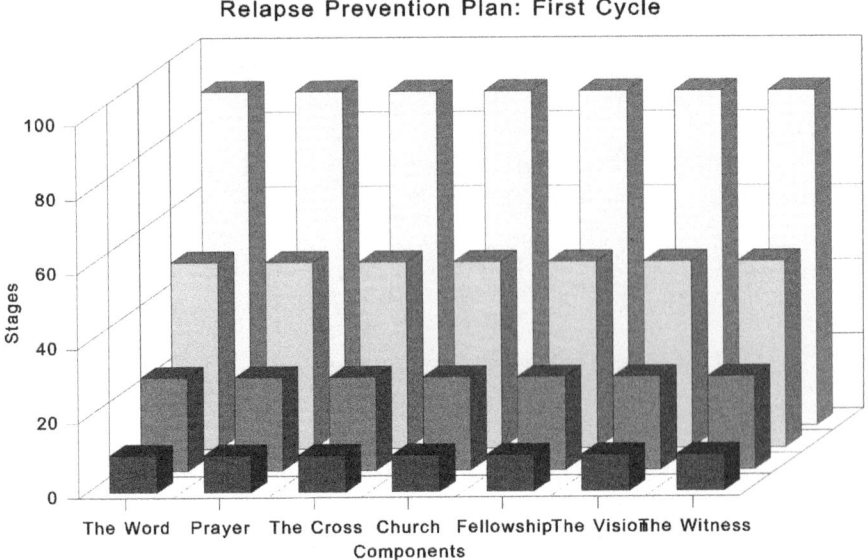

Exercise #1: Study and read the profile of a recovered person. (pg142) For each component on the chart, evaluate your strength according to the appropriate numerical stage by coloring the bar. Seven columns of bars should be colored---one for the Word, Prayer, the Cross, the Church, Fellowship, the Vision and the Witness. List any bar colored at the less then 50% stage.

Restoration

How do you intend to make improvements? For those bars that show a 60% rate or more, how do you plan to increase and maintain your progress?_____
_____
_____
_____
_____
_____
_____
_____
_____
_____
_____
_____
_____
_____
_____

Exercise #2 Review the 7 doorways to demonic activity. List those areas that may have affected you. Explain the circumstances in your own words.

_____

Exercise #3 A part of taking back control of your life is self examination. Casting down imaginations and high thoughts is a good start. Negative thoughts can bind you to hopeless pessimism that will block your recovery. Take the following test by reading the statements below. Choose the term which best describes your thoughts and feelings over the last 30 days. Put the number above that term in the blank beside each statement. Retake this test every 30 days.

1-2-3-4-5-6-7
ALWAYS VERY OFTEN OFTEN SOMETIMES SELDOM VERY SELDOM NEVER

___I think about past failures or experiences of rejection.
___I feel that the past has ruined my chances for a better life.
___I perceive myself to be an immoral person.
___I think that God is waiting for me to mess up again.

To Curse The Root

___I cannot speak about my past because it is too shameful.

___I think that I am not fit to be used by God.

Exercise 4: When God delivers you from your past, He will cause your family, neighbors and associates to witness it. He will do this to manifest His own glory to the people. Read Act. Chapter 9.

How did Paul overcome His past as a persecutor of the early church and as a murderer of Christians? Select the correct response.

1. Paul heard the word and he _____ it. (received/rebelled against)

2. Paul_____on the next step. (searched for/waited for)

3. The next step was that he_____ (went on his missionary journey/was baptized and healed.

4. How did Paul learn of his purpose and assignment?

EXERCISE 5: Do you know what your purpose and assignment is? If you do, write it down._

___

What priorities have you set that show that you have accepted the Lord's purpose for your life?

___

EXERCISE 6: Look up each of the following scriptures: Ephesians 1:4-6, John 15:16, Galatians 4:4 According to these scriptures, God chose his people before the foundation of the earth to fulfill His purposes. How does your personal destiny fit into the overall purposes of God? How has the Lord revealed Himself and His purposes to you relative to your past failures?__

___

Restoration

EXERCISE 7: Meditate on II Chronicles 16:9. " For the eyes of the LORD run to and fro throughout the whole earth, to shew himself strong in the behalf of them whose heart is perfect toward Him." As you reflect on your own life, take a moment to write down a specific situation where the Lord Jesus Christ used you to manifest his glory or "show Himself strong" as a witness to someone else in recovery.

Also, write down how you would define a heart that is "perfect toward Him." Do you have such a heart?

EXERCISE 8: Were you abused as a child? Why do you suppose that Satan took such a vicious stand against you so early in life? Did he know something that you didn't know?

EXERCISE 9: In the midst of the abusive situation, how did the Lord God show you His grace and mercy?

APPENDIX:

Blessed Are the "Poor in Spirit"

I understand now why the Lord Jesus Christ declared that John the Baptist was the greatest born among men. With the exception of the Lord's own mission of bringing salvation to the world, John the Baptist's mission was the most important, as the only way to rebirth is through repentance. No one can come to the Father except by Jesus. Even so, no one can come to Jesus accept through John's message of repentance.

In spite of the fact that John the Baptist did not heal, nor did he cast out devils, John's ministry was indeed the doorway to the supernatural. Through the preaching of repentance and through baptizing the sinner in water, John's job was to prepare the way for the Lord to the sinner. Only through repentance and baptism in water is the sinner prepared to receive the Lord. The charismatics have amplified the meaning of repentance as a "change of mind" or a "turning in another direction." However, the repentance that saves is to experience godly sorrow. Godly sorrow is an experience of the soul's grief for having no worthiness to approach God on one's own merit.

It should not be mistaken for human shame or guilt due to wrong doing. The truth is that most people are already convinced in their minds that they are sinners. They reason in their minds "well, yeah, I have sinned, but so has the next guy and when I look around at others, my sins are nothing compared to his, so I believe I'm going to heaven because I am not that bad." People in the world repent every day for this sin or that sin, yet without the leading of the Holy Ghost, they will not repent of being in the depths of their soul, "an alienated sinner, without God in the world."

Godly sorrow of this kind is a deeply emotional experience where the sinner is brought face to face with his own inner darkness. It is the dark night of the soul. It is no longer a

Appendix

comparison to the "next guy." It becomes "it's me Lord---and compared to You, I am a wretched being, a poor excuse of humanity. My heart cries out to You to save me."

Brokenness is an important aspect of achieving repentance toward God. When we are broken, we become ready to be forgiven for our sins and to be sanctified or set apart for His use. Brokenness is symbolized in the baptism in water, in that "the Lord is near to those who have a broken heart, and saves such as have a contrite spirit." (Psalm 34:18) The brokenness of repentance feels like someone came into the room of our lives and suddenly turned the light switch on and exposed us. Jesus said that unless a seed falls to the ground and dies, it cannot become what it was destined to be, and that is "a child of God and a son of God." We cannot cry out "Abba, Father" until we become aware in our hearts how our sin has separated us from Him and that the Lord's Jesus Christ's sacrifice at the cross has brought us into right relationship with Him.

Repentance is a walk of humility into the valley of brokenness. Unless we take this walk, we are too rigid and hard to be molded in the hand of God. More than just simply being powerless before God, repentance leads to a brokenness before Him where we have been made to see our sins as God sees them. Repentance is the process whereby we have come to realize deep within, that our sins have hurt the Father. Only then, does the sinner receive salvation.

Recently, I have been shocked to have been exposed to persons who have responded to Jesus through the "believe, confess, and receive" gospel---persons who are now severely demonized. Then there are also those who went to a Pentecostal altar, repeatedly chanting "Jesus, Jesus, Jesus" or "Hallelujah, Hallelujah, Hallelujah," only to walk away demonized. The case of Maria is only the tip of the spiritual iceburg where charismatic witchcraft is concerned. Sometimes it has taken years for the demonic torment to manifest.

The sad part of the situation is that in every case, these believers have been sincere seekers of the Lord Jesus Christ. I ask myself "how could this have happened?" Reminded of several scriptures in this regard, I have wondered how could sincere seekers of the Lord Jesus Christ---those who have responded to the preacher's invitation,--- walk away from a church altar having received a religious demon instead of the Holy Ghost? Even Jesus Himself said that if we who are sinners know how to give good gifts to our children, "how much more shall your Heavenly Father give the Holy Spirit to them that ask Him?" (Luke 11:11) I believe the message is found in the message of John the Baptist. The word is "repent!"

I have found in my counseling practice that several on my caseload who are severely demonized today are believers on the Lord Jesus Christ who did not repent at the moment of their salvation. They simply responded to the "good news" and came to the altar. Some repeated a sinner's prayer. Others simply confessed their belief that Jesus Christ was raised from the dead. Others tarried for long hours and eventually spoke in an unknown tongue. Even others received the right hand of fellowship from a denomination and were placed on the church rolls. It is clear to me that none of the captives in question were ever really saved simply because they did not understand the depth of their sinful nature and that if it were not for the price paid by the Lord, that they were headed for hell.

Blessed Are the Meek
UNCOVERING STRONGHOLDS

A part of being meek is to identify stumbling blocks to fruitfulness. A stumblingblock is an interconnection of a person (s), a place or surrounding, an event, a personality defect or a thing that demons continue to employ to cause the captive to fall. Often there is something in the captive's personality or character that draws him either by attraction or seduction to perform an act that proves to be detrimental, by acting as a doorway for particular demons. Usually the stronghold is upheld by a particular sin, serving as a stimulator to the weight that continues to beset the captive.

A stronghold may consist of one demon or a constellation of demons. The bigger the stronghold, the more unproductive the client's spiritual life will be. Upon searching for strongholds, you should prepare the captive to face them squarely by recognizing factors and issues that may lie in either his subconscious or even the unconscious mind. In this regard, dream interpretation will be an important tool in uncovering subliminal strongholds. As a deliverance counselor, you should seek the Lord in prayer, asking Him to uncover that which is hidden so that the captive can receive a powerful insight that might be earth shattering. For example, consider a captive who was raised in the church. She strongly believes that she is saved because of her church affiliation and the fact that she speaks in tongues. The captive in this example never suspected that her inability to contend with demons is because she never got saved while attending church. However, the Lord has revealed to you that He has allowed the demons to torment her because her eternal salvation was in the balance. In other words, the torment drove the captive to you for help, so that the Lord could open up the captive's eyes so that she could perceive her true spiritual condition.

Some captives are very invested in maintaining the power of their stronghold, even though they would like to be relieved from torment. Consider a person who is out on the ledge of a highrise apartment house, trying to get into the window of her apartment which is several feet to the left of her. In order to reach her destination, she must avoid looking down or to the right to avoid getting dizzy or distracted and end up falling to her death. Similarly, a person bound by a stronghold may try to avoid any deviation from his usual patterns for fear that he may fall. The course that the captive has developed over time consists of unconscious defense mechanisms, designed on a subliminal level to keep the captive on his path, even though the captive would agree that the path he has chosen is destructive.

As an example, a female captive who is dependent upon an abusive partner will be hindered from making any independent moves of her own. As such, those in the bondage to a stronghold most likely lack spontaneity of feeling, thought and or willpower, making his soul weak and unstable. Each stronghold will create a specific fear or doubt as well as an accompanying behavior of his self concept and pride system.

Captives who are in bondage to their own self created stronghold will often attribute the strength of the stronghold to demons, when in fact, casting out the demons will not bring any relief. In a case of this kind, the stronghold is embedded in the captive's personality defect.

A STRONGHOLD IN THE AFFECTIONS

When the captive seems to admire what in truth he resents, he is alienated from his own true feelings. In such cases, the captive will be out of touch with his own likes and dislikes, fears and resentments, longings and motivations. Furthermore, the captive has lost the capacity to assert his own wishes. Without adequate knowledge of his own desires, the captive will be blocked from receiving the Lord's desires. Delighting in the Lord through worship, praise and devotionals will be fruitless because the captive is out of touch with his true affections.

Jesus said that we shall know them by their fruit. Therefore, as a deliverance counselor, you should search for the fruit and build upon it. When attempting to consider what fruit actually is, I can reveal to you what fruit is not. It is not church attendance, tithing, or praise and worship. It is not even going from door to door to witness, casting out devils, the power gifts, street ministry or even winning souls. How could these things be "fruit, when Jesus Himself declared that there will be those who have cast out devils, those who have said, "Lord, Lord", and I will say that I did not know you. In other words, these

Appendix

people that Jesus is referring to were worshippers. Apparently they were not worshipping in spirit and in truth. They were probably worshipping "in soul and in deception." It seems that soulish worship does not count with the Lord---AT ALL!!!

What then, is fruit?

I believe that fruit is the manifestation of the power of the resurrection in a person's life. In other words, does an individual demonstrate in his or her life that Jesus Christ is alive? As Jesus said, "if we abide in Him, then we will bare fruit." So in order to manifest fruit, we must abide in Him. To abide is "to live in" or "to dwell." Jesus also said that He came that we might have life, and have it more abundantly. So, abundant life is a synonym for "fruit."

Since the just shall live by faith, if we walk in faith, then our lives should be fruitful. Our faith is our evidence of the power of the resurrection. In other words, because we believe on the resurrection, we believe that Jesus is alive. Therefore, to bare fruit, is to consistently live by faith, in a manner that demonstrates that Jesus Christ is no longer in the tomb. It is a power that is demonstrated without even the necessity of quoting a scripture. Demonstration of power can be recognized by those who have it and felt by those who do not have it.

Demonstrations of power are obtained by building one's foundation upon the Rock. Jesus declared that if we built our house upon the rock, and not upon sand, when the storms of life attack us, we will remain standing. In this context, then once again, the 9 fruit of the Spirit represent "the rock." From an architectural, natural standpoint, when we build a house, we would like to have confidence in its foundation. Therefore, when we look for fruit that will demonstrate the resurrection power of the Lord Jesus Christ, we should examine where the client or captive has placed his or her confidence.

There is such a thing as "fake fruit." I am sure that you have at one time been fooled by plastic or rubber fruit sitting in a bowl as the center piece on a dining room table. Sometimes these plastic replicas look even better than the real thing from a distance. However, up close, you can see that there is no life in fake fruit. This is also true of fake spiritual fruit.

Take for example the fruit of meekness or humility. Those who are "fake", may appear to have a lack of self confidence. However, at the root of their apparent meekness is compulsive modesty. In such instances, the captive's pattern is to overlook his own needs, suggesting that the thoughts and ways of others are more reliable than his own. False humility of this kind will lead the captive to not feel safe unless a significant other in his life will protect, defend, advise or nurture him. In such cases, the captive loses the capability to take responsibility for his own life. With women, the Adam's Rib Syndrome develops, where she does not view herself as a whole person without a mate to help her feel complete.

False meekness also manifests itself when clients who have low self concept develop techniques and processes whereby the self is placed in the background by losing self regard. In an attempt to avoid anger at all cost, the captive will repress hostility and will become self effacing. Some captives will merely adjust their behavior to adapt to the stronger personality, while others will allow their personalities to be changed by stronger people. People like this are often wrongfully perceived as having the fruit of meekness.

To illustrate, women suffering from the "Adam's Rib Syndrome" tend to build their foundation upon the sand, where their partner is at the center. The woman will undoubtedly expect the partner to fulfill all of her expectations, becoming a ready victim to a demonic soul tie, as addressed in SEW IV. She is left vulnerable to manipulation and domination, where the fruit of love is also fake and without power. Love is a fruit of the spirit that is liberating, for as the scriptures indicate, perfect love casts out fear. However, the Adam's Rib Syndrome is not based upon true, solid love. In fact, carnal love canbecomes in itself a stronghold that leads to fear of desertion and a fear of being alone. As an example, a woman who is dependent upon an abusive partner will be hindered from making any independent moves of her own. As such, those in the bondage to such a stronghold are most likely to lack spontaneity of feeling, thought and will power.

Each stronghold will create a specific fear or doubt as well as an accompanying pride system that will be difficult to break through. Captives so bound, will often attribute their strongholds to demons, when in actuality, casting out a demon will not bring any lasting relief. This is because the stronghold is embedded in the captive's personality and is therefore a stronghold in the soul. In cases where there has been little to no personality change, it will seem as though deliverance has failed when in reality, the root of the problem was not so much demonic as it was "soulical." Casting out demons may bring a momentary sense of freedom or joy. Even so, a substantial, solid deliverance is one where the fruit of true meekness has been planted and nurtured.

THE FRUIT OF MEEKNESS

Since Meekness is the doorway to blessing, (Matthew 5), any captive in need of deliverance must become poor in spirit. To be poor in spirit is to be emptied of one's character defects. Deliverance will empty the captive from demons, but these demons and others will ultimately return if the conditions that provided them a safe haven still remain. Therefore, your job as a deliverance counselor is to seek the help of the Holy Spirit to sensitize a conscience that has been hardened by the pride of life.

Meekness is manifested when the captive comes to the realization that his thoughts are not as high as the Lord's thoughts, nor his ways higher than the Lord's ways. Furthermore, as a deliverance counselor, your own meekness should sustain you with the following truth. This is a simple, yet a profound truth and that is, "whatever does not originate in the inward parts of the captive himself, will not bring him life." Therefore, deliverance counseling is more than bringing the client a great idea, quoting a scripture, or coming forth with an insightful revelation. Such a thing may provide a temporary stimulation but it will not leave a lasting result. Even false or counterfeit spirituality may appear to produce a beneficial result but it cannot grant authentic, resurrection life. You, as a counselor then, must yourself labor by the revelation of the Holy Ghost. If you do this yourself in your everyday walk with the Lord, eventually the captive will be convinced and his spirit well be touched by the unction of the Holy Ghost that is within him and "he will need no man to teach him." Then he will truly be ready for deliverance.

THE RELIGIOUS DEMON AND THE SUBSTANCE ABUSER: A CASE IN POINT

George has never been my client. However, all sides of his personality have been exposed to me and I probably know him more intimately as his pastor and his friend since 1989. George has heard me preach more often than any other person, except of course, my immediate family. For five out of 15 years of knowing George, he was incarcerated, and even then, I remained his pastor. In fact, George was instrumental in opening the door to my preaching in a prison ministry that lasted for 8 years. So, to make a long story short, I know George very well.

If I were to ask myself which of the sheep that I have pastored I would find to be the most disappointing, without a doubt, the first to come to mind would be George. For a person to know the word of God and love preaching and teaching as much as George does, the bottom line is to wonder why after all of these years, there has been no fruit for Christ at all. George's spirituality is an excellent example of "having a form of godliness but denying the power thereof."

To truly understand the longstanding fruitlessness of George's religious experience, an assessment of his background

Appendix

is important. George's situation is comparable to a cycle or even a circle of juxtapositions: religious piety versus drug and alcohol abuse; sexual piety versus sexual perversion; caring and giving versus violence and even murder; lasciviousness of all kinds and then back to religion and constant church going. While George has a semblance of control over addiction, his pattern was to partake of either drug or drinking episodes during the week and come to worship service and bible study sober, until his drug abuse became too difficult to hide from the church. The intensity of these episodes increased at check time, wherein his monthly allotment would be squandered in two days. The rest of the month, he would borrow into his next check. This kind of behavior would continue until at least once or twice a year, he would go into a local hospital for detoxification and then spend 28 more days in rehab. Once involved in a secular recovery program, George once again becomes "religious." George's life resembles the character "Dr. Jeykl and Mr. Hyde.

One of the ways that the "Mr. Hyde" side of George's personality would attempt to resolve his inner conflicts while he is religious and somewhat sober is to repress the dark aspects of his personality by bringing its opposite to the forefront. On one hand, George is mannerly, respectful and gentle. Sometimes he can be very compliant, always willing to share and to offer a helping hand. However, under the influence of drugs, George turns into a kind of werewolf, entirely devoid of all human beings, at times, even bent on maiming or killing. In fact, when I met George in 1989, he revealed that he had served 13 years in prison for murder. It has always been clear to me that George never repented of this murder, primarily because the family of the murdered man retaliated for the death of their brother by murdering one of George's brothers.

Then while a professing Christian, George himself was stabbed by a woman while he was on one of his drunken sprees. I advised him to report the woman to the police but he answered me very "religiously" and piously professed that he was required by the Lord to forgive this woman and not take her to court. A month later, George was arrested for stabbing this same woman an inch from her heart. His claim of not guilty by reason of self defense was overturned, and at the age of 64, George went to prison and served 5 years. While in prison, George became very religious once again, attending worship and bible study whenever offered in the prison. Once released from prison, George joined my church. As a result of his outreach and advocacy for our ministry, he became known in the community as "Preacher Man." For the next five years, George continued to travel through the revolving doors from church to the crack house until his health became damaged with alcohol related diabetes. Now he is living in an independent living situation within a drug free residential program. As such, George has been totally clean and sober for the last five months, longer than he has been drug free for the last fifty years, not counting a total of 18 years behind bars.

Needless to say, George has been a thorn in my side in ministry. A two-edged sword works both ways. Although I could see no fruit in my ministry to George, George was used as a pruning fork to bare fruit for Christ within me. For example, my own spiritual pride was confronted, in that as previously stated, George is the person who has heard more of my sermons than anyone other than my family, and yet the word that I preached and taught bore no fruit in him. Where was the demonstration of power? Where was the resurrection life? So I myself began to "project." I thought that I heard in the spirit that the devil had sent George to me to serve as a hindrance to my ministry. In other words, how could I deliver those captive to alcohol and drugs if I could not deliver someone who is an integral part of my own ministry?

In other words, I began to believe that the devil was trying to mock me by seating George in my midst. With thoughts like these, the next line of thinking of course would be that George either "cease to exist" or not exist around me. So Satan began to send me threatening dreams of George's demise. I believed that

Appendix

these dreams were from the Lord, and so I began to strongly warn George that if he did not stop being a religious hypocrit, the Lord was going to "wipe him out and send him to hell." Well, the threats did not work. Briefly George joined another church and I was momentarily relieved. But, he couldn't stay away, and so after Mr. Hyde ran his course, Dr. Jekyl was back.

While sober, George was not the easiest personality to take. In spite of his "nice guy" image of helpfulness an feigned gentleness of spirit, George's high opinion of himself was extremely distasteful. For example, the women could feel the perverse sexual energy behind the façade of politeness and everyone repelled from his handshake or his "holy kiss." The men were turned off to him because their attitude was "old man, why don't you go sit yourself down somewhere and just be quiet!!!" The pompousness and bravado of George's rather proud and puffed up nature was a bit much to take from a man now 70 years old but who can still pass for 50. Before this last drug episode, he was assumed to be a man in his early 40's--- that is how good he looked until this last episode of crack use.

Furthermore, George's vanity has caused him to overlook in himself his own advancing years. Yet like a child, anything that his mind desired, the lusts of his flesh always demanded immediate fulfillment. In other words, George could not wait for anything, not could he withstand a disappointment. The underlying stronghold in his personality is a lack of any enduring satisfaction. Whereever he found himself to be, George always longed to be somewhere else. Not able to spend time alone, yet George was only momentarily grateful for his present company and soon desired to be among others. This lack of satisfaction was most apparent by his rather short attention span. For example, he would make an unexpected visit to an acquaintance, stay for 15 minutes an then either make a phone call to someone else. If no one else was available, then he would make frequent "in and out" trips through the front door.

To Curse The Root

So, for the most part, we all tolerated George. Pastoring him was difficult because I suspected for some time that George was not saved. This would explain the constant wavering between two opinions, two personalities. I suspected that his spiritual life was based upon either foolishness, fakery, or a combination of both. George could speak in one of the most beautiful tongues that I had ever heard, yet how could he truly be speaking in a tongue from heaven if he continued to wallow in the muck and mire of filth and uncleanness of hell on earthEven more, I had George to take me back to the day he believed that he got saved. Even though his description of what happened was supernatural, there was no indication that the experience was a result of repentance. . It was very simple. No fruit, no salvation. However, I did not realize that what I was to do about it was also simple.

When I saw that nothing at all seemed to work with him, I ceased from my own works and just extended him compassion. I offered support and help as long as he wanted to stay clean and sober. In other words, forgiving him, seventy times seven, even though for the last five years he chose the Easter season to backslide. In spite of how offensive this was to both my spirit and my flesh, I refused to judge him. After much tireless effort of reprimand, warning and rebuke, I decided to simply not have any expectations of George, and to just love him without condition or requirement.

One day, I was on the telephone with the church member who finds George most repulsive. Mozelle complained, "Pastor, what we going to do about George? I get so tired of hearing his stupid, phony testimonies that every time he opens his mouth on a Sunday morning, my skin crawls. What shall I do? I just can't stand feeling this way." I responded by saying "Mozelle, all we can do for George is to just love him." Within two hours of this statement I made to Mozelle, after 15 years of seeking the Lord Jesus Christ, George was marvelously and simply saved. What was impossible with men was possible with God.

Appendix

So, how did it happen? Well, first let me say to you that Jesus makes it clear in His discussion with his apostles about the rich man, that there are human conditions within the pride of life system that will hinder salvation and make coming to Him as impossible as a camel being able to go through an eye of a needle. The condition that Jesus uses in this particular case is wealth and material riches. I believe that there are other conditions which are mentioned by Paul to the Corinthians and to the Galatians. These include fornicators, idolators, adulterers, homosexuals, sodomites, thieves, covetous, DRUNKARDS, revelers and extortioners. Besides this list to the Corinthians, the list to the Galatians include sorcery, selfish ambitions, uncleanness and lewdness, and such conditions as outbursts of wrath, dissensions, heresies and MURDERS.

George's primary hindrances to salvation include DRUNKARDS and MURDERS. There are even a few more from this list that could be added, particularly those that suggest sexual lasciviousness. The entire list of hindering conditions to salvation are doorways to demonic infiltration. As Paul warned, if the message of Christ is hid, it is hid to those who are lost and perishing because those the god of his world blinds their eyes to the gospel message, lest the light of the glorious gospel of Christ Jesus should shine on them. (II Corinthians 4:3,4) Any and everyone who partakes of any one of these conditions is indeed perishing.

Although it is difficult, it is not impossible with God to save even these. For as Paul also wrote to the Corinthians "And such were some of you, but you have been washed, cleansed and sanctified by the blood of Jesus Christ. (II Corinthians 6:10) With men, it was impossible to save me, one who had practiced idolatry through sorcery, necromancy and divination. I was also a fornicator. Therefore, what was impossible with men, by the divine sovereignty of the Lord, He Himself intervened to save me.

Such also was the case with George. In a nutshell, Mr. Hyde made the acquaintance of Dr. Jeykl and said "look, you are no different from me. You are as evil and sinful as I am." The introduction was made in a way that I myself would never have thought of. As is his manner when sober, George brought a resident of the recovery program to church. I could see that this was a work of George's religious flesh. The man was in no way seeking after the Lord but simply was coming to church to be entertained. Anyway, back at the residence, George began to feel very disdainful and critical of this man. Apparently, the man was a buffoon, one who likes to tell raucous jokes in his attention seeking efforts among his peers. So the day before George got saved, he called me on the phone. "Pastor, I just can't stand Victor. He is such a busybody, running his mouth like a fool. He is always up in people's business. I don't get in people's business. I mind my business. Pastor, I just felt like walking up to Victor today, and smashing glass all in his face. I just wanted to tear his face off."

I rebuked him. "George, that is the most awful thing I have ever heard. You bring the man to church because you claim you want his soul to be saved yet you have a murderous feeling in your heart toward him. How can you want to save his soul yet you also want to destroy his body. What has he ever done to you? The NERVE of you!!! Who do you think you are---God Himself!!! The violence in your heart that you used to blame on drugs is still there. Right in your heart---- yet you are sober!!!! You are a murderer still and you call yourself a Christian. Who gave you the right to want to hurt somebody just because YOU don't like him? I have never heard such evil pride in all of my life."

Well, these words penetrated George's soul like a knife. For the first time in his life, he could literally feel his own evil. He could feel the evil that he had been hiding in the Dr. Jekyl part of his personality. He could not blame Mr. Hyde any longer. George ran to his AA counselor to "take the knife out of his chest." All his counselor could say was "Man, you've got some character defects that you've got to work on." The knife remained and George could find no rest so he called me again. Crying and sobbing he said "Pastor, I tried to take this to the cross but I didn't know what to do. I didn't know what to say." So, I led George through repentance to the cross. And the knife came out. He had finally repented. He is now saved. What was impossible with men was possible with God.

FOOTNOTES

1. Taken from "The Twelve Steps of Alcoholic Anonymous"

   Step #6. Were entirely ready to have God remove all these defects of character.

   Step #11 Sought through prayer and meditation to improve our conscious contact with God as we understood Him, praying only for knowledge of His will for us and the power to carry that out.

2. Step #4: Made a searching and fearless moral inventory of ourselves.

   Step #5: Admitted to God, to ourselves, and to another human being the exact nature of our wrongs.

3. Taken from "The Twelve Steps of Alcoholic Anonymous"

   Step #2 Came to believe that a Power greater than ourselves could restore us to sanity.

   Step #3 Made a decision to turn our will and our lives over to the care of God as we understood God.

4. Taken from "the Twelve Steps of Alcoholics Anonymous"

   Step #1 We admitted we were powerless over (problem)--that our lives had become unmanageable.

   Step #2 Came to believe that a Power greater than ourselves could restore us to sanity.

Step #3 Made a decision to turn our will and our lives over to the care as we understood Him.

5   Taken from Joyce Myer's casette tape series entitled, "Birthing A Vision."

6   Surely he has borne our griefs and carried our sorrow; yet we esteemed Him stricken and smitten by God, and afflicted. But He was wounded for our transgressions, he was bruised for our iniquities; the chastisement of our peace was upon Him, and with HIS STRIPES WE ARE HEALED. (ISAIAH 53:4,5)

ABOUT THE AUTHOR

Formerly a psychic medium and an astrologer, Pastor Pam had a Damascus Road type of experience with the Lord Jesus Christ while she was an atheist. Converted in her living room on March 29, 1977, she was sent by the Holy Ghost to the African Methodist Episcopal Zion Church in 1979 where she served as a local preacher, a pastor and an evangelist over a 22 year period. She obtained both a BA and a Masters Degree in Social Work, conferred by the State University in Albany, New York.

Along with her daughter, Zonnita Banks, she is the co-founder of Healing Waters Christian Center, a non-traditional ministry and assembly of believers in Jesus Christ of Nazareth.

As senior pastor of Healing Waters, Pastor Pam is also an anointed counselor and teacher of the word of God.

To hear her anointed sermons and teachings, or to learn more about the author, the Spiritual Bootcamp Sessions, (SBS) the Recovery in Christ Program, (RIC) and the Spiritual Empowerment Workshop (SEW) visit her website at http://www.healingwaterscc.com You can also email her directly at pastorpam911@yahoo.com, particularly if you are seeking deliverance counseling by telephone. Rev. Sheppard is also available to conduct conferences, workshops and seminars anywhere in the world.

Made in the USA
Monee, IL
30 April 2023

32745179R00218